AMMAN UNITED
RUGBY FOOTBALL CLUB

AMMAN UNITED
RUGBY FOOTBALL CLUB

Copyright © Amman Rugby Club, 2003

Published in 2003 by
Amman United RFC
Club House
32, Cwmamman Road, Glanamman
Telephone (01269) 822147

All rights reserved. No part of this book may be reproduced, stored in a retreval system or transmitted, in any form or by any means, electronic, mechanical, photocopying, recording or otherwise, without clearance from the Amman Rugby Club.

ISBN 0-9546177-0-3

Printed and bound in Wales by
MWL Print Group LTD
Unit 10-13, Pontyfelin Industrial Estate
New Inn, Pontypool NP4 ODQ

Designed by
The Info Group
The Village Studio
Heol-Y-Coed, Rhiwbina
Cardiff CF14 6HP

Cover designed by The Info Group
Photograph by John Vince Williams

Canmlwyddiant Clwb Rygbi Yr Aman

*To all men who have loved this Club
And all the Women who have let them*

THE CENTENARY HISTORY OF AMMAN UNITED RUGBY FOOTBALL CLUB 1903 - 2003

Edited by
Howard Gabe Davies

"Life's happiness and rarest joys
Are not in wealth or fame
But in the friendships that we make
And the way we play the game."

George Boots
(Newport and Wales)

DEDICATION

To Past and Present Amman United Players
And Enthusiasts of Rugby Football

*Height, weight, proportion, strength and speed are all good things
For a rugby player to poses, but I have known tall men who were
reeds in the wind, heavy men who were soft as dough, strong men who
were clumsy bunglers, and perfectly proportioned men with the speed
of the antelope who had no real football qualities –*

*The rarest quality in rugby football is the quality of mind: The
power to see, to understand and to do. How often we see hesitancy on
part of a player. He is not master of himself because he is not
master of his mind. It is the mind which controls hands and feet and the whole body.
It is as the fruit of thought that players do the right thing at the right moment.*

Dromio
South Wales Argus
15.10.1932

INTRODUCTION

To relate a hundred years of history is never a simple task; to attempt to do for a rugby club in a venture of this kind has been a mammoth task. It has been impossible to check on the authenticity of all the information included, and we should also apologize in advance for anybody whose part in the history has not been properly recognized. For as time passes memories are less vivid, truth becomes harder to unearth and as in the autumn, some colour inevitably fades. In the early days in the industrial small villages of Cwmamman with their mines and tin works, many of the rugby players faced death every day in the coal mines. Hunger and deprivation followed in the 1920s and 1930s for themselves and their families. The mines have long gone; we have gone from colliers to college boys but good players continue to appear and many of them at the end of their career stay on to help in the administration of the game which gave them so much.

To function efficiently a rugby club needs many people behind the scenes, from the people who look after the kit, and the committee men to the ladies who provide the food. They are all part of the team and without them Rugby would be the poorer. Today it is becoming increasingly difficult to get old players and individuals in the community to hold office as treasurer or secretary in the club and it is equally difficult to find ladies in the supporters club and hard working committee men.

The centenary book team are made up of such old players, it seemed the best way to show our gratitude to this club for the enjoyment we have experienced both on and off the field and I would have to say personally that they were "The Best years of my Life," especially with the friendships that were forged on the field and that have been consolidated as I have grown older.

We are delighted to have participated in the publication of the book and I as editor must thank the centenary book committee team of Alan Thomas, Lyn Roberts, John Vince Williams, Hywel Roberts and Martin Luther Jones for the enormous task of compiling the history in the short period of nine months. I would also like to record my admiration and thanks to Eurof Walters who has such an amazing memory on the history of Amman United and has helped me and the other members of the team in their pursuits. Also to David Jones for copying over 300 photographs to such a high quality, some of which are 100 years old. Finally, to our proof readers Gwyneth Davies, Gwyn Davies and especially to Linden Evans for their hard work.

The club's search for the oldest living player brought us to Rees Price (Cardiff) at 86 years old. This was amended to Eddie Ward (Brynamman) at 89 years old and finally the honour went to Tom Bowen (Gorseinon) at 90 years of age.

Our oldest supporter, Mrs Doreen Rees who lives in Garnant, is 83 years of age and is still regularly seen at home games.

As we celebrate our centenary year we hope that our contribution of the

centenary book, with contributions by many people who have had close associations with the club, will be enjoyed by players and supporters both past and present. It will probably create as many arguments as it will solve. I shall leave it to others to try and solve them.
Good luck to the Amman United RFC in its next hundred years.

Howard Gabe Davies - Editor

FOREWORD

I am honoured to have the privilege of writing this foreword. This book takes you on a fascinating journey from the humble beginnings in the long room of the Amman Hotel in 1903 through two World Wars, the depression years and the loss of outstanding players to rugby league, the post-war boom through to the introduction of professionalism into rugby union.

As one would expect, it has been a rollercoaster ride both on and off the field. From the highs of winning championships and cups, of playing Llanelli, Swansea and Newport to the lows of struggling to find fifteen players to play on a Saturday. There are accounts of splendid victories on the rugby field, tales (albeit censured!!) of tours to Southend, Nottingham, Manchester and even Germany. You can read articles on famous players who donned the scarlet jersey of the Amman and then went on to gain fame (and fortune?) on foreign fields. There are fascinating articles on famous rugby league players and on the exceptional contribution that certain families in the area have made to the club.

As well as the history of the first XV, there is, quite rightly, a detailed account of the history of the Amman Quins, and the central role played by a club's second XV. Again, the many successes of the Quins make interesting reading, and confirm the significant impact that a successful second team has had on Amman United.

The Junior and Youth teams are not forgotten, and there are articles on the development of rugby for the young people in the area.

When one reads this fascinating history, it is interesting to ponder on the dedication and enthusiasm of those involved in the first hundred years. Officials who have given freely of so much of their time for the benefit of the Club, together with the invaluable contribution of various ladies' committees. The Amman has also enjoyed wonderful support, and it is interesting to read accounts of large crowds attending matches throughout the history of the Club.

The contribution of Amman United to rugby football is well known, and I am sure this book will provide pleasure and informative reading with interesting facts, features as well as a historical review with statistical details. There is a wealth of facts and figures to delight not only followers of Amman United but rugby people everywhere and the whole of the community of the Amman Valley.

A Centenary year is not just a time to reflect on the glories of the past but also to prepare, with eagerness, for the future. Good luck to Amman United for the next hundred years, may the Club continue to flourish and provide opportunities for the young people of the area.

I would like to thank the people who have worked tirelessly, fact-finding, collecting and collating information for the book, in particular we owe a huge

debt of gratitude to the Editor for his splendid work.
Pob lwc am y dyfodol a chofiwch - "Yr Aman yw y gore".

Owen Jones
20.08.03.

CLUB PRESIDENT
Trevor Evans

Looking back can help you see forward.

As recently appointed Club President of the Amman United Rugby Football Club, I was surprised to be informed that there have only been four Presidents since the club's formation in 1903 with DT Jones 1903-11, Lord Dynevor 1911-71, Marcus Roberts 1971-88 and Tommy D Williams 1988-2002.

The honour is an even greater privilege as we enter into our centenary year.

The lack of resources rears its head at regular intervals throughout the history of many clubs, including the Amman. Financial resources, the resources of facilities, organisers and obviously players are the resources essential for the formation and continuation of any club.

Probably the first major contributor to the facilities of the club was Lord Dynevor, who generously provided a level area of ground, a valuable commodity at any time of the century, and this has ensured there would always be a venue for the Amman United.

If another piece of land becomes available, that could be the catalyst to initiate the provision of an all-weather area, an essential facility of the 21st century for the sports people of Cwmamman and surrounding areas.

The financial ledgers show times of adversity but again the generosity of the members, and usually a bank manager, has ensured the Amman was still there for the next season.

This adversity pales into insignificance when one considers the Depression years of the 1930s when unemployment was catastrophic in the South Wales valleys. I cannot begin to imagine the hardships endured by the families of the Amman Valley but again the records confirm the club continued and hopefully contributed to the resilience and support of the community spirit of the time. And, moving on today, we have the young people experiencing different pressures, the worst obviously being drug-related. I cannot underestimate the importance of the Junior section, which usually has about 5 age groups. This is the first step to the future of the Amman United and the Amman Valley. The juniors have the undaunted support and "corrective" hand of loyal organisers and parents plus a ready supply of hot dogs!

However, the committee for the senior side has, in my opinion, to consider restraint in our involvement with the professionalism of rugby players due to our financial limitations; further progress in the improvement to the clubhouse and ground facilities is essential to ensure a growth in the number of members and players.

I have dwelled perhaps on the difficulties endured in the past because the following pages contain numerous successes of the teams over the years. The achievements of individual players at representative level, characters of different eras and numerous anecdotes remind us that there is as much enjoyment after the game as on the field.

Finally, I wish the players and organisers every success and prosperity in this centenary year and for the long-term future of the Amman United.

Pob lwc am y dyfodol.

CHAIRMAN'S NOTE

To be Chairman of the Amman United Rugby Club is a great honour and a position that I will never forget.

I feel especially honoured to be Chairman in its Centenary Year. With the enthusiasm of the players, the help of the committee and officials, the goodwill of supporters and the people of Cwmamman in general, I look forward to a very successful year for the Amman United.

The history of this club speaks for itself and the contents of the centenary book will verify this fact. In the late fifties, as a youth player, representing the club was a thrill, but when progressing to the senior side in the early sixties and wearing that scarlet jersey, it was as if you were representing your country. Amman United was everything to us!

At this time, the club was based at the Half Moon. Selection was made on Thursdays and the teams for Saturday's games would be displayed on the notice board outside the entrance door of the Half Moon. If for some reason your name did not appear on the 1st XV sheet and you were selected for the Quins XV there would be no moans and groans; you just got on with it and battled for your position back in the 1st XV.

Owing to work commitments, I left the valley in 1965 and returned in 1981 when again I became involved with the club as a committee member - what an eye opener! I did not realise how much work was involved on the administrative side of a rugby club but through the highs and lows, I have enjoyed the challenges.

I wish to thank everyone for their support, patience and tolerance over the years, my thanks go to all who have helped and supported the Rugby Club in any way during its long history.

To close, I would personally like to thank all contributors who have worked so hard in compiling this centenary book and I'm sure it will be interesting reading.

Roll Along Amman United, Roll Along.

Diolch yn fawr,
Edgar Morris

YR AMAN YN FY NGHALON
Gan Darrel Campbell – Is Gadeirydd

Mae'r Aman wedi bod yn rhan bwysig o'm bywyd ers blynyddoedd. Dechreuodd fy niddordeb pan oeddwn yn ddisgybl yn Ysgol Gynradd Garnant, ac yn cael fy hyfforddi i chwarae rygbi gan Alan Thomas a Peter Williams, athrawon yr Ysgol. Roedd Alan Thomas yn hyfforddwr i dîm Yr Aman ar yr un pryd, dechrau da!

Pan yn grwtyn ifanc, dechreuais wylio'r Aman yn chwarae pob dydd Sadwrn gyda fy nhad a'm brawd. Roedd chwaraewyr Yr Aman, y pryd hynny, yn gewri i mi ac roedd eu steil o chwarae yn denu nifer fawr o wylwyr i weld pob gêm. Roedd nifer o'r chwaraewyr yn enwog drwy rygbi Gorllewin Cymru – chwaraewyr fel Dennis Davies, Hugh Harries, John 'Bach Manora', Cen 'Glynmoch', Hywel Evans, Owen Jones, Gordon 'Butch', Jeff Thomas, Ryan Bartlett, Martin Jones, Peter Griffiths, Adrian Jones, Malcolm Davies, Colin 'Talley' Davies, Ian Wagstaff a nifer o chwaraewyr eraill.

Dechreuais chwarae i dîm cynta'r Aman yn syth ar ôl gadael ysgol yn ddeunaw mlwydd oed ym mis Medi 1979. Datblygodd y tîm dros y blynyddoedd ac roeddwn yn ffodus i chwarae mewn cyfnod eithaf llwyddiannus. Ond i mi, y pleser mwyaf, oedd chwarae rygbi gyda fy ffrindiau i dîm y pentref – doedd dim yn cyffroi'r galon mwy na chwarae yn erbyn yr hen elynion fel Brynaman, Llandybie neu Rhydaman. Rhaid diolch i'r clwb am roi cyfle i mi gael chwarae safon uchel o rygbi yn erbyn timoedd fel Caerdydd a Chasnewydd dwy waith – ac yn siomedig i golli'r ail gêm o 6 – 8 pwynt. Roedd yn anrhydedd mawr i fod yn Gapten ar y tîm dair gwaith.

Yn ystod un o'r blynyddoedd 1992-1993, aeth y tîm drwy'r tymor heb golli gêm, ac yn ennill y West Wales Bowl – y tro cyntaf ers 1972 pan oedd Hywel Evans yn gapten.

Oni bai am Yr Aman, fe fyddai nifer o chwaraewyr lleol ddim wedi cael cyfle i ddangos ei doniau, Trefor Evans, ac yn ddiweddar Shane Williams yn ddau sydd wedi cael cyfle i chwarae ar y llwyfan rhyngwladol.

Gan bod y Clwb wedi rhoi gymaint o foddhad i mi dros y blynyddoedd, yr wyf yn gobeithio'n fawr y bydd y Clwb yn parhau i roi cyfleoedd i fechgyn ifanc yr ardal am ganrif a mwy eto.

ACKNOWLEDGMENTS

This book is not a definitive history of Amman United Rugby Football Club, the loss of records over the years have made that task impossible.

It is however a sincere attempt to place on record the contribution Amman United have made to Welsh Rugby over the century.

The preparation for the publication of this book would however have been a much harder task without the assistance of a great many individuals and organisations.

If we have inadvertently omitted to name any individual or organisation we express our sincere apologies. It is not deliberate and must be attributed to collective memory loss.

In a task of this magnitude there will be errors and omissions and again we ask that the reader accept our apologies.

All photographs included in the publication have been borrowed from private and public sources and we are confident that no copyright has been infringed.

WELSH RUGBY UNION
Minutes of Meetings of the Welsh Rugby Union General Committee
Welsh Rugby Union Schools Handbook
Welsh Rugby Union Youth Handbook
Welsh Rugby Union Handbook

THE REFERENCE LIBRARIES:
Ammanford, Cardiff, Carmarthen, Llanelli, Neath, Swansea, The Welsh Rugby Union and National Library of Wales, Aberystwyth

NEWSPAPERS:
The Western Mail - The South Wales Daily Post - The South Wales Evening Post
The Carmarthen Journal - The Amman Valley Chronicle
The South Wales Guardian - Y Llais Lafur (South Wales Voice) – Llanelli Star – Glo Man

BOOKS:
David Evans/Huw Walters – The Amman Valley Long Ago
Brian Lewis – Photographic Portrait of the Amman Valley
Harry Slocombe – Amman United Rugby Football Club Fiftieth Anniversary Book 1903-1953
David Jarman – The Life and Times of Swansea RFC
Gareth Hughes – The Scarlets, Phil Melling – Man of Amman
Stephen Wild – The Lions of Swinton, Robert Gate – Gone North
Graham Morris – Wigan RLFC
John M Jenkins, Duncan Pierce, Timothy Auty – Who's Who of Welsh International Rugby Players
Guardian Newspapers

CONTRIBUTORS
Gwilym Ward - Terry Ward - Bobby Hunt - Nevin Anthony - Hywel Williams - Norman Bevan - Tom Bowen – Winston James –Iwan Gabe Davies - Owen Jones - Howell Cousins - Eric Jones (Twyn) - Jeff Thomas - John Gwyn Jones - Rhys Price - Vince Jones – Hubert Jones - Griff Evans - Mike Price – Ian Penman - Peter Williams – John Llewellyn – Malvern Evans – Peter Owen (WRU) – Hywel Evans – Trevor Evans – Patrick Davies – Martin Luther Jones – Clive Williams – Alban Morgan – Ogwyn Evans – Mrs Pugh – Janet Wynne Evans – Dewi Davies – Wyn Lloyd – Arwyn Williams – Gelli Plant

PHOTOGRAPHS
David Jones - Dairy Crest - Arvan Williams - Ryan Peregrine - Danny Richards - David Power - Mark James - John Vince Williams – Arwel Davies – Grogg Shop

PROOF READERS
Gwyn Davies – Gwyneth Davies(Welsh) – Linden Evans

In conclusion we Howard Gabe Davies, Eurof Walters, Alan Thomas, Lyn Roberts, John Vince Williams, Hywel Roberts and Martin Luther Jones would categorically place on record that despite the hard work it has been a pleasure and an experience, as well as a duty, to record and write this Centenary History.

CONTENTS

1	Dedication	4
2	Introduction	5
3	Foreword	7
4	Notes: President - Chairman - Darrel Campbell	9
5	Acknowledgements	14
6	Contents	15
7	Club Officials and Committee 2003	16
8	The Early Years 1903 - 1914	17
9	Between the Wars 1918 - 1939	27
10	The Oldest Amman Player - Tom Bowen	45
11	Experiences of Rees Price	47
12	From Amman Junior to Welsh International	49
13	The Early Post War Years 1945 - 1950	53
14	The 1950s	61
15	The 1960s	66
16	Welsh National 7s Final - Sevens Glory for the Amman	76
17	Sine Die	85
18	Profiles: Bobby Hunt - Dennis Davies - Martin Luther Jones	89
19	Amman United 1971 - 2003	101
20	Profiles: Graham George - Darrel Campbell	131
21	Amman Harlequins 1947 - 2003	135
22	History of the Amman United Youth 1949 - 2003	145
23	Amman United Juniors 1971 - 2003	159
24	Cwmamman Schools 1975 - 2003	175
25	The Rugby League Connection	179
26	Rugby Family Connections - Bevan - Rees - Ward	191
27	Tours: Southend 1967 and Germany in Fallingbostel 1971	203
28	Recollections: Hywel Evans - Eurof Walters - Ian penman Jeff Thomas - John Gwyn Jones	209
29	History of the Amman United Badge	227
30	A Tribute to the Amman United	228
31	Profiles: Trevor Evans - Shane Williams - David Jones	231
32	Amman United's Welsh Internationals	249
33	Honours List	254
34	Amman United President and Club officials	263
35	Vernon Pugh Q.C. Chairman of the International Rugby Board	265
36	Congratulations	269
37	Caneuon yr Aman	275
38	Montage of Amman Players and Administrators	277

AMMAN UNITED R.F.C. 1903 – 2003

Affiliated to: Welsh Rugby Union
Carmarthen County Rugby Union
West Wales Rugby Union
Llanelli and District Rugby Union
Welsh Youth East Carmarthenshire Youth Rugby Union

CLUB OFFICIALS 2003 – 2004

President	**Chairman**	**Vice-Chairman**
Trevor Evans	Edgar Morris	Darrel Campbell
Secretary	**Treasurer**	**Quins Secretary**
Martin Luther Jones	Rowland John	Ken Davies
Youth Secretary	**Junior Secretary**	**Social Secretary**
John V Williams	Gerwyn John	Nigel Pawson

Committee
Darrell Campbell Edgar Morris Mal Davies
Nigel Pawson Eric Jones

Club Captain
Alun Rees

Coaches
Phil John and Pat Nolan

Team Manager
Lyn Roberts

Life Members
Nevin Anthony Hywel Williams Eurof Walters
Clive Brooks Martin Luther Jones Trevor Evans
Shane Williams

Trustees
Peter Williams Eurof Walters Martin Luther Jones

Patrons
Dr. F Powell Dr. A Jones Dr. D Rowlands

THE EARLY YEARS
By Eurof Walters

1903 to 1919

The location of a community, its geographical and geological environs, must of necessity be instrumental in moulding and developing the character of its inhabitants.

Cwmamman, consisting of Glanamman and Garnant on the valley floor, Penybont, Twyn and Tircoed on the side of the Black Mountains, located at the north-western boundary of the South Wales Coalfield and crossed by the drovers' North to South route, bounded on the North by the ominously named Black Mountains, is a case in point.

Since the valley became the centre of anthracite coal production and indeed the tin plate industry in the mid 1880s, its inhabitants have proved to be durable hard-working and uncompromising in the face of adversity.

Allied to these characteristics have always been a sense of adventure, and a willingness to attempt anything.

Put all these virtues together and you have the makings of a rugby team. The big fly in the ointment, however, was and still is parochialism and inter-village rivalry. These were present in no small way in Cwmamman prior to 1903 and might still be so today but for the intervention of Rees Dukes, the landlord of the Amman Hotel, who called a meeting in the tavern's long room in order to bring the two villages – Garnant and Glanamman - together to form a rugby team representative of Cwmamman to play teams as far away as Llanelli, Neath, Llandovery and Swansea.

The meeting duly agreed to form a committee – 10 from each village with Rees Dukes, a native of Clydach, as Chairman. The number of committeemen has continued to be part of the constitution of the club until the present time. Mr David Thomas was the first Secretary with Mr Willie Camber Thomas taking the post of Treasurer. Headquarters of the new club was to be the Amman Hotel and games were to be played on the Brynlloi Field where Bryn Seion Chapel now stands.

The Club would be named AMMAN UNITED RUGBY FOOTBALL CLUB and an advert was duly placed in the South Wales Daily Post requesting fixtures for the coming season.

All members, committeemen, and players would contribute five shillings per season to allay the cost of jerseys and all players were to supply their own boots, shorts and stockings.

The colour SCARLET was chosen for the jersey and with the exceptions of 1912 – 1914, 1924 – 1925 and 1946 – 1947 has always been the Amman colour.

These exceptions were when the colours cherry and white were used for these three years. The jerseys used in 1946-47 were supplied by Ted Ward and were a set of Wigan RLFC jerseys. Expulsion from the WRU would surely have followed had this been discovered.

In order that the complete harmony apparent in the initial meeting be apparent to all the residents of the two villages, it was unanimously decided that a "SMOKER" be held in the Raven Hotel, which proved to be resounding success.

All players were to be responsible for their own laundry and would also contribute to travelling costs until such time as the club's finances were on a firm footing.

Billie Jones became the club's first captain and in the inaugural season games were played against Ammanford, Pontardawe, Pontardulais, Llangennech, Llandybie, Llandeilo, Felinfoel, G.C.G United, Neath Excel and Half Way.

A total of 23 games were played during this season with fifteen being won, two drawn and 6 lost.

Parochialism, however, was still rife within the valley with two games cancelled due to quarrels within the club.

The players who represented the Club in that inaugural season were:

Full back: Willie Jenkins
Left Wing: Evan Basset
Left Centre: Arthur Jones
Right Centre: Phillip Rees
Right Wing: Emrys Griffiths
Outside-Half: David John Rees
Inside-Half: Tommy Smith
Forwards: Evan Bevan, Jim John, William Arthur Rees, Evan Jones,
John Thomas, Billie Jones (Capt.), John Llewellyn, Jack Day, William Pike

Amman United RFC 1903-04 the First Amman Team.

Far Left: Billy Jones, Amman United RFC's First Captain and First Life member.

Left: David Thomas. Amman United RFC's First Secretary.

Below left: Season Ticket 1904 - 05

Below right: Season Ticket 1904 - 05 Reverse side

BILLY JONES
Amman's First Captain

LIST OF FIXTURES.

Date.	Opponents.	Where Played.	For	Agst.	Scores.
1904					
Sept. 3	Pontardawe	Home			
,, 10					
,, 17	Pantyffynnon	Home			
,, 24	Half-way	Away			
Oct. 1	Llangennech	Away			
,, 8	Pontardawe	Away			
,, 15	Pontardulais	Home			
,, 22	Harbour Lights	Home			
,, 29	Pontardulais	Away			
Nov. 5	Felinfoel	Away			
,, 12	Half-way	Home			
,, 19	Pontardulais	Home			
,, 26	Llangennech	Home			
Dec. 3	G.C.G. United	Away			
,, 10	G.C.G. United	Home			
,, 17	Pontardulais	Away			
,, 24	Llandebie	Home			
,, 27	Carmarthen	Away			
,, 31	Gowerton	Home			
1905					
Jan. 7	Felinfoel	Home			
,, 14	Pantyffynnon	Away			
,, 21	Half-way	Away			
,, 28					
Feb. 4	Neath Excels	Home			
,, 11	Ammanford	Home			
,, 18	Neath Excels	Away			
,, 25	Llandebie	Away			
Mar. 4	Carmarthen	Home			
,, 11	Wales v. Ireland	Swansea			
,, 18	Half-way	Home			
,, 25	Llandilo	Away			
April 1	Llandilo	Home			
,, 8	Bettws	Away			
,, 15	Ammanford	Away			
,, 22	Bettws	Home			

- AMMAN UNITED -
Football Club
SEASON 1904-05

President - Mr. D. T. JONES, D.C.

Chairman of Committee

Mr. E. Ceidrim Rees

Vice-Chairman: Mr. W. Thomas

Captain: Mr. D.J. Rees

Vice-Captain: Mr. Evan Bassett

Hon. Treasurer: Mr. Willie Thomas

Hon. Sec: Mr. D. Thomas

Member's Name

E. Ceidrim Rees

Vaughan, Ammanford

Interestingly, Billie Jones's career was cut short by injury but he gave many years' service to the club as a committeeman and became the club's first Life Member. Evan Basset and Willie Jenkins both served the club as treasurer and Evan Bevan became a Life Member after becoming Captain and then committeeman, eventually serving the Club faithfully for 40 years.

His duty done, Mr Rees Dukes handed over the chairmanship to

Amman United season 1908 - 09

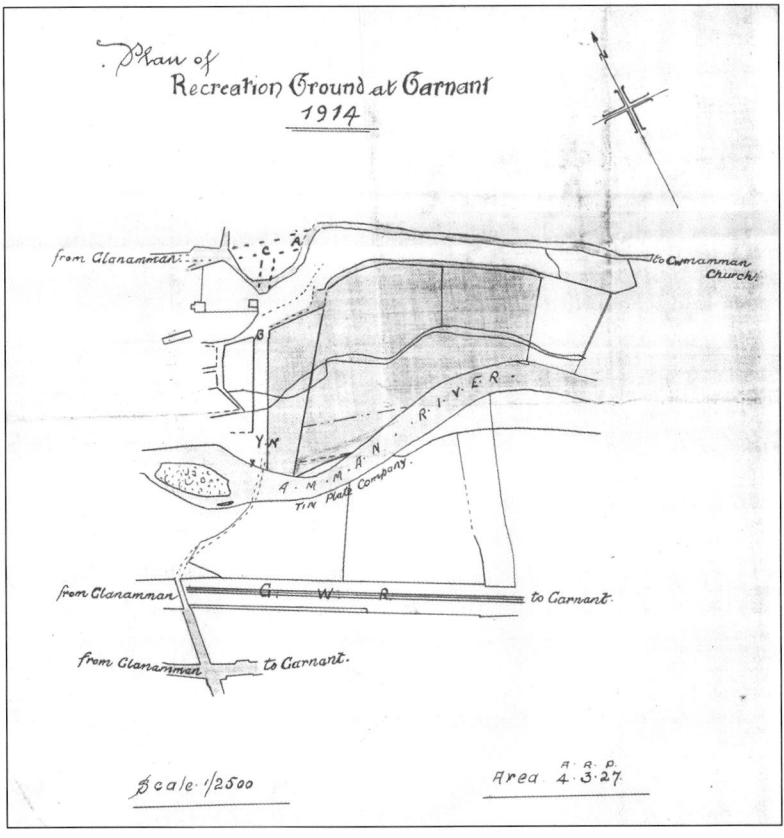

Plan of Cwmamman Park 1914

Mr E Ceidrim Rees and D.J. Rees took over the captaincy 1904 – 1905 with a full list of fixtures, 29 in all. The newly-formed side was beginning to make a reputation for themselves as a team with hard, uncompromising forwards and clever backs.

The team came to the notice of Llanelli R.F.C., primarily due to playing Felinfoel, Llangennech, Harbour Lights, Half Way and Pontardulais – all in the Llanelli area.

Twenty-one games were won and nine lost with Captain D.J. Rees being in outstanding form throughout the season, scoring in all games bar three.

His form interested Llanelli and he joined them the following season and during that season scored 12 tries for Llanelli; he was chosen as a Welsh reserve and at the end of the season joined Aberdare as a professional for the very substantial signing-on fee of £50.

Emrys Griffiths, 'the flying wing', became the club's third captain and was followed by Phillip J Rees.

These were not very successful seasons with more games being lost than won.

Committee members, however, were very busy during this time and were making huge efforts to become members of the Llanelli and District Rugby Union. As members of the league, Amman quickly became known as a formidable force and were responsible for taking Mynydd Bach's three-year-old ground record in 1907, causing the team and supporters to be chased from the ground.

Season 1909 – 1910 was one to remember, when the team was unbeaten and were winners of the Llanelli and District League Championship and the League Cup. They beat New Dock Stars in the Cup Final and Llangennech in the League Championship Final. The captain of this victorious team was Evan Bevan, who had been a member of the first team in 1903 and was later destined to give over 40 years' service to the club as committeeman and treasurer. Amman were to wait until 1950-51 season to repeat the feat of being unbeaten.

This was also the season when the club moved headquarters to the 'CUSTOM BUILT' premises erected at the rear of the HALF MOON HOTEL and started playing on Cwmamman Park, with the first game against Llangennech and first try being scored by Dan James (Prince).

Lord Dynevor presented Cwmamman Park to the people of Cwmamman for an annual rent of £10, of which the Amman was responsible for the payment of £6 p.a.

The Parks Committee of the time had incurred substantial debts and the promise by the club to clear this debt was instrumental in the Amman being given preference over the Garnant Association Football Club to use the ground for Rugby Football.

The huge success enjoyed by the club during their membership of the Llanelli and District League was instrumental in the increase in the formation

Copy of the original lease of Cwmamman Park 1909

of other rugby teams in the valley.

Teams such as Garnant Rangers, Garnant Rovers and Amman Rovers were the foremost of these; all three acted as feeder teams for Amman United but were responsible for attracting huge crowds and indeed also had a fife and drum band present when playing at home.

Gate receipts of £5 were recorded during these local derbies – a huge crowd when admission was 3 old pence per person.

Roller-skating and foot racing were two popular pastimes in the valley during this period and Amman produced champions in both events. Oswald Rees, a future Amman wing, came second in the 'Professional' Powderhall Sprint Championship in Scotland and Wat Gwilym Williams, another flying winger, was West Wales Roller Skating Champion.

Cricket was also popular throughout the valley and many Amman players were fine cricketers.

Garnant Cricket Club 1911

Back Row: A Cole, W Rees, J Bevan, WJ Grey, D Jones, H Fuller, F Barry, WH Morgan, WA Jones, J Rees.
Middle Row: D Thomas, E Griffiths, T Bevan, J Morgan, GH Davies, WA Hay, JS Evans, W Jenkins, WJ Williams, E Thomas.
Front Row: Master C Bevan, JH Hughes, W Thomas, DJ Bevan.
This team contains a WRU Referee, WRU Selector, 4 Amman Captains and 4 Amman United players.

Amman's success on the playing field was also attracting players from other villages, notably Brynamman, with such illustrious future Amman players as Handel Isaac, Joe Evans, Oliver Roberts, Wat Gwilym and Will Thomas Corner House. There is no doubt that the club owes a debt of gratitude to Brynamman for the service given by these fine players. Although, it is interesting to note that according to Bertie Davies – Amman's most infamous chairman of later years - 'that the only two good things that ever came out of Brynamman was my mother and the road'.

In season 1910 – 1911, Dick 'Bach' Thomas was elected as captain and became the second Amman player to achieve national recognition, when he was selected as a reserve inside-half for Wales v Scotland during that season.

This was the season that Amman became members of the Welsh Rugby Union on their first application and gained the right to play against stronger opposition. Their six-year reign in the Llanelli and District League had resulted in 3 League Championship titles and 2-Cup Winner trophies.

Joe Rees, at 16 years of age, became the youngest player to represent the club and commenced the association of the Plough family with Amman United, which lasted 50 years.

The Season is to be further remembered as the one when the Amman Anthem was first performed. It happened in the Dimpath Hotel Headquarters of

Amman Rovers 1912 - 13

Furnace RFC after the Amman took their ground record by 9pts to 3pts. "Yr Amman yw y Gorau" has been sung by all Amman players to the present day.

Season 1912 – 1913, with Evan Bevan again as captain, was the start of a short golden era, unfortunately disrupted by the First World War.

The team contained such magnificent players as Joe Rees, Rees Rees, Garfield Phillips (the youngest ever Amman player at 14 years and 8 months), Will Thomas (Maesteg), Gilbert Davies (later Major), Dick (Bach) Thomas, Alun and Ellis Williams (Danybryn), Willie Jenkins and Wat Gwilym Williams. Their record for the season speaks for itself. Played 28 games, won 26, and lost 2.

The following season was one of the best in Amman's history to date. 1913 – 1914 was the inaugural season of the Welsh Hospitals Cup, open to both first and second class teams. Having beaten Skewen, Resolven, and Ystalyfera on the way, they met Aberavon in the semi-final on Cwmamman Park. A capacity crowd contributed £166-10 shillings to the Amman coffers and saw the home team narrowly lose by 3 points to nil. Present watching the game was WRU Secretary Mr Walter Rees and members of the General Committee.

Season Ticket 1912 - 13

This season also saw the start of a long association between the cub and the proprietors and management of various collieries. Mr W.J. Hay was club secretary and manager's clerk at Gellyceidrim Colliery.

In order that the playing area on the park be deemed to be up to a good standard after five weeks of dry weather, he dispatched a pump and two men for the day to pump water from the river Amman, resulting in a magnificent playing area that impressed the WRU hierarchy watching the semi final.

The season can indeed be counted as one of the best with 26 victories out of 32 played.

Outbreak of war in September 1914 brought an end to rugby for 4 years and

25

many players volunteered their services and served in France.

The committee was busy during this period diverting the river from its old course to its present position, giving the park much needed extra width.

Despite hostilities, plenty of unofficial rugby was played during these years. Teams such as the All-Whites, Raven Rovers, Grenig Rovers and Prospect Stars flourished, and by the end of hostilities produced such players as Evan Phillips, Billo Rees, Joseph Hay, Frank Griffiths, Dan and Dai Evans, Gomer Griffiths, D.M. Davies, Evan Jones, and Bob Davies, who were to give sterling service to the club for many years.

Amman United RFC 1913 - 14
Semi-Final Welsh Hospitals Cup Amman United 0 v Aberavon 3

Amman United, 1913–1914. Semifinal Welsh Hospitals Cup:

Back Row: GH Davies, R Owen, MC Williams, WD LLewellyn, E Bevan, D Jones, E Rees, W Ward, WH Thomas.
Middle Row: G Phillips, R Rees, DB Rees (Capt) J Rees, E Williams, A Williams, D Evans.
Front Row: Dick (Bach) Thomas, Will Thomas, A Price Interestingly there are three Rees's (Plough) in the photograph with the young Billo Rees seated next to A Price.

BETWEEN THE WARS
By Eurof Walters

1919-1939

The period between the wars was bereft of organised rugby but there was no let up in playing the game, and the period saw the emergence of so-called junior sides, which filled in the gap and indeed bred quality players who would be Amman regulars for many years.

Many Amman players remained at home due to being employed in reserved occupations, but among the players who fought in France and elsewhere were Major Gilbert Davies, Joe Rees, John Thomas, Dick Bach Thomas, Ellis Williams, WD Llewellyn, T.J. Thomas, Evan Evans, Arthur Price, Evan Phillips, Tom Evans, W.R. Thomas, Luther Evans, J.H. Griffiths, Frank Griffiths, Bob Morris, Evan Jones and Gomer Griffiths.

All were lucky to return unharmed but Evan Evans died at home from wounds received in the Great War.

At the re-union parade on the 20th September 1919, all discharged volunteers from Cwmamman attended and it is recorded that 400 men from villages did volunteer for service, of whom 54 paid the supreme sacrifice.

There was one Military Cross, five Military Medals, and one Distinguished Service Cross Medal, and one Cross of Saint Stanislau awarded during this period to men of Cwmamman.

This period also saw the emergence of Raven Rovers, The All-Whites, Grenig Rovers and Prospect Stars as teams in their own right, and all in turn supplied some magnificent players to Amman United.

Resumption of games by the club started in September 1919 with Llangennech being the first visitors to Cwmamman Park. Will Thomas (Maesteg) was the first captain after the war and a new management team was also in office, with three officials from Gellyceidrim Colliery in charge - W Hay as secretary, J Enoch James as chairman and TW Gunning as a committeeman. These three ensured that jobs were available for Amman players and also had a team representing the colliery entered in the Amalgamated Anthracite Collieries Shield Competition, which they duly won in 1927-28-29 seasons and were cup winners in 1924-25 season.

Joe Rees, having been capped for Wales in a War International, was still appearing for the club and playing on permit for Swansea.

His brothers Billo, Rees and Nathan were also making their mark and were all being contacted by both Swansea and Llanelli to sign for them. The committee finally snapped and put a moratorium on transfers and permits unless submitted to committee by Monday evening.

An interesting feature of rugby reporting in these days was that, at the start of every season, the reporter at the time, "Old Sport", would apologise in

Gellyceidrim Colliery Team Season 1924 - 25

Back Row: E Jones, G Morris, WH Williams, DG Edwards.
Second Row: C Williams, J Owen, EJ Powell, H Joshua, E Jones, R Evans, EJ Davies, DR Roberts, L James.
Front Row: D Jones, CJ Davies (Manager) D Evans, D Davies, DW Evans, E Griffiths (Capt), J Hay, S Griffiths, WA Hay. Capt. Edwards.

Wales v England 1919

Joe Rees left centre row

28

advance for any criticism printed of individual players during the season. One report of a game between Amman and Pontardawe contains a reference to the "unpleasant feature of the amount of talking amongst the visitors"; presumably they should have saved their breath to play as they lost the game. A further note of interest was that Amman at this time played a few games against a team named the Carmarthen Mental Hospital. I wonder whether the team contained any patients?

Players who had started their careers with the Junior sides during the war were now maturing into Amman regulars and Evan Phillips (who started his career as a wing three -quarter), Tom Evans, Garfield Phillips, the Style brothers, Stan Jeremiah, D Benjamin Rees together with Joe Rees, Gilbert Davies and MC Williams, were making Amman a force to be reckoned with in West Wales.

Amman, under the captaincy of Major Gilbert Davies 1919-20, and Garfield Phillips in 1920-21, had two excellent seasons, in spite of losing Joe Rees to Swansea and the miners and railway strikes of that time causing players to leave the area to look for work.

The reporter, " Old Sport", had arranged a testimonial match to be played on 4th December 1920 with proceeds going to Arthur Jones whose health had failed due to silicosis. The Old Contemptibles played Amman on a Thursday afternoon before a large crowd, which resulted in a gate of £126-5s-6d, which was duly handed over to Arthur Jones.

The team representing the Old Contemptibles was:

Joe Rees

E Basset   HM Fuller   Ellis Williams   D Elias Thomas

W Thomas   Dick Thomas

E Bevan   WD Llewellyn   Evan Rees

DJ Hughes   D Evans

WH Williams   J Protheroe   W Llewellyn

With substitutes – Yes, SUBSTITUTES - WH Williams, Bob Shaw and Evan Rees.

DB Evans, a future Welsh full-back and Jack Elwyn Evans, a future Welsh wing both commenced their career in 1920, and Billy Rees was picked for a Welsh final in Aberavon in December 1920.

March 1921 was a month to remember in Garnant for two reasons.

Firstly, Billo Rees was chosen as Welsh reserve against Ireland. He missed selection by the chairman's casting vote – because he came from a second class team (Amman's moratorium on permits was still operational).

Secondly – "The Star Stores Murder", a still unsolved crime 83 years later.

Prospect Stars were proving themselves to be something special at this period and during the season took long standing ground records from six teams.

Llanelli were now a regular team in the Amman fixture list and in 1920-21 Amman lost 3 points to nil against Llanelli, drew with Swansea and beat Neath 10 points to 3 on their own ground. To round off an excellent season, Amman entertained Tumble when the proceeds were passed to the Cwmamman Distress Fund. It also marked the first appearance in Amman colours for a Prospect Stars scrum-half who was heavily criticised in the press report for his unorthodox play. Who was he – DM Davies of course!

Swansea RFC made a further visit to the park on 14th April and after the game, Joe Rees was presented with a gold hunter watch to mark his selection for Wales.

Joseph Henry Griffiths was chosen as club captain for 1921-22 season. A cousin of the Plough family, he proved a popular choice but the season was not particularly successful with more games lost than won. He was followed in 1922-23 season by Tom Evans, probably one of the best forwards ever produced by the Amman conveyor belt; In April 1922, Tom became the Amateur Boxing Heavyweight Champion of Great Britain. He later joined Neath and was their captain during their invincible years of 1928-29-30; a deliberately broken leg put an end to a promising career.

These were the halcyon days on Cwmamman Park with Resolven, Ammanford, Skewen, Cwmavon, Carmarthen and Llandybie being regular visitors as well as Swansea, Neath and Llanelli becoming regular home and away fixtures in 1921; when they played at Cwmamman Park on 21st April 1921, the game was entered in the Llanelli season ticket as versus Glanamman.

Evan Phillips, who had made a reputation as a wing-three-quarter, joined Llanelli and was converted into wing-forward and was immediately chosen as Welsh reserve after being presented with the "Porter Jersey" – the New Zealand captain's jersey was presented to the finest back row forward they had met on tour.

Interestingly in 1925, when Llanelli appeared on Cwmamman Park, the game was held up for 6 minutes whilst a herd of cows were removed from the playing area. Evan Phillips represented Llanelli on that day. To finish a memorable day the game was abandoned 10 minutes early as all four-match balls had been kicked into the River Amman in flood.

Joe Rees finally transferred to Swansea and his brothers Billo and Rees joined the professional ranks with Rees leaving for Hull in January 1922 and Billo joining Swinton in 1921, and becoming the finest stand-off in league till 1934.

Jack Elwyn Evans joined Broughton Rangers after being capped against Scotland in 1926 at the same time as DM Davies and Garfield Phillips, who had departed Cwmamman to give sterling service to Neath RFC. Evan Phillips, whose career was cut short by injury, joined them both at Broughton. Jack Davies brother of DM Davies had left Amman for Ammanford before going North to Keighley. Interestingly, Billo Rees earned the princely sum of £500 when he joined Swinton, most of which was spent on a new Norton motorcycle which, so the story goes, lasted 14 weeks.

Amman United 1922 - 23

Amman United RFC Second XV 1922 - 23

M Evans, J Evans, C Lloyd, B Davies, L Jones, S Davies, W Goss, T Rees, S Evans, I Lloyd,
D Richards, E Evans, D Williams, P Rees, DM Davies.

Grenig Rovers Season 1922 - 23

Back Row: DR Roberts, E Jones, G Williams, R Evans, WD Davies, D Evans, C Thomas.
Second Row: WD Richards, J Thomas, L James, W Watkins, B Bowen, G Fuller, D Davies.
Front Row: M Jones, G Grice, E Slocome, J Jones.

The loss of such players as these must have had an enormous effect on Amman United, but such was the talent available within the valley that Amman proceeded to show West Wales how rugby should be played.

They showed disdain however for financial stability; it seems that committees never change. In spite of drawing regular gates of £110 on Cwmamman Park with admission at one shilling (5p), the club found themselves being called to task and were obliged to meet their bank manager, and to avoid foreclosure were obliged to give an undertaking to clear the debt at the princely sum of £12 per annum. It was finally cleared in 1945.

This financial crisis meant changes in personnel with Joe Bevan taking over as treasurer and Harry Slocombe as secretary, a post he relinquished to DB Evans who returned to serve on the Amman committee after his international career ended.

Sports of all kinds thrived in Cwmamman in the 1920s with cycling being very popular and the round ball was well represented by the thriving Amman Rangers.

Harry Slocombe eventually became a reporter for all Amman Valley sport under the by-line H.S. Running was still a popular pastime during the summer months and DM Davies freely admitted that he returned to the Amman Valley during the summer months to make pocket money to last until Xmas.

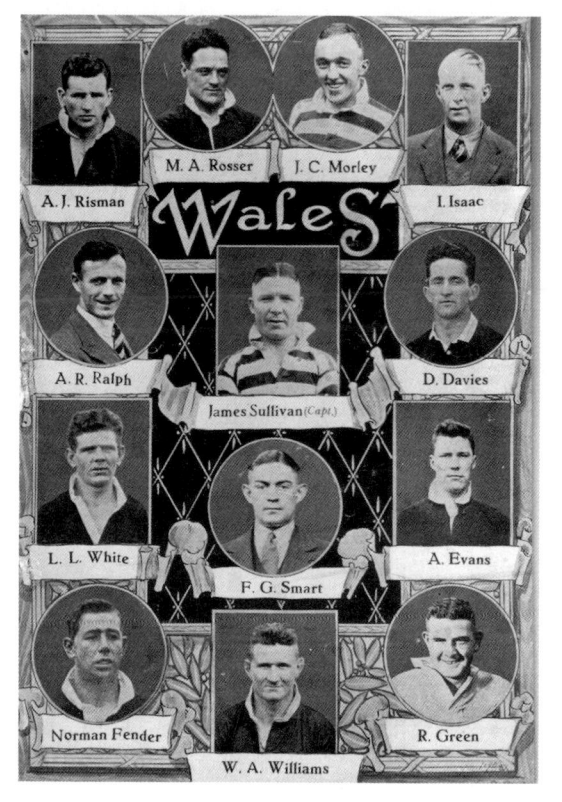

Fixture list and Season ticket 1922 - 23

Wales Rugby League Team
DM Davies in 1932

Amman United 1924 - 25

Amman United RFC 1927 - 28 - 29 *Amman Valley Shield Winners*

Back Row: EB Rees, L Jones, C Davey, G Griffiths, W Watkins, J Evans, B Bowen, EK Jones.
Middle Row: J Quick, W Davies, R Noble, I Williams, H Jones, N Rees, F Bevan.
Front Row: E Jones, D Evans, S Evans, EJ Jones, J Marshall, A Price, B Roberts.

The Junior sides in the Amman Valley were still producing rugby players of note with a great many moving on to represent Amman.

DB Evans took over as full-back for the Amman and later for Swansea and Wales.

Percy Rees filled a gap at half-back and DW Evans was a shining light at centre.

In season 1927-28, DW Evans became the first Amman player to score 100 points in a season when he scored 127 points, a record that stood until 1948.

Amman continued to attract players from other areas as well as nurturing local talent, and Cwmgorse supplied Ben Rees Jones, E Kelly, Claude Davey, Will Davies and EJ James. The first connection with Penybanc was Jim Quick, Ron Noble and Joe Marshall. Local players who gave sterling service during this period were Nathan Rees, Bertie Bowen, Mal Jones, Wally Watkins, Freddie Bevan, Bryn Roberts and Arthur Price.

In July 1927, the Amalgamated Anthracite Collieries Ltd announced that they were prepared to sponsor a trophy named "The Amman Valley Challenge Shield".

The competition proved to be a popular one with gates of £150 being recorded in Ammanford, Llandybie and Amman.

Amman won the trophy in the first two years 1927-28 and 1928-29, and 1927 was also the first season for Claude Davey who had been capped by the Welsh Secondary Schools the previous season and was also the first Welshman to score against the French Schoolboys. He joined the Amman from Curwen Stars as a scrum-half together with Will Davies as outside-half.

The presence of Arthur Rees, Percy Rees and Bryn Roberts ensured that they were unable to hold their places and they were converted to centre and loose-forward respectively. They both moved eventually to Swansea and were capped by Wales, with Claude having the distinction of being captain of Swansea and Wales.

WA Hay, a member of the club committee, became a Welsh Rugby Union Selector in 1922-23, a post which he held with distinction until 1934.

The seasons 1928-29-30 were not particularly successful for the club, with Amman having probably their worst seasons since inception. Other pursuits were being followed; with greyhound racing becoming a major leisure activity in the valley.

On the 24th August 1929, the first mechanical hare greyhound meeting took place in Glanamman. 48 dogs took part in 8 heats with the final race being won by Tell Me Not with Jock second and Penrhiw Lad third.

The clerk of the course was the Neath captain Tom Evans, Jonah Griffiths being secretary and judges being Evan John Evans Glanamman, W Cook Craig Cefn Park and Tom Rees Garnant.

The season 1929-30 was to see the continuation of the Bevan dynasty, with Freddie Bevan elected as captain. He was to be followed into the next decade by Eddie Bevan and Mal Bevan.

35

Welsh Rugby Union Selection Committee 1922 - 23

WE Rees (Sec), J Jarrett, W Rees, E McGregor, DB Jones, D Jones, WW James, WA Hay (Amman United) H Packer, RP Thomas, TD Scholffield, HS Line, JS Jones, JB Williams, AS Barge.

WRU Committee Match Ticket 1929

Shortage of funds within the club was the reason for DB Evans organising a concert in the Workman's Hall during January of that year and it is interesting that a Swansea XV attended after playing on Cwmamman Park. Rowe Harding was the chairman of the evening as reward for the services given by Amman United players to Swansea RFC.

The artists were: Jack Fowler – singer and comedian
DJ Evans - pianist
Stepney Glee Party

Mr Waldron gave a gramophone recital of HMV records.

The undoubted star of the evening was a "youthful young whistler" named Mr Eddie Jones, who happens to be the father of the long serving Amman Secretary Martin Luther Jones.

Edryd Jones, a Swansea policeman and a worthy successor to Joe Rees and DB Evans as Amman's custodian, also followed the same path and joined Swansea RFC as full-back and was ultimately chosen as Welsh Reserve full-back. Strange additions to the Amman fixture list during this period were teams such as Ogmore Vale, Aberamman and Weston- super-Mare. It is interesting that DW Evans ultimately left Amman to join Weston-super- Mare, from where he was awarded a Somerset County Cap before joining Llanelli and going North to Halifax RLFC.

Moving pictures were also being developed and December 1930 saw them introduced in the Workman's Hall and in January 1931 in the Palace.

Interest in the round ball was still strong in the locality and it's a strange phenomenon that even in those days there were reports on 1st Division soccer games appearing in the Amman Valley Chronicle on a weekly basis.

Will Davies, prior to his departure to Swansea, captained the club in season 1930-31 and Jim Quick of Penybanc, the first "foreigner" to captain Amman, in 1931-32.

Eddie Bevan followed Freddie Bevan by being captain in 1932-33 and again the club had a poor season and was heavily criticised in the local press.

The report on the Ammanford v Amman game on 24th February 1933 was particularly damning with regard to the Amman supporters:

"The behaviour of the crowd on Saturday was outrageously disgusting and shameful. Stenoureously they urged on their men to commit acts unpardonable on a football field, acts that were diagonally opposed to the spirit of our great national game".

Players coming to the fore during this period were Cliff Harry, Bryn Edwards, Mal Bevan, Stan Noble, Emrys Evans and Gwilym and Mock Ward.

It was also the year that Cwmamman Silver Band became West Wales Champions and Cwmamman UDC were warned of financial irregularities by the District Auditor.

Severe unemployment was still present in the valley and the Cwmamman Distress Fund was still diligently collecting and distributing funds. To assist this

Claude Davey being presented to the King, Wales v England 1933

worthy cause the Amman Patron, Mr Dudley Folland brought a team of first class players to Cwmamman Park to assist the fund.

Amman United:

                                  C Harry

E Treharne   B Bowen   F Bevan   C Daniel

        Ifor Jones   M Morris

H Davies   L James   G Meredith

          W Thomas   R Davies

J Williams   D Evans   RH Morgan

Dudley Dudley Follands XV:

Allen Tayler (Briton Ferry) Walter Lewis (Swansea) Willie Davies (Swansea)
J Gwilym (Pontardawe) D Folland (Swansea) WJ Trew (Swansea) Cliff Evans (Neath)
Tom Day (Swansea) E Jones (Llanelli) Dai Thomas (Swansea)
T Hollingdale (Swansea) D Parker (Swansea)
Arthur Lemon (Neath) Dai Evans (Neath) D Richards (Swansea)

The officials were B Palmer referee with DB Evans and HM Fuller as touch judges.

Programme Wales v Ireland 1936 (*with Claude Davey as captain*)

MASTERS'
GREAT ANNUAL SPRING TAILORING OFFER
IS NOW PROCEEDING

The Newest Designs in Worsted Suitings **63/-** To Measure

The dominant feature of this remarkable offer is **VALUE AT ITS BEST AND GREATEST** AND IS ONLY MADE POSSIBLE BY HUGE PURCHASES OF THE CLOTH DIRECT FROM MAKERS.

You will save money if you investigate and ORDER NOW.

Every suit cut and tailored throughout in first-class style in our own Workrooms!

MASTERS & CO., LTD.
40 ESTABLISHMENTS.
Headquarters: 28, 29, 30, and 31, St. Mary Street, Cardiff
Also at 28, QUEEN STREET, 292, BUTE STREET, 228, CITY ROAD, — CARDIFF
Phones 1445 and 1446 Cardiff
Branches throughout South Wales and the West of England.

The Welsh Rugby Union.
OFFICIAL PROGRAMME
Walter E. Rees

IRELAND
CARDIFF ARMS PARK, CARDIFF.
MARCH 14th, 1936.
VERSUS
KICK-OFF 3.30 p.m.

WALES

WHY NOT "TRY" BOVRIL?

This Programme is the Copyright of the Union of Junior Leagues and Welsh Schools Rugby Union and Published by them for the Welsh Rugby Union and Printed by Western Mail & Echo Ltd., Cardiff

---

D. J. DAVIES, Wheatsheaf Garages
MERTHYR TYDFIL — Phone 47
South Wales Distributor for ... **DENNIS**
GOODS-CARRYING MODELS — 35-Cwt. to 12 Tons.
PASSENGER CARRYING-MODELS — 20 to 56 Seats.
A DENNIS Doesn't Cost — It Pays!

THE GILBERT MATCH RUGBY BALL
FAMOUS SINCE 1823
(when the Rugby Game originated) AND STILL THE BEST BALL
May be obtained from all Sports Dealers.

Try **MORLEY'S UNDERWEAR** — you'll be converted

AFTER THE MATCH
Come to Tea at
DAVID MORGAN LIMITED CARDIFF

After-Match Teas **9d.** and **1/6** or A-LA-CARTE

The Restaurants, situated on the Second Floor and served by a Lift, are beautifully appointed and are famous for the high quality of the produce used in the preparation of the various dishes.

IRELAND
Full Back	L. M. MALCOLMSON (15) — North Ireland
Right Wing	C. V. BOYLE (11) — Dublin University
Right Centre	A. H. BAILEY (12) — University College, Dublin
Left Centre	L. B. McMAHON (13) — Blackrock College
Left Wing	J. J. O'CONNOR (14) — University College, Cork
Outside Half	V. A. HEWITT (10) — Instonians
Scrum Half	G. J. MORGAN (9) — Clontarf

Forwards:
R. ALEXANDER (1) — North Ireland & R.U.C.F.C.
S. WALKER (2) — Instonians
C. E. BEAMISH (3) — North Ireland & R.A.F.
H. J. SAYERS (4) — Landsdowne and Army
S. J. DEERING (5) — Bective Rangers
J. E. SIGGINS (Capt.) (6) — Collegians
C. R. GRAVES (7) — Wanderers
J. RUSSELL (8) — University College, Cork

Referee: Mr. C. F. GADNEY (English R.U.) Leicester.
Irish Touch Judge: Mr. S. T. IRWIN, M.B., B.S., President, Irish Rugby Union.
Welsh Touch Judge: Mr. HARRY PACKER, Welsh R.U., Newport.
NO NEW INTERNATIONALS — ALL PLAYERS ON BOTH SIDES PREVIOUSLY "CAPPED."

WALES
(A) VIVIAN G. J. JENKINS — London Welsh	Full Back
(B) B. E. W. McCALL — Welch Regiment	Left Wing
(C) WILFRED WOOLLER — Cambridge University	Left Centre
(D) CLAUDE DAVEY (Capt.) — Swansea and Sale	Right Centre
(E) J. IDWAL REES — Swansea and Edinburgh Wand.	Right Wing
(F) CLIFF W. JONES — Porth and Cambridge University	Outside Half
(G) HAYDN TANNER — Gowerton County School and Swansea	Scrum Half

Forwards:
(H) T. J. REES — Newport
(I) BRYN EVANS — Llanelly
(J) TREVOR WILLIAMS — Cross Keys
(K) HAROLD THOMAS — Neath
(L) GRIFF WILLIAMS — Abersovon
(M) A. M. REES — London Welsh
(N) JIM LANG — Llanelly
(O) EDDIE LONG — Swansea

● exclusive reports by **ASTRAL & CLEM LEWIS** in Monday's **NEWS CHRONICLE**

Something NEW and GOOD
ELLIMAN ATHLETIC 'RUB'
For Superb Physical Fitness

Promotes — AGILITY, ELASTICITY, FLEXIBILITY.
Prevents — STIFFNESS and STALENESS.
Guards Against — MUSCLE TEARS and Strains.

POPULAR PRICE **1/-** CLUB SIZE **2/6**
Of BOOTS, TAYLORS, etc.
Made by
ELLIMAN, SONS & CO., Ltd., SLOUGH

BUY YOUR **FORD 8 h.p. SALOON or VAN**
At **£100** To-day or £30 Deposit
INCLUDING INSURANCE, TAX, DELIVERY, &c.
A. E. HARRIS, LTD. - **FORD HOUSE, CARDIFF**

ALEC WARD
64, Queen Street, CARDIFF
NO LIMIT — LINCOLN & NATIONAL
Phone 5801
RACING & FOOTBALL ALL THE YEAR ROUND

Programme Wales v South Africa 1931 (*with Claude Davey and Will Davies*)

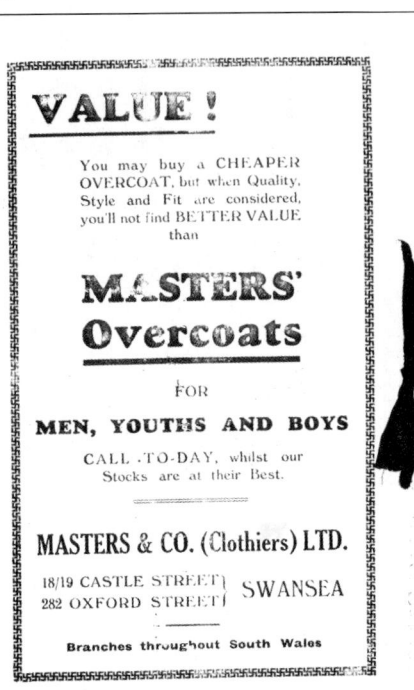

PRICE THREEPENCE

THE WELSH RUGBY UNION
OFFICIAL PROGRAMME

Walter E. Rees

South Africa (SPRINGBOKS) v. **Wales**

ST. HELEN'S GROUND, SWANSEA
SATURDAY DEC. 5th, 1931
KICK OFF AT 2.30 P.M.

Drink Bovril and Enjoy the Game

VALUE!

You may buy a CHEAPER OVERCOAT, but when Quality, Style and Fit are considered, you'll not find BETTER VALUE than

MASTERS' Overcoats

FOR MEN, YOUTHS AND BOYS

CALL TO-DAY, whilst our Stocks are at their Best.

MASTERS & CO. (Clothiers) LTD.
18/19 CASTLE STREET
282 OXFORD STREET
SWANSEA

Branches throughout South Wales

DEAFNESS Overcome by the almost invisible British Acoustiphone. Posted on 14 days home trial for 21/- prepaid (to be allowed off price of instrument) or 2/1- month for six months—no deposit. Cash Price 5 Guineas. CALL TO TEST IT. Only Address—E. T. RICH, as below.

RUPTURE RICH'S Hand Pressure Binder—the most natural and comfortable support. Single, 21/-, Double, 30/-.

Call personally to be fitted or write privately for Consultation Form. Only Address:

E. T. RICH, Surgical Chemist, 30, High St. SWANSEA
(Just below Mackworth Hotel).

THE GILBERT MATCH RUGBY BALL
FAMOUS SINCE 1823 (when the Rugby Game originated) AND STILL THE BEST BALL
May be obtained from all Sports Dealers.

Morley's take the field in every match played by the Springboks. Jerseys, scarves and socks have been supplied to them by I & R MORLEY ever since the year 1896.

I & R MORLEY MANUFACTURERS, HOSIERY, UNDERWEAR, GLOVES

BUY a BRITISH cruise

BUYERS of a White Star Winter or Easter Cruise ARE BUILDERS of the most important thing of all — their health and fitness to cope with the exacting demands of to-day.

S.S. 'LAURENTIC' cruises to the **MEDITERRANEAN**

FEB. 6 from Liverpool £30, 19 days from
FEB. 27 from Liverpool £30, ten 14 days from

Easter Cruise
MAR 24 from Liverpool £25, 16 days from

WHITE STAR

Full particulars from White Star Line 18a, High St. Cardiff, or Local Agents

---

*SOUTH AFRICA.

Full Back	G. BRAND (29) or J. C. TINDALL (28)	
Right Wing	M. ZIMMERMAN (25)	
Right Centre	B. G. GRAY (26)	
Left Centre	J. WHITE (6)	
Left Wing (from)	F. VENTER (2) G. BRAND (29) or J. H. van der WESTHUIZEN (24)	
Outside Half	BENNIE L. OSLER, Capt. (21)	
Scrum Half	D. CRAVEN (19)	
Forwards selected from	L. STRACHAN (1)	
	F. BERGH (7)	
	P. J. NEL (8)	
	H. G. KIPLING (11)	
	G. M. DANEEL (12)	
	C. "BOY" LOUW (13)	
	A. van der MERWE (15)	
	PHIL MOSTERT (17)	
	J. A. MacDONALD (18)	

Referees:
Mr. E. HOLMES, Roydon-on-Tyne, Durham. (English Rugby Union)

Touch Judges:
South Africa— Mr. THEO. B. IPENAAR, Manager.
Wales— Mr. A. WYNDHAM JONES, W.R.U., Merthyr Vale.

WALES.

(A) ‡ J. BASSETT, Capt.	Penarth	Full Back
(E) R. W. BOON	Cardiff	Left Wing
(D) FRANK WILLIAMS	Cardiff and Headingley	Left Centre
(C) CLAUDE DAVEY	Swansea and Sale	Right Centre
(B) J. C. MORLEY	Newport	Right Wing
(F) A. R. RALPH	Newport	Outside Half
(G) W. C. POWELL	London-Welsh	Scrum Half
(H) A. SKYM	Cardiff	Forwards
(I) F. A. BOWDLER	Cross Keys	
(J) T. DAY	Swansea	
(K) †W. DAVIES	Swansea	
(L) A. LEMON	Neath	
(M) T. ARTHUR	Neath	
(N) E. M. JENKINS	Aberavon	
(O) WATCYN THOMAS	Swansea and St. Helen's	

† Denotes First International, all others previously capped.

* At moment of going to press the Springboks' team was only provisionally chosen as above, the final choice depending on ground and weather conditions at mid-day to-day. Readers will please distinguish the playing fifteen by the numbers appearing below their names.

ELLIMAN'S EMBROCATION
Invigorates the Muscles

INVALUABLE FOR LUMBAGO, STIFFNESS, SCIATICA, MUSCULAR RHEUMATISM, SPRAINS, BRUISES, CHEST COLDS, SORE THROAT FROM COLD.

At all Chemists, 1/3, 2/- & 4/-

Free booklets on "Training," by T. Whittaker (the Arsenal Trainer), and on "Massage," may be had on application.

ELLIMAN SONS & CO., LTD. Dept. FO, SLOUGH.

Fullest Reports of all Matches — **Sunday Times** — By D. R. Gent and "Forward"

Published by the Union of Junior Leagues and Welsh Schools Rugby Union for the Welsh Rugby Union and Printed by Rees' Electric Press, John Street, Cardiff.

Amman United RFC 1932 - 33

Back Row: B Llewellyn, WH Morgan, OD Evans, WH Jones, TE Howells, J Rees, R jones, C Harry, D Davies, W Davies, S Noble.
Front Row: E Bevan, E Mathews, G Ward, M Bevan, M Ward, F Lewis.

Amman United RFC Season 1935 - 36

Back Row: WH Thomas, WD Ward, W Thomas, W Davies, JH Davies, E Walters, E James, JC Evans, T Bowen, L James, WR Thomas, T Christopher, C Llewellyn.
Middle Row: R Williams, J Lewis, C Harry, Dudley Folland, F Bevan, DP Thomas, E Bevan.
Front Row: M Ward, C Davies.

Season Ticket 1936 - 37

AMMAN UNITED RUGBY FOOTBALL CLUB
FIXTURES—SEASON 1936

				R	Points F | A
Sept	5	Llangennech	Home		
,,	12	Skewen	Away		
,,	17	Brynamman	Home		
,,	19	Briton Ferry	Away		
,,	26	Llandebie	Home		
Oct.	1	Brynamman	Away		
,,	3	Hendy	Home		
,,	10	Ystalyfera	Away		
,,	17	Penclawdd	Away		
,,	24	Swansea University	Home		
,,	31	Penclawdd	Home		
Nov.	7	Tumble	Away		
,,	14	Briton Ferry	Home		
,,	21	Swansea Unversity	Away		
,,	28	Abercrave	Away		
Dec.	5	Aberystwyth Varsity	Home		
,,	12	Cwmavon	Away		
,,	19	Tumble	Home		
C.D.	25	Brynamman	Home		
B.D.	26	Skewen	Home		

AMMAN UNITED RUGBY FOOTBALL CLUB
FIXTURES—SEASON 1937

				R	Points F | A
Jan.	2	Loughor	Away		
,,	9	Cwmllynfell	Home		
,,	16	Llangennech	Away		
,,	23	Swansea United	Away		
,,	30	Ogmore Vale	Home		
Feb.	6	Cwmllynfell	Away		
,,	13	Ammanford	Away		
,,	20	Ogmore Vale	Away		
,,	27	Cwmavon	Home		
Mar.	6	Aberystwyth	Away		
,,	13	Swansea United	Home		
,,	20	Llandebie	Away		
,,	27	Abercrave	Home		
E.M.	29	Carmarthen	Away		
E.T.	30	Loughor	Home		
E.W.	31	Ammanford	Home		
April	3	Gowerton	Away		
,,	10	Hendy	Away		
,,	17	Ystalyfera	Home		
,,	24	Gowerton	Home		
May	1	Carmarthen	Home		

42

Both teams were then entertained to a meal in Garnant Primary School.

Amman United won the game by 11 points to 8.

Ivor Jones became captain in 1933-34 season and, with a magnificent squad of 20 players, proved to be one of the most successful of Amman captains.

They had a magnificent cup and league run with games against local teams in all rounds.

Llandeilo were beaten 10-6 in the first round of the cup, then Brynamman were routed 16-0. They met Llandybie in the semi-final and were lucky to draw, with Fred Lewis, Emrys Evans and Stan Noble outstanding. They won the replay, with Cliff Harry and DP Thomas giving magnificent displays.

They met Penclawdd in the final at Pontardulais and lost by the odd try to nil, Bryn Edwards having a perfectly legitimate try disallowed by the Penclawdd touch judge.

This final, before a capacity crowd, is still recognised as the finest West Wales Rugby Union Cup Final of all time. The cup run was equally successful before losing to Tumble in the final at Llandybie on the 28th April 1934 by 6 points to 3.

In the season 1935-36, after having an early exit in the cup, Amman were again consistent in the league and, after many close encounters, kept a ground record into the second season. They met Ystradgynlais in the league semi-final at Ystalyfera and went on to beat Tumble in the final by 8 points to 3.

A report of season 1936-37 gives the playing record of: played 46, won 33, drawn 8 and lost 5, points for 303 and against 104. A credit balance of £18.00 was declared. The team under the captaincy of Mal Bevan again lost in the cup final to Felinfoel.

To bring these sections to a close it must be placed on record the exploits and contribution of Amman Juniors to Cwmamman Rugby.

Formed in 1932, and disbanded in 1939 due to the Second World War, they were formed under a separate committee to enable the Amman to have a nursery and included players from all other clubs in the locality.

Mr Dudley Folland became their President and the committee members, as well as players, graduated to the senior ranks. Chief amongst these was Bertie Davies, later to become Amman chairman, and Frank Dallavalle, who gave sterling service in organising wartime rugby in the valley. The team was unbeaten from season 1933 to 1938, and during that time also won the Tinplate Cup, donated by their president, and the Swansea and District Cup and League.

24 players were presented with pullovers for their feats and of the 24, sixteen went on to play for the senior side; they also supplied future captains in Cliff Llewellyn, Eddie Slocombe and Ivor Jones.

The team played Vardre in a Cup Final at St. Helens in 1934 and were successful by 3 points to nil.

The following poem was written at the time to commemorate the victory; by Dickie Evans.

AMMAN JUNIORS v VARDRE JUNIORS
Roedd Bertie Davies Chairman,
Y sec, ac Ifan John,
Yn gweiddi nerdd ei chegau,
"Now juniors come along."
Ond oedd captain Cliff Llewellyn,
Fel ebol ar y cae,
Yn gweiddi ac yn crio
Fod y juniors yn chwarae dda.
Busnes Lyn a Tali, Gwyn Bartlett a Dai Madge,
I basio mas I Ifor ac intai chwarae dda.
Ac intai rhoe I Dilwyn
Ac intai pasio mas I Sibie.
Ond oedd Sibie mynd fel sebra,
Gan ddweud wrth pawb "GOODBYE."
A pawb yngweddu Llawen,
"It was a rattling try."

Amman Juniors RFC Team Season 1935 - 36 *(unbeaten from 1933 to 1938)*

Back Row: D Madge, E Pugh, E Morgan, D Rees.
3rd Row: E Slocombe, C James, W James, I Williams, G Bartlett, WR Thomas, S Davies, L Lewis.
2nd Row: R Price, D Morgan, DJ Morgan, C Llewellyn, C Bartlett, WH Morgan, S Bevan, C Evans.
Front Row: I Evans, I Jones, E Ward, D Hammer.

TOM BOWEN - THE OLDEST AMMAN PLAYER
By Howell Cousins

Tom was born in October 1912 and played for the Amman from 1929 – 1936. He was born in Caeswllt Cottage, Llandeilo Road, Garnant, overlooking the Hendre fields, one of the best spots in the valley, according to Tom, with fine views of Garnant and the Betws Mountain. When we talked to Tom about his youth and playing days with the Amman we got an interesting insight into the social life of the valley in the 1920s /1930s.

He was one of 9 children, 6 of whom survived into adulthood. His father worked in the mines but did not want his sons to work underground. As a result Tom was directed to work with his uncles who were builders and stonemasons, and his first job with them was working on the Workmen's Hall in 1926. In the late 20s he also worked in the Tin works in Garnant and remembers 72-hour weeks for 7s 6d pay (37.5p).

He started playing for the Amman in 1929. The Amman did not have a youth team in those days, but the Gelli Pit ran a youth team, and Tom played for the Raven Stars before joining the Amman. The Raven Stars changed in the stables of the Raven Inn, and played on the riverside field below the Raven works.

He first played for the Amman in 1929 as an open-side wing forward and played through until 1936. There was not much work in the valleys in the early 30s and he remembers many periods of unemployment. They may have been difficult days but he remembers them fondly because of the friendship and camaraderie.

The rugby team was very successful in that period, culminating in winning the West Wales Championship in the 1935/36 season. The successful team were presented with blazers by Henry Folland.

The final was played against Tumble in Stradey Park, and it is a game that he will always remember. It was also his last game for the Amman. In 1936 the work position improved, and in the week after the final he got a job in the Maerdy tin works in Gorseinon. He moved into lodgings in Gorseinon and thereafter found it too difficult to continue playing for the Amman, but he did play a few games for the local team.

During his playing career, like many local players, he was offered to go

"North". He remembers playing with and against Claude Davey, who played for Swansea against the Amman. The best player that he played against was the Penclawdd outside half, Willy Davies, who could run rings around any wing forward. Tom was a West Wales referee for 10 years from 1953 –1963, and he refereed many a game on the Park.

The move to look for work in 1936 proved to be permanent, apart from 2 years in Birmingham during the war, he has lived in the Gorseinon area ever since, working for ICI or AlCOA until he retired. He still has a great interest in Rugby and has strong opinions on the current problems in the national game. Of one thing he has no doubt, the players of today have it a lot easier than they used to in his day!

EXPERIENCES OF REES PRICE
by Howard Gabe Davies

Amman Stars, Amman Juniors, Amman United, Loughborough, Llanelli and Harlequins.

Rees Price was born on 13.12.1916 near the Glanarafon Farm and first played for the Amman Stars, and then Amman Juniors, before playing for the Amman United.

Amman Stars played on a field at Neuadd Road and used the Lamb in Garnant to meet and change. Every Friday, 6d was collected for the privilege of playing; the money was used to pay the rent of the field and for the red jerseys worn with a star sewn on to the shirt.

Amman Juniors played on Cwmamman Park, had the famous Ted Ward in the team, and had an unbroken run of victories at the time. The Amman Stars 'Big' match of the season was against the Amman Juniors and both teams eventually amalgamated as the Amman Juniors.

Rees remembers playing for the Juniors on a very wet Saturday at Tycroes. The team changed in a garage, the rugby field was on a slope and at the bottom there was a ditch full of water; towards the end of the game, one of our players, Pascal Thomas, chased after the ball and then disappeared. Pascal was not seen for a while and the team had to go and look for him, eventually rescuing him from the waters.

While still at Amman Valley Grammar School, Rees would play for the school in the morning and for the Amman United in the afternoon.

Rees was 16 years old in 1932 and started to play for the Amman United – 'far too young' remarked the two referees in his first season. The first referee asked, "How old are you?" Rees replied, "16." The referee said, "Too young but you're doing damn well."

The second was the international referee Ivor David. Rees had played for the school in the morning, and the Amman had an away cup game at Llandybie, playing by the limeworks. Rees caught the ball and called for a 'mark'. Ivor David said, "I know you didn't call for a 'mark' Rees, but I blew up because I thought you would be killed."

The Ward brothers were a large element in the team at that time. They were Eddie, Mock, Gwilym, Iau (a brilliant hooker) and Ted, who went north to play Rugby League and ended playing for the Great Britain rugby league team. Ted was a very accurate kicker of goals.

In 1937 Rees went to Loughborough College for his training as a Physical

47

Education Teacher and played for the Amman during the holiday periods. While in Loughborough, He played full back for the university and in 1939 played in the U.A.U final against Swansea University and lost. The Swansea team contained the famous Welsh International half-back Haydn Tanner, who played in the victorious 1935 Swansea team that beat the All Blacks.

Rees joined the Royal Navy when war broke out and served most of the war on destroyers in the 'Battle of the Atlantic', and was part of the search for the German pocket battleship the 'Bismarck'. Rees played one rugby match during his five and a half years in the war and that was in Bermuda, where the frigate 'Afflick' had been picked up at Boston and was undergoing sea trials. The frigate 'Afflick' was later torpedoed and sank off the French coast near Cherbourg. Rees was rescued and spent the next three weeks in hospital, suffering from the effects of chemicals discharged from the damaged depth charges; he still suffers today from these after-effects.

After the war Rees resumed playing for the Amman and also had an occasional game for Llanelli.

Rees started teaching in Reditch, Worcestershire and came back to play for the Amman in their Cup Final against Tumble in 1945 as 'Bertie Clerk' wanted to play the best possible team; that was the last game that he played for the Amman United.

Whilst teaching in the Twickenham area, Rees played a few games for the Harlequins and did not encounter any snobbery. The home games were played on the Twickenham ground; for these games only one stand was opened and it was quite eerie playing there. The present Harlequin ground near the Twickenham stadium is called the 'Stoop' after the famous Adrian Stoop. After the match ended, the team took baths under the stand. The whole place would be full of steam but Stoop's face would appear beside each bath and would inform each Quins bather (player) of the mistakes they had made during the game. Adrian Stoop was then fairly advanced in years, and took a particular interest in the Harlequins, watching all the matches from behind the goal on a seat provided by the groundsman, who then moved it to the other end at half-time. While playing full-back for Quins against Cambridge University he noticed to his amazement that the Cambridge full back was Hugh Lloyd Davies from Tycroes, who had followed him into the Amman Valley County School team. The Quins' touch judge was also the secretary, Ken Chapman, the son of the famous Arsenal Manager, Herbert Chapman.

Rees retired in 1948, due to his age and the school commitments of refereeing and coaching rugby on Saturday mornings. Rees left the teaching profession in 1953 to take up farming in Cwmamman and has now moved to Pentyrch, Cardiff, to be near his daughter.

Rees follows rugby today and feels that payment to rugby players has spoilt the game; he was never paid anything in his rugby career.

FROM AMMAN JUNIOR TO WELSH INTERNATIONAL
By Howard Gabe Davies

Gwyn Evans can claim to be the only Amman United Welsh International to have only played for the Amman Juniors.

Born in Treherbert 17.8.1918, the son of a coal miner, he was brought up in Clydach, Swansea.

His connection with the Amman Juniors started with an apprenticeship with the Amalgamated Anthracite Company at Ammanford Colliery, which he had through his uncle, David Jefferies, the General Manager of the company. As a 16-year-old, he was working on the installation of Concordia Electric Lamps at Gellyceidrim Colliery, Glanamman. He would travel by bus from Clydach in the winter and would cycle to work in the summer. He clearly remembers the beauty of the valleys; it was glorious way to go to work in the morning, cycling up the Tawe Valley and then across, and down the Amman Valley to Glanamman and he also saved the 2s 6d weekly bus fare.

Gwyn was always a big boy for his age and started playing rugby in school as centre three-quarter.

He was approached by Mr Price, the manager's clerk at Gellyceidrim Colliery, (a big man he remembers) and also a Mr Evans, both of whom were connected with the Amman United Rugby Club, to play for the Amman Juniors.

The Amman Juniors team was a very good nursery for the senior side Amman United. They had a good team and it was very difficult to get into the first team. The West Wales League was also very competitive in those days and playing standards were very high.

He joined Swansea RFC in 1936 after playing one Christmas morning; the match was at Vardre RFC. He went to the match as a spectator and there was a shortage of players. He was asked if he wanted to play and cycled home to get his kit a mile away. At the match, there was a Swansea Police Sergeant, Dai Thomas, who commented on his play and that he had a good game in that he ran all day and would he be interested in playing for Swansea RFC. He heard nothing for two weeks and then received an invitation card to play for the Swansea club the following Saturday.

His first game for Swansea was against Leicester as a prop, his first in that position and clearly he has never forgotten the experience of that day. After the game, he went to the Plaza cinema and was so tired that he slept throughout the film show and was awakened by the playing of the organ at the end of the show. Neath was his next game and he played flanker, playing against Cyril Challinor (Welsh International 1939) and he learnt so much from the game. Gwyn the rookie was shown by Challinor the subtleties of the wing-forward game – holding of the jersey – sticking his foot out and the backside - coming around the scrum; they were later to become the best of friends.

Gwyn played for Swansea for one and a half years; he was then a big lad and even today, in 2003, he is still an imposing figure at 84 years of age.

Gwyn had applied for a job with the Glamorgan Police Force and went to Cardiff to sit the examination papers. He left Neath at 5.30am for the 10.00am test and eventually arrived home in Clydach at 12.00 that night. He did not receive the job with the Glamorgan Police Force but to his surprise was offered a job with the City of Cardiff Police Force. He started on the 8.4.1938 and the policemen were made up of university graduates; they were nearly all English from Gloucester and Somerset and they didn't like the Welsh. His father, a collier, was earning £2. 4s. 6d and Gwyn's starting wage was £3. 12s as a 19-year-old recruit; his father told Gwyn to take the job.

Gwyn played soccer for the police force, as there was no rugby being played by the city police force.

The Second World War had started and he saw more injuries in the bombing of the city than in his later active service in North Africa and Italy. Police officers under 25 years of age were being called up for duty and Gwyn joined the Royal Artillery in 1942. He played some rugby during this period, whilst doing his basic training and, being Welsh, you were automatically expected to be able to play rugby. Gwyn found that, even with the war being fought in Italy, rugby was played whenever the possibility arose, and most importantly that, in the army, if you played rugby you were in the 'Freemasons Rugby Family - playing rugby opened doors for you! while reading the forces' newspaper, 'the Union Jack' Gwyn read a request for rugby players to which he replied. Later, he received a phone call from a colonel who was looking for players for his team, the REME. Gwyn was transferred from the Royal Artillery in Solerno to the Royal Electrical and Mechanical Engineers (REME) in Naples. This led to him playing rugby in his army boots with studs inserted. After one rugby match, the colonel was going to the officers' mess in Naples for a few beers. Gwyn being a sergeant, a non-commissioned officer was not allowed in the officer's mess. The colonel told Gwyn to take off his tunic and then took off his own colonel's tunic for him to wear, which resulted in Gwyn being saluted by officers and soldiers, and entry into the officers' mess, and he had a very good night.

Gwyn was re-called to the police force in 1945 and flew home in a Lancaster bomber; he remembers it as a horrendous flight back to the UK.

After the war, he did play rugby for the Cardiff City Police Force as their new Chief Constable Price was from Brecon and had started a city police rugby team.

At the beginning of season 1946/1947, there was an advertisement in the South Wales Echo that trials were being held by Cardiff RFC, which he attended and he received an invitation card to play for Cardiff Athletic v Cilfynydd. Gwyn, at the time, lived with his wife in Penarth and on the day of the match had finished his night shift at 8.00am and asked his wife to get him up at noon. Gwyn cycled from Penarth to Cardiff to play for the Athletic and at the game none of the officials or players spoke to Gwyn. He was told later that he had looked much older than his age of 28 years due to his baldhead and that he had had a good game, a feature of which was that he hadn't stopped running during the entire match. The following Saturday, he was picked for the Cardiff v Newport game and 5 weeks later was picked for the Welsh Rugby Trial.

In January 1947, he was picked to play for Wales against England and the critics said Gwyn Evans was too inexperienced a player to be picked to play international rugby against England. In the match itself, Gwyn scored a try; running 40 yards to score and went on to play 12 consecutive games for Wales.

During his time in the city police force, he was never given any time off to play rugby and retired from first class rugby at 32 years of age, when he was placed on the regular night shift. However, he continued to play rugby for the police force until he was 42 years of age and later became the Chairman of the South Wales Police RFC.

Gwyn retired from the police force at 61 years of age as Chief Superintendent.

He feels that when he started as a young police constable, that his superiors looked down on their men (constables), whilst Gwyn saw every trainee and was lucky to have a photographic memory and could remember their names; years later, he would be able to speak to any one of his men on point duty and be able to address them by name, which brought enormous loyalty from his men.

Gwyn lives in Cardiff with his wife, has a son and daughter and watches Welsh rugby with interest; he can still be seen at 85years of age in the Cardiff Rugby Clubhouse enjoying a pint of beer.

AMMAN UNITED RFC
1945-1970
By Alan Thomas
The early post-war years

The early post-war period was a time of rebuilding for the club. In this respect they were fortunate in having a good mixture of pre-war players and some promising new ones available. This difficult period also called for competent and conscientious administrators. Two of the most notable were Bertie Davies (known to all as Bertie 'Clerk'), who was Chairman for most seasons between 1945 and his passing in 1962, and Percy Thomas, a star outside-half of the 1930s, who was Secretary during the early post-war years.

Bertie was a renowned character, famous (and indeed infamous in some parts!) throughout the world of West Wales rugby, and was not averse to poaching a player or two from nearby clubs if he thought they were good enough for the Amman. It cannot be said that he was a great lover of Brynaman or its Rugby Club. Indeed, one of his best-known sayings was, "Only two good things ever came out of Brynaman - my mother and the main road." Bertie still keeps a close eye on proceedings - his is the portrait in the Clubhouse lounge bar whose eyes follow you wherever you go!

MR. BERTIE DAVIES
Chairman who reformed Team after War II.
Now a Life Member.

In Amman's 50th Anniversary booklet, editor Harry Slocombe wrote:

"An honour worthily bestowed in this Jubilee year is that upon Mr. Bertie Davies, Amman United's chairman. Mr. Davies, who has held the office for the seven past years with but one short break, has done more for Amman Rugby than many enthusiasts realise. Six years ago he was elevated to the office of chairman, after serving for 18 years as a committeeman, so this year sees him completing 30 years service. Mr. Davies followed Mr. David Thomas, who retired through illness. The chairman had a long-playing career covering 19 seasons.

He commenced his career as a member of the Prospect Stars R.F.C., of which he was also a pioneer. He next joined the Amman Rovers, which side he eventually captained, and in the same season captained the Amman Valley representative XV in their game against the Swansea All Whites. For nine seasons he assisted the United, and after 18 years as a player retired, to be accepted as a committeeman on his first candidature. Since then he has served continually, and has been an invaluable asset to the club. When, some years ago, the club reached its lowest ebb, and when abandonment was suggested, he refused to countenance the abolition of such a famous club. He therefore set seeing the club again established on a sound financial basis.

With a few faithful friends, he took up the reins after the war, and without funds or a team they set about resuscitating the team. He enjoyed the pleasure of knowing that the team had one of its most successful seasons. During the War he was entrusted with the organising of all War charity rugby and in this again his efforts resulted in the raising of large sums for the funds. For a number of seasons he has been the club's delegate on the West Wales Rugby Union, and their representative at various conferences.

His election to the chair, in this, the Jubilee year, is only befitting after his valuable work for the club".

Outside-half Percy Thomas was one of Amman's star players of the 1930s, and one local newspaper of the time claimed that he would have played in Welsh Trials if Amman had released him to play for Llanelli. Unfortunately, his playing career was curtailed through ill-health, but what the club lost on the playing field they gained on the administrative side.

Harry Slocombe wrote in the 50th Anniversary booklet:

"Mr. Percy Thomas, the club's secretary since it re-formed after World War II, has been appropriately entrusted with the arranging of the 50th Anniversary celebrations. Mr. Thomas joined the club as a player in the 1933-34 season, when his County School coaching served him and the United in good stead. For a number of ensuing seasons he played a big part in Amman's Cup and League Tournament successes. For a while he was engaged as a clerk in London, in which season he assisted Edgware R.F.C. who, during his term of office, defeated most of the leading London clubs. In each game he scored two or three tries, in addition to cutting out openings for many more."

MR. D. PERCY THOMAS
Club Secretary

Mr. Percy Thomas, the club's secretary since it re-formed after World War II, has been appropriately entrusted with the arranging of the 50th Anniversary celebrations.

Mr. Thomas joined the club as a player in the 1933-

So successful was the post-war recovery that the team reached the final of the West Wales Cup competition twice in three seasons, in 1945-46 and in 1947-48.

The first of these, which was lost against Tumble, was a great disappointment as it was a match that most people thought the Amman should have won.

It's interesting to note that three of the renowned Ward brothers played in this match. Wat Jones, the scrum-half, played cricket for Glamorgan for many seasons. The captain, Will Haydn Thomas, was, in later years, a prominent official of the N.U.M. at Abernant Colliery.

Amman Team v Tumble - *West Wales Cup Final 1946*

Standing: Glen Jones, T.J. Paddock, D.J. Lewis, Dennis Cochram, Eddie Ward, Bobby Hunt, Eddie Smith, S. Nelmes.
Seated: Gwilym Ward, Rhys Price, W.H.Thomas (Capt.) W.D. (Iau) Ward, Griff Evans.
Front: Wat Jones, Mal Bevan.

Amman United 1947-48 *(Not the Cup-final team)*

Back row: Mike Rosser-Davies, Iau Ward, Len Brown, Gordon Thomas, Dennis Cochram, Bobby Hunt, Danny Williams, Dai Rees, Elvet Lewis, Bill Styles.
Seated: Cliff Owen, Doug Thomas, Gwilym Ward, Bertie Davies (Chairman), Eddie Slocombe (Capt.), Percy Thomas (Sec.), Wat Jones, Ron Brooks.
Front: Terry Ward (Mascot).

The following is an account that appeared in the South Wales Voice ("Llais Llafur") on May 9th 1946:

"Amman United, whose splendid performance was loudly applauded by the 10,000 spectators at Stradey Park, Llanelly, were defeated after extra time by Tumble. Although they failed to lift the cup, the United demonstrated that they are a side that play typical Welsh Rugby, despite the fact that their backs failed by far to reach their best form.

The fact that the United have failed in four finals tends to the belief that despite their classical football, they are no cup-fighters."

The Amman Valley Chronicle reported on May 9th 1946:

General opinion was that Amman United should have won in the final of the West Wales League Cup, played at Stradey, Llanelly, before a large crowd on Saturday last. Extra time was necessary for Tumble to score 9 points to Amman's 3 points.

Consider the fact that 10,000 people turned out for a match between two village sides. These days Llanelli would be pleased to have a crowd like that at Stradey for a European Cup match.

In later years, when discussing this match in the Amman clubhouse, "Iau" Ward remained convinced that the drop-goal scored by Tumble scrum-half Jimmy Wiltshire from under the Amman posts was indeed a punt. In a recent conversation, Griff Evans ("Carreg Isaac"), who played on the wing in that match, was of the same opinion. Incidentally, Griff, at 22, was the youngest player in that team.

Griff remembers an incident in a particularly rough and tough match during that season down in Penclawdd. A woman shouted out, "You dirty bloody colliers!"

Iau Ward shouted back, "If it wasn't for our coal, you wouldn't be able to boil your bloody cockles."

This immediate post-war period was still a time of food rationing and considerable food shortages, and because of this Griff remembers particularly a match against R.A.F. Fairwood Common, where the airmen were extremely well-fed. Not only were the Amman boys feasted after the match, but also they were each given a packet of sugar to return home!

Amman reached the final of the West Wales Cup again two years later, where they played against Felinfoel, at Stradey Park. This had proved to be a very tough campaign, as Briton Ferry were beaten only after a second replay, and in the semi-final a second replay was again necessary to defeat a very tough Abercrave side.

The Amman team in the 1948 West Wales Cup final against Felinfoel was as follows:

John Rees; Terrence Jenkins, DJ Lewis, PC Wat Jones, D. Thomas; Gwilym Ward, Eddie Slocombe (Capt.); Dennis Cochram, WD Ward, Bobby Hunt, Danny Williams, Will Hopkin, Len Brown, Will Styles, Dai Rees.

Only six of this Cup-final team had played in the last Amman final just two years previously. Three of them, Gwilym Ward, Wat Jones and Dennis Cochram showed their versatility by playing in completely different positions.

Amman v Abercrave 1948

This picture was taken during one of the semi-finals against Abercrave at the old Brynaman ground. The prominent Amman players are Griff Evans and Will Hopkin on the left and Iau Ward on the right.

Will Styles, who had kicked three huge penalties from half-way in an earlier round to beat Briton Ferry 9-6, was to become secretary of the Amman in later years.

The following account by "The Scout" appeared in the Amman Valley Chronicle on Thursday May 6th 1948:

"When the teams came on the field, one of my colleagues remarked on the difference between them. The one came on in faded jerseys, and with one of the centres even having his stockings down around his ankles. The other side trotted on to the playing arena spick and span, looking as if they were trained to the minute."

"The Scout" goes on to dissect the game in a long account in surprising detail, the general conclusion being that the forwards gave a very good account of themselves, but the backs were not quite up to scratch, with many of them playing out of position. The forwards who were given special mention were WD Ward, Len Brown, Danny Williams and Will Hopkin.

Other reports also mention Amman's faded jerseys. Apparently, the lady who washed the jerseys had inadvertently soaked them in parazone, and no replacement kit was available at short notice!

If you've wondered how people coped before the days of the mobile phone, perhaps this little account from the South Wales Evening Post on May 3rd 1948 will help you:

FROM STRADEY TO AMMAN 'PAR AVION'

There must have been a mournful gathering around a certain pigeon-loft in the Amman Valley late on Saturday afternoon. There was certainly a sad 12-year-old pigeon-fancier in the Stradey stand at the end of the West Wales Cup-final, in which Felinfoel beat Amman United.

This youthful Amman fan arrived at Stradey with a box containing a pair of pigeons. The first of these, released at half-time, bore north-eastwards a slip of paper upon which was pencilled the state of the game at that stage.

With 'Foel' ahead by five points at the final, it was noticed that the second pigeon was allowed to become airborne without a bulletin of any kind. This was obviously a case where no news would be interpreted as bad news.

The young lad mentioned in the above story was Gwynfor Bartlett, whose father was well-known local pigeon-fancier Johnny Bartlett.

Amman United 1948-49

Standing: Will Hopkin, Dai Rees, Iau Ward, Will Rees, Elvet Lewis, Vaughan Davies, Wat Jones, Ivor David (Referee).
Seated: Reggie Bevan, John Rees, Gwilym Ward, Dennis Cochram (Capt.), Mal Bevan, Griff Evans.
Front: Carwyn James, Eddie Slocombe.

Dennis Cochram the captain, although relatively small in stature, was a hard, tough front-row forward; who served the Amman well for many, many seasons. He was a regular selection for the West Wales Representative teams of this period. Iau Ward and Mal Bevan were real veterans at this stage, having played for many years before the war.

Of course, the most famous player in this photograph is Carwyn James, who was a student at Aberystwyth University at the time. Very few people owned cars at the time, so, for every game, the Amman used to send a taxi to fetch him and to take him back.

The referee is Ivor David, who was the most celebrated of Welsh international referees during this period. He made quite a name for himself when he sent off Colin Windon, a star back-row forward with the touring 1947-48 Wallabies, in their match against Llanelli.

Denzil Jones

Denzil Jones was the finest outside-half produced by the Amman during this period and probably throughout its existence. Born in 1925, Denzil attended Garnant National (Church Primary) School and Amman Valley County School, where he captained the First XV. He played first-class rugby in war-time matches for Llanelli while still a schoolboy. Playing outside him at centre at the time was Ted Ward, as Union and League players were allowed to play together during the war.

He remembers playing in a war-time Sevens tournament at St. Helen's Swansea, when his team consisted of the five Ward brothers, Tom Paddock and himself. Ted told the team to forget their boots and to play in "daps", as the ground was so firm. Denzil recalls that Ted still managed to kick all his goals – even though goal-kicking in those days was "toe-kicking" rather than "round the corner". They lost in the final to a team captained by Rugby League legend Jim Sullivan. Denzil speaks warmly of Ted's support and encouragement during this period.

After school, Denzil attended Cardiff University, where he captained the University Rugby team and the University of Wales team. He recalls playing a match for a University Past and Present team, when his scrum-half was the great Haydn Tanner. At the first scrum, Tanner threw out a pass so hard and fast that Denzil hardly saw it, and it carried to the outside-centre!

Denzil joined the Swansea club in 1947 and played in the team that lost narrowly by 11 points to 8 to Australia. In 1948, he was selected as reserve in a Welsh Trial at Carmarthen. He travelled down to Carmarthen by bike, but still claimed his bus travelling expenses. If the powers-that-be had found out, he would probably have been professionalised and banned forever!

He later joined the Aberavon club, which he captained in the 1951-52 season. In November 1951, he captained a Combined Neath/Aberavon team against South Africa.

In 1949, Denzil was selected as a reserve for Wales. Unfortunately, this was in the pre-substitute era, otherwise; surely, he would have won a well-deserved Welsh cap.

Towards the end of his career, Denzil returned to play for the Amman for a couple of seasons, to delight both players and spectators with his great skills.

Denzil's professional career was spent with the Mining Inspectorate, mainly in various parts of England. He and his wife Nina, who hails from Glanaman, are now enjoying their retirement in Doncaster, close to their daughters and their families.

Amman United 1949-50

Back row: Elvet Lewis, Glyndwr Jones, Gordon Thomas, Dai Rees, Wat Jones.
Middle row: Bobby Hunt, Moc Ward, Iau Ward, E. James, Danny Williams, Eirwyn Davies.
Front row : Denzil Jones, Denzil Griffiths, Griff Evans, Eddie Slocombe.

Although Gwilym Ward was the captain during the 1949-50 season, he does not appear in this team photograph. Front row left is that fine outside-half Denzil Jones, who does not appear in many team photographs because of his involvement with first-class clubs. Middle row right is E.B. Davies, who later became secretary of the Welsh Youth Rugby Union for many years, and also became President of the Welsh Rugby Union.

The Jones Brothers

The late 1940s was the period when the three Jones brothers from Penybanc joined the club. The eldest of the three, Gwyn, joined in 1948, to be followed a year later by Vince and Hubert, who was a Youth player.

The three gave the Amman sterling service up until the mid-1950s. Gwyn captained the club the last time the Amman won the West Wales Championship in the 1953-54 season. A strong, fast winger, Gwyn had periods with the Llanelli and Swansea clubs, and played for the All Whites against the Springboks in 1951. After his playing days were over, Gwyn was the hardworking secretary of Betws Rugby Club for many years.

Vince clearly remembers the time he was "persuaded" to join the Amman. He was playing for Llandybie at the time. One afternoon, he was returning home from work at Saron Colliery, when he saw a man helping his mother hang the washing on the line. It was Bertie, the Amman chairman, who had come to ask for his services! I ask you, how could he refuse! Bertie's efforts were well spent, as Vince proved to be one of the best flank forwards ever to play for the Amman. He captained the team in season 1951-52, and, at 20 years of age, is the youngest ever to have done so.

The youngest of the three, Hubert, started playing for the first team at outside-half when he was 17 years old, and played four full seasons before he was 21. A fine all-round player, he moved to scrum-half, where he played for most of his career.

The 1950s

The 1950's began in tragic circumstances, when three people closely associated with the club were killed in the Llandow Air Disaster. The plane-returning supporters from the international match in Ireland crashed on landing, killing over eighty people. At the time, it was the world's worst air disaster.

The three from the Amman who died were:

Gomer Griffiths, a former captain of Amman United,

Freddie Schofield, treasurer of the Quins,

Elwyn Davies, treasurer of Amman United Supporters Club.

The first Amman captain of the 1950's was Bobby Hunt. Bobby was a member of that most formidable and renowned long-term Amman front-row whose other members were Iau Ward and Dennis Cochram. He was also a very prominent local boxer.

In 1951, Vince Jones became, at the age of twenty, the youngest captain in the history of the club, and remains so to this day. The photograph shows the team that took part in a memorable win over Aberavon at Cwmamman Park during that season. Only three of these players played in the cup-final only three years previously, so it was clear that Bertie was on the prowl and changes were taking place. Apart from local players, the team includes the three Jones brothers from Penybanc, Godfrey Hitchings from Pantyffynnon, Arwyn Evans from Cwmgors and Peris James from Caio.

In 1950, stories had been reaching the Amman Valley about the rugby prowess of young Peris, so Ammanford RFC decided to send two of their committeemen to his home to try to persuade him to join Ammanford. As they were approaching the house, who was coming out of the front door but Bertie, who said to them, "Too late, boys. He's playing for the Amman on Saturday." Peris was to serve the Amman for many seasons, and also had a prolonged period with Swansea RFC.

Although Amman United RFC was formed in 1903, and the Centenary is being celebrated in the 2003-04 season, the 50th Anniversary was celebrated in the 1952-53 season.

61

Amman United 1951-52

Standing Glyn John, Will Hopkin, Arwyn Evans, Godfrey Hitchings, Jackie Harries, Gwyn Jones.
Seated: Peris James, Reggie Bevan, Kendrick Lewis, Vince Jones (Capt.), John Jones, Norman Bevan, Bobby Hunt.
Front: Hubert Jones, Eddie Slocombe.

Amman United - *50th Anniversary 1952-53*

Back row: Viv Rees, Ieuan Evans, Godfrey Hitchings, Vaughan Davies, Nev Anthony, Esmond Williams.
Seated: Gwyndaf Walters, Norman Bevan, Glyn John (Capt.) Viv Williams, Vince Jones, John Jones.
Front: E. Jones, Gwyn Jones, Hubert Jones.

To acknowledge this event, a booklet was produced that gave "A Brief History of the Club's Progress". Harry Slocombe, who reported the club's matches on local newspapers, wrote it. It has proved of great value in the production of this book, as it provided a wealth of information.

A Gala Dinner was held at the Garnant Constitutional Club to celebrate the occasion.

The honour of leading the Amman during its Jubilee Season fell to Glyn John, a teacher who had previously captained Gidea Park in the London area. His vice-captain was Norman Bevan. Norman, a very versatile player who could play in most back positions, is the nephew of Joe and Evan Bevan, who had served the club with such distinction.

During one match, Amman found themselves a player short, and Mal Bevan (of the same clan) came to the rescue, although well into his forties. According to the Amman Valley Chronicle:

The outstanding feature of the game was the resuscitation of that old and well tried servant of the club – Mal Bevan. He gave a demonstration of how the head should control the foot, and a player's actions generally. His display was an object lesson to the younger players who played alongside him on Saturday.

Although this team contained many talented players, the club had to wait until the following season to achieve real success. The photograph, incidentally, is the only known one in existence where Nev Anthony has hair!

50th Anniversary Committee

Back row: Glen Thomas, Lewis James, Cis Jones, Evan Davies, Ted Cole, Albert Pike, Raymond Morgan.
Middle Row: Dai Rees, W.D. Evans, Tom Morris, D.F. Morgan, Tom George, Harold Davies, Sid Davies, Phil James.
Front Row: Percy Rees, Jack Davies, (Vice-Chairman), Percy Thomas (Secretary), Bertie Davies (Chairman), Tom E. Howells (Treasurer), Amman Rees (Asst. Secretary), Fred Hughes.

Elwyn Davies is the father of Stuart Davies, the Swansea and Wales back-row forward of the 1990's who is now a television Rugby pundit. Elwyn himself was an excellent centre who played for Swansea for many seasons.

This was the season when Amman was to win its first West Wales Championship since 1936, and, as it turned out, the last time it ever won it. At that time, the top four teams in the Championship table played off in semi-finals and a final to decide who the champions would be.

They had started the season very badly, and they had soon reached the situation where they had to win every remaining match if they were to make the top four. Things improved dramatically, and consecutive wins against Llandybie, Ammanford, Briton Ferry, Gowerton, Tumble, Hendy and Pontardulais enabled them to scrape in at fourth place.

"Sentinel" wrote in the South Wales Voice on April 2nd 1954:

"Amman United stumbled badly at the beginning of the season but a wonderful recovery enabled them to gain a place in the West Wales honours list.

A big factor in their success has undoubtedly been the skill of that grand old warrior, Ieuan Evans, playing as well as ever in the full-back berth.

Amman's attractive, open-type football will make them favourites with the spectators in the games to come."

The other three teams to Qualify for the top-four were New Dock Stars (1st), Seven Sisters (2nd) and Crynant (3rd).

In the semi-final, Amman beat Seven Sisters by 3 points to nil before a record attendance for West Wales matches at the Gnoll, Neath.

The final against New Dock Stars was played at Stradey Park and, in a hard-fought match, Amman won by 6 points to 3 with Peter Williams scoring the winning try.

The following report appeared in the South Wales Voice on April 30th 1954:

A salvo to Amman United on their West Wales Championship win! According to some critics it was not a good game, but I saw it as an interesting struggle between two very determined sides, and who can blame them from trying to avoid errors?

"Give nothing away" was the order of the day for each side.

The United finished strongly and there is no doubt of their worthiness as champions of the West for this season. They were very well served by Ieuan Evans at full-back, and by two good wings, Peris James and Peter Williams.

Unfortunately, no match or playing records are available for the remainder of the fifties, and the only photograph I've managed to come across is the one of the 1956-57 team captained by Evan James ("Ianto Gorsto")

Six of this team were newly-arrived from the very successful Amman Youth team of the previous season, and two of them in particular were to have an immediate impact on the West Wales scene. John "Cisco" Francis was a hard-running centre and devastating crash-tackler whose reputation went before him. Glyn James, who was later to captain the Amman in seasons 1960-61 and 1963-64, was a superb scrum-half who was renowned for his bravery, particularly when he was behind a beaten pack. This resulted in Glyn suffering a broken nose on more occasions than Henry Cooper.

West Wales Champions 1953-54

Back row: Peris James, Cyril Rees, Ceryl Barnett.
Second row: Peter Williams, Jarvis Styles, Godfrey Hitchings, Vince Jones, Viv Rees, Hubert Jones (injured).
Seated: John Jones, Gwyndaf Walters, Bertie Davies (Chairman), Ieuan Evans,
Gwyn Jones (Club captain - injured), Elwyn Davies, Billy Bowen.
Front: Norman Bevan, Con Mathias.

Amman United 1956-57

Back row: Dennis Davies, Jarvis Styles, Glyn Jenkins, Peter Gerrard, Malvern Evans, Trevor Jones.
Middle row: Neville James, Ken James, Evan James, Ieuan Evans, John Francis.
Front row: Ritchie Bundock, Glyn James, Emrys Davies, Elwyn Owen.

The 1960s

For the Amman, the 1960s got off to a wonderful start with the official opening of the Grandstand on April 26th 1960. With the concrete terracing on the opposite side, this made Cwmamman Park the best venue in West Wales.

The Committee had worked extremely hard, mainly through the selling of "Tote" tickets, to raise the necessary funds. The stand cost £6,000 pounds, which was a very large amount of money in those days. At the time, the average price of a house was about £2,000.

The following appeared in the South Wales Evening Post on Wednesday, April 27 1960:

AMMAN GET THEIR NEW £6,000 STAND

The new stand at the Amman United ground was officially opened yesterday by Mr. F.G. Phillips, past president of the W.R.U. and life president of the W.W.R.U. He said that the stand stood as a monument to the untiring efforts of club committee members.

At an estimated cost of £6,000 the stand is equipped with dressing-rooms for the players and referees, showers and committee rooms.

Other speakers at the opening ceremony were Major Gilbert Davies, the architect, Major W.H. Clement, secretary of the W.R.U. and Mr. D.L. James, chairman of the W.W.R.U. Mr. Bertie Davies Amman United chairman introduced them.

Also present were Messrs. Ivor Jones, Ewart Davies, V.J. Parfitt and Dr. Rocyn Jones of the W.R.U., and Messrs. Eurof Davies, W.W.R.U. secretary, Lewis Davies, member of the W.W.R.U. management committee, and Hermas Evans, ex-secretary of the Welsh Youth R.U.

Referee at the celebration match which followed was Mr. S.J. Williams, of Newport, who although born only a stone's throwaway, was handling his first match at the Amman United ground.

First player to pass through the door was Onllwyn Brace, of Llanelly and Wales, who skippered an Amman Valley XV against the Amman Valley side. Amman's skipper, Hugh Harris, followed him.

Players and guests were entertained after the match which the Valley XV won 17 – 13, by Cwmamman Workingmen's Club and Institute, Garnant.

The Amman Valley XVs points came from tries by Cennydd Hopkins (Ammanford) 2, Peter Thomas (Llandeilo) 2 and a self-converted try by John Elgar Williams (Brynamman). Amman United's points came from a try each by Martin Jones, Raymond Edwards and Tony Lodge, with one conversion by Tony Richards.

Generally, throughout the sixties, Amman's results varied from just below average to just above. Even in their weakest season, 1963-64, 11 matches were won and 4 drawn out of the 31 played. Their best season was 1966-67, when, of the 35 matches played, 21 were won and 6 drawn. During this season, Amman also won the C.C. Evans Cup for the first time when they beat Llandybie at Ammanford by 14 points to 5.

Throughout most of this period, the administration of the club was in the safe hands of Chairman Phil James, Secretary Nev Anthony, Treasurer Brian Lloyd and a hard-working committee.

Freddie Phillips and Beatie Davies at the official opening of the stand

Amman XV at Official opening of stand

Back Row: Sam Williams (Referee), John Jones, Tony Richards, Mel Griffiths, Aneurin Williams, Raymond Edwards.
Middle Row: Dai Howells, Hywel Williams, Nev Anthony, Trevor Jones, Colin Lodge.
Front Row: Hywel Jones, Martin Jones, Hugh Harris, Glyn James, Rowland Jones.

Amman United 1962-63

Back row: Rowland Jones, Jeff Butt, Hugh Harris, Aneurin Williams, Clive Brooks, Tony Richards, Randall Williams, Ken Davies, Phil James (Chairman).
Middle row: Ritchie Bundock, Edgar Morris, Dennis Davies (Captain), Raymond Edwards, Griff Morris.
Front row: Glyn James, Keith Hughes, Martin Jones.

Amman United 1963-64.

Back Row: Colin Davies, Dai Howells, Jeff Butt, Hugh Harris, Aneurin Williams, Peter Gerrard.
Middle Row: Dennis Davies, John Howells, Edgar Morris, Brian Davies.
Front Row: Andrew Matthews, Eirian Jenkins, Glyn James (Capt.), Martin Jones, Ken Davies.

Amman United v Carmarthen *Quins West Wales Cup Semi-Final – April 1966*

Back row: Clive Brooks, Gethin James, Randall Williams, Rowley Phillips, Jeff Butt, Ken Davies.
Seated: Martin Jones, Keith Hughes, Alan Thomas (Capt.), Rowley Davies, Hywel Evans.
Front row: Dai Thomas, Ritchie Bundock. Rowland Jones, John Thomas

Amman United 1966-67

Back row: Ian Penman, Howard Davies, Gethin James, Hugh Harris, Gordon Thomas, Trevor Evans, Randall Williams.
Middle row: Colin Davies, Alan Arnold, Huw Joshua, John Thomas, Alan Thomas (Capt.), Dai Lloyd, Dai Thomas, Martin Jones, Dennis Davies.
Front row: John Williams, Owen Jones, Len Jones, John Pugh.

Although we were having an average season, winning half of our league matches, we did manage to reach the semi-final of the West Wales Cup after wins against Trebanos and Cwmgors.

The semi-final was played at Ammanford against Carmarthen Quins. Quins had a huge pack of forwards against our lightweight eight, and after a mighty struggle we lost by six points to three.

The 1966/67 team was the most successful of the 1960's and I regard it as a great honour and privilege to have captained it. There are so many outstanding individuals that I thought it only right that I should write a short pen-picture of each.

Ian Penman: A Scotsman, capped for Scottish Schoolboys at Soccer. Strong-running winger who became a member of our great sevens team. Ian has kindly written an amusing memoir for this book of his time with the Amman.

Howard Davies: "Howie" joined the Amman from his beloved Penybanc Tigers. Uncompromising front or second-row forward, he gave many years of loyal service to the club, and maintains a very close contact in spite of now living on the Gwent border. He has been the driving force behind the production of this book.

Gethin James: Very fit and mobile prop forward who was good enough to become a member of the very successful 1966 sevens team.

Hugh Harris: One of the club greats on and off the field, Hugh started playing for Amman Youth when he was fourteen, and was capped for the Welsh Youth in 1958. After Youth rugby, he went straight into the Neath team in spite of being very slimly built. During the sixties and early seventies he played many games for Llanelli, and was the regular outside-half for Aberavon for many seasons despite periods of ill-health. When not involved in first-class rugby, Hugh was in his element back with the Amman, and captained the club in the 1961-62 and 1964-65 seasons. He was an inspiration on the field, and always brought out the best in those playing outside him. He was also the catalyst for so much of the enjoyment in off the field activities. Sadly, he died in his early forties after a long, brave fight against his illness.

Gordon Thomas: Superb No. 8 forward, "Butch" came straight into the Amman pack after playing centre in youth rugby, where he came close to winning an international cap. Very skilful and deceptively fast, he was the first to captain the club on three occasions. A member of the great sevens team of 1967.

Trevor Evans: (see elsewhere) I would merely like to comment that Trev's last cap was the same size as his first.

Randall Williams: Rugged second-row forward who thrived on a physical challenge. Not a pacifist. Known as "Coch" for obvious reasons, but his full nickname is used only by close friends and those with a death wish.

Colin Davies: An excellent attacking full-back, "Talley" could play in most back positions, and spent a couple of seasons with Swansea. His greatest moment came during one of the annual Easter matches against the Barbarians. Swansea were losing heavily when their scrum-half was injured (no subs in those days). Talley was moved to scrum-half, and, with bravura performance, won the game for them. While at Swansea, he also developed an interest in Roman law.

Alan Arnold: Although a lightweight as second-row forward, Alan was a very durable and mobile player and an excellent lineout jumper.

Huw Joshua: A versatile player who played mostly at outside-half or centre. Huw was also a very good sevens player.

John Thomas: "John Bach" started playing rugby at the age of 18 after being the local soccer star. He immediately stepped into the Amman team as an outside- half, and started making a name for himself. He starred in the great Amman sevens teams of 1966 and 1967 and soon drew the attention of Llanelli. Later, he was to win the Bill Everson Trophy as the outstanding player in the tournament when Llanelli won the Snelling Sevens Competition. John played at centre for Llanelli for many seasons and played against the Springboks in 1970. Although small in stature, John was a superb tackler.

Dai Lloyd: An excellent hooker who had previously played for Penarth, Dai captained the Amman in the 1968-69 season.

Dai Thomas: Capped by the Welsh Secondary Schools as a centre, "Dai Manora" was an extremely fast, elusive and well-balanced runner, who was capable of tearing defences to shreds. Appeared for many first-class sides, and played for the star-studded Cardiff College of Education side when they beat the Amman in the famous sevens final at Aberavon in1967. The previous year he had been a member of Amman's sevens team.

Martin Jones: (see elsewhere)

Dennis Davies: (see elsewhere)

John Williams: John was a classy scrum-half with an excellent service. He had a Final Youth Trial as an outside-half. John captained the club in season 1967-68.

Owen Jones: Owen was a very versatile player who played mainly at centre or outside-half, and was a key player in the 1967 sevens team. He won a Rugby Blue at Oxford University in each of the 1969,1970 and 1971 seasons, and was on the winning side on each occasion. In1969, he scored all the points (3 penalties), and in 1971 he captained the side. He was also in the Oxford side that defeated the Springboks in 1969. He was the Amman captain in season 1969-70.

Len Jones: Mobile front or second-row forward. Hard scrummager and good lineout worker.

John Pugh: Fine all-round rugby player who was equally at home in the back row or at centre. Superb sevens player and a member of the 1967 side.

The clubhouse

Unquestionably, the most important development that took place in the club during this period was the acquisition of a clubhouse. The committee had considered several premises before deciding that the most suitable would be the Salutation Hotel on Cwmamman Road, Glanaman.

Salutation Hotel, Victory Carnival, 1945, The jockey is well-known local character "Rhys Steaks".

After negotiations with Buckley's Brewery, a long lease on a peppercorn rental was arranged. After much redecoration and refurbishment, The Amman United Clubhouse opened in October 1967. This was a very proud and satisfying moment for all concerned with the well-being of the club. At long last, Amman United R.F.C. had a home to call its own.

Although all the officials and other committeemen had their parts to play in ensuring the success of the clubhouse, direct responsibility fell on the shoulders of the new Social Secretary, Peter Williams. An ex-player, who played in the last Championship-winning side, he fulfilled his responsibilities with a great deal of hard work and high competence. The club owes him a great debt of gratitude for his efforts.

Amman United RFC Clubhouse

A ladies Committee was formed at this time and organised many successful events at the Clubhouse. It consisted of the wives of committeemen, players and ex-players, and also of some enthusiastic women supporters. Officials of the first Ladies Committee were Agnes James (Chair), Avril Williams (Secretary) and Yvonne Williams (Treasurer).

Amman Ladies Committee 1968

Back row : Glenys Jones, Gwennie Evans, Mair Timothy, Jean Jones.
Middle row : Mair Howells, Maureen James, Mary Walters, Nina James, Edna Evans.
Front row: Betty James, Gillian Thomas, Agnes James, Avril Williams, Yvonne Williams.

The Clubhouse was an immediate success. It was well-supported during the week and packed to the rafters on weekends. This ensured the financial security of the club for many years to come.

Many changes and adaptations of the building have taken place over the years, and recent refurbishments will ensure the continuing comfort of members.

Amman United Committee 1967

Back row: Donald Evans, John Evans, Hywel Williams, Raymond Morgan, Will Harse, Dil Williams, Sid Davies, Arthur Rees, Gareth Jenkins, Cis Jones, Bill Murphy.
Front row: Peter Williams, Eurof Walters, Brian Lloyd (Treasurer), Phil James (Chairman), Nev Anthony (Secretary), Jack Evans, Lewis James, George Heathcote, Max Williams.

In Welsh Rugby, the late Sixties was a period when serious coaching became the order of the day, and the game, to a large extent, lost its innocence. In its way, this development probably had as much of an impact on the game as did the advent of professionalism in the late Nineties.

Life, for the Amman and the rest of Welsh Rugby, would never be the same again.

Amman United 1969-70

Back row: Howard Davies, Dai Jones, John Rees, Hywel Rees, Dai Jenkins, Graham George.
Middle row: Alan Arnold, Colin Davies, Owen Jones (Captain), Dai Thomas, Dennis Davies.
Front row: Alan Rogerson, Ryan Bartlett, Ieuan Bevan, Harry Davies.

WELSH NATIONAL SEVENS COMPETITION FINALS

Held at the Abaravon, Talbot Ground, May 6th, 1967

Western Mail, Saturday, May 6, 1967

Small clubs will tilt at rugby giants

By J. B. G. Thomas

It is the ambition of the smaller clubs in Wales to play the larger ones, and while it is not always possible to do this at 15-a-side level, progress will be made today in the staging of the first full national seven-a-side tournament at Aberavon by the Welsh Rugby Union.

Although the national sevens have not yet captured the imagination of rugby followers in the manner of the Snelling sevens with its record crowd of 40,000 last week it will be interesting to see whether the clash of the "big and little fish" of Welsh rugby swells the gate receipts today.

Unfortunately the draw finds four of the leading senior clubs in opposition: Bridgend play Newport in the third match of the first round and Llanelli play Pontypool in the last match of the first round.

The meeting of Bridgend and Newport a repeat of the semi-final tie in the Snelling tournament could have a vital effect upon the final for one of these teams must surely go through to the final in the top half of the draw.

Points scorers

Bridgend should be a stronger side than they were last Saturday because two of their international players and prolific scorers Keith Bradshaw and R. Evans hope to return to the side.

However, their speedy wing A. Morgan is suffering from a heavy cold and may not be available.

Newport have a complete seven in the field apart from G.R. Britton. Several of their leading players are injured.

Britton will be supported by K. Poole, V. Perrins, G. J. Treharne, W. J. Morris, K. Jarret and S. J. Watkins.

Following their disappointing showing last Saturday the Neath club held special training sessions this week and N. Rees replaces R. Davies as hooker. Neath meet Cwmavon in the second match.

Glamorgan Wanderers who beat Abertillery in extra time last week meet Caerphilly while Whitland meet Ruthin in a West v North Wales clash.

The fittest seven in the tournament could well be that from Cardiff Training College who have been engaged for some time in special practice and who won their district preliminary rounds quite convincingly at Landfall. However, today they will be without John Jeffrey who is attending a wedding.

There should be an interesting struggle between Felinfoel and Pontypool United, who are holders of the WRU trophy. The United have been trained by B. E. Jones the former Pontypool outside half who has earned a considerable reputation as a schoolboy coach.

Finally, Llanelli meet Pontypool and if Llanelli field a full side they may challenge the Training College in the second semi-final.

If one had to forecast two finalist, although the situation is not clear cut as it was for the Snelling tournament, it is likely that the winners of the Bridgend v Newport tie and Cardiff Training College will meet in the final.

Newport would like to win the trophy to prove themselves undisputed sevens champions of Wales but I expect they like several other clubs are disappointed that Cardiff have not been allowed to field a seven in the tournament since a very good one could have been drawn from the highly successful Athletic XV.

1.30-	*Glamorgan Wanderers v Caerphilly*
1.50-	*Neath v Cwmavon*
2.10-	*Bridgend v Newport*
2.30-	*Ebbw Vale v Amman United*
2.50-	*Whitland v Ruthin*
3.10-	*Cardiff Training College v Cwmllynfell*
3.30-	*Felinfoel v Pontypool United*
3.50-	*Llanelli v Pontypool*
5.30 and - 6.10	*Semi-finals of WSSRU sevens (Newport H.S. v Llanelli G.S.; Ystalyfera G.S. v Quakers Yard G.S.*
5.50 and - 6.30	*Semi-finals of national sevens*
6.50-	*WSSRU final*
7.15-	*National final*

SEVENS GLORY FOR THE AMMAN
By Owen Jones

[Collage of newspaper clippings with headlines including: "Ebbw Vale, Bridgend and Neath Toppled by West Wales side....", "SALUTE UNITED", "JOHN THOMAS SCORES 17 POINTS", "Magnificent village seven k.o. the top clubs", "Amman lose final", "Amman win all the glory", "Shock for Vale, Sunk by last kick of match", "Amman Utd. go giant killing"]

In the modern professional and semi-professional era of rugby, seven-a-side rugby tournaments have lost their appeal and attraction for players and therefore, for the public. When one looks at the names of the players playing for Wales on the International Sevens Circuit, it's obvious that the priorities for the present generation do not include sevens. In many ways, I think this is a mistake, for the skills developed when playing sevens, particularly for the younger players, would improve their performances generally.

During the 1960s, in the halcyon days for sevens, the Snelling Sevens, featuring the so-called First Class Rugby Clubs, attracted large crowds and were hugely popular. International players regularly featured in the tournament and the standard was very high.

In 1966, the Welsh Rugby Union organised a National sevens tournament at Aberavon, where the winners of each of the Districts' sevens competitions took part. Amman United won the District 'F' Competition and the proud record of the club in sevens had started. Unfortunately, the First Class clubs did not participate, but in 1967 they did join the competition. Thus the qualifiers for the Finals Day at Aberavon on Saturday, 6th May were the nine winners of the District Competitions held on 22nd April and the quarter-finalists from the Snelling Competition held on 29th April. This was the era before leagues and cups, and it was the only opportunity for the Davids and Goliaths of Welsh rugby to meet for the title of National Sevens Champions. The programme notes suggested that biblical history could repeat itself I doubt if the writer of the programme anticipated the shocks, which were in store for the major clubs.

We won the District 'F' sevens again at Ammanford and took our place in the finals at Aberavon. We all looked forward eagerly to the big day and there was great anticipation as we travelled on the bus. The team was a mixture of youth and experience, and contained players who could play in a number of positions. Captain of the team was Hywel Evans, later to become famous as the actor Dafydd Hywel. Playing at hooker, he was the talisman and led from the front. Hywel went on to play for Bridgend in the following season. The props were John Pugh and Gordon (Butch) Thomas, two expert ball winners and very good all-round footballers. At scrum half was the gifted John (Manora) Thomas. An outstanding natural footballer, John went on to have a successful career at Llanelli and indeed won the player of the tournament when representing Llanelli at the Snelling Sevens in 1971. Playing at centre was Martin Jones who was Mr Reliable. In all the tournaments I played with Martin, he never had a bad game, playing equally well at prop or centre. Martin was, and still is, Amman United through and through, and has given excellent service to the club as a player and secretary. On the wing was the flying Scotsman Ian Penman. A strong and powerful runner Ian scored important tries for the team. It was my good fortune at nineteen and the baby of the team to play outside half. Colin Davies played splendidly at centre in the tournament at Ammanford when John Pugh was not available and Martin played prop.

There were no coaches to help prepare us, the only coaches were buses to take us to and from games! However Hywel, John Pugh and I had been fortunate in having the excellent John Elgar Williams to coach us when we were pupils at Amman Valley Grammar School. We had achieved considerable success in sevens at the school, losing in the final of the Welsh Secondary Schools Sevens at what is now the Millennium Stadium in 1964, and winning the final in 1965 at St. Helens Swansea. The final was played before the final of the Snelling Sevens tournament and gave us invaluable experience of playing in front of large crowds.

There was a large crowd for the finals at Aberavon and we were due to play Ebbw Vale in the fourth match. The first three matches went according to plan with Glamorgan Wanderers, Neath and Bridgend winning comfortably. No-one outside our loyal band of supporters gave us a chance, but we were quietly confident and, in an exciting and pulsating match with the lead changing hands many times, we beat Ebbw Vale by 15 points to 14. Bridgend, with their galaxy of stars and renowned sevens players, were our next opponents. Tackling like demons and refusing to yield to intense pressure, we won by 6 points to 3 (a try was 3 points and we outscored them two tries to one). Into the semi-final and the All Blacks of Neath stood in our way. In another close and exciting encounter, we managed the unthinkable and beat Neath by 10 points to 8. Our opponents in the final were Cardiff College of Education (now UWIC) who had a much easier run to the final having beaten Cwmllynfell, Ruthin and Llanelli. We were desperately unlucky to lose, but we had certainly put the Amman on the map. There was very little rugby on the television in those days, but on the Monday evening highlights of the tournament were shown on BBC and headlines such as "the Magnificent Seven" were common features in the newspapers.

We won the District 'F' sevens again in 1969 and played in the finals at Cardiff, but, unfortunately, we were reduced to 6 players because of injury early in the game. Substitutes were not allowed during the game and we lost to Bridgend. We also reached the final of the District 'F' sevens in 1968 and 1970, and we won a number of other tournaments. Numerous trophies won are a constant reminder of the splendid times we had in playing sevens for the Amman United.

Western Mail, Monday, May 8, 1967

Magnificent village seven k.o. the top clubs
Amman lose final – but win all the glory

By John Billot

Seven players from the obscurity of village rugby walked into the headlines as they trudged off the pitch at Aberavon. Amman United were a beaten side, but this team will be talked about long after everyone has forgotten just who beat them in the exciting final of the Welsh Rugby Union National Sevens competition.

Cardiff College of Education took the cup – Amman United stole the glory, and the crowd cheered them every inch of the way. It was very nearly a fairy-tale ending as they led 10-8 until college wing Gary Laycock raced away to complete his hat-trick of tries and pip gallant Amman 11-10.

When College skipper Derek Jones was handed the cup he said, "At one stage I did not think we were going to do it." Those words could have been used by Amman to describe every one of their first three games.

To reach the final Amman had to beat Ebbw Vale, Bridgend and Neath-and each time after being behind. This "impossible" task would have been enough to make Hercules quit his labours. Amman beat them all.

Neath beaten by last kick.

A superb conversion from the touchline by scrum half John Thomas gave them a sensational 15-14 first-round win over Ebbw Vale one of the semi-finalists of the Snelling Sevens.

I had already written Ebbw Vale's name in my programme as going through to the second round as they led 14-10. I was to make another mistake in the semi-final-and had to scratch out the name of Neath the champion Welsh club of the season just ended.

But first it was Bridgend who found Amman irresistible. Having put out Newport 13-8 in the first round (Newport fielded only one of the team Gordon Britton that had won the Snelling Cup the previous week). Bridgend had high hopes of adding the sevens cup to the Welsh Floodlight Alliance trophy they won this season.

John Lloyd gave them the lead with a try, but, John Thomas with a penalty goal, and Owen Jones with a try mad it 6-3 for Amman-and a place against Neath in the semi-final.

John Thomas top scorer.

No team should expect a reprieve after being down 8-0 to Neath with barely five minutes to run. Yet Amman turned this fantastic match into a 10-8 win with the last kick of the match-another John Thomas conversion from out near the touchline in the rain.

This match was so dramatic that referee Ken Morgans forgot the conversion kick would decide the result and whistled for the end after Owen Jones's try put Amman level.

Amman players protested; the crowd booed and Mr. Morgans suddenly realised. He turned, dashed back and indicated the spot from where scrum half star John Thomas would try his conversion.

What a roar when the ball curled between the posts! What a hat-trick of wins over Wales's top teams by the village boys!

This magnificent seven comprised of Ian Penman, Martin Jones, Owen Jones, John Thomas, John Pugh, hooker Hywel Evans and Gordon Thomas. Martin Jones and Penman each scored three tries in the tourney and John Thomas was the top scorer of the day with 17 points from a penalty goal and seven conversions.

Cardiff College of Education were bigger, fitter and faster-but better by only one point against these Amman boys!

Derek Jones converted one of Laycock's three tries for the 11-10 verdict after John Thomas had goaled tries by Martin Jones and Penman.

College six hold out

The College had two easy first games. Yet they looked in serious trouble in the semi-final when prop Steve Thomas was kicked on the shin in a scrum before the ball had been put in. Thomas had a deep cut and was of for most of the first half.

But the six College players snatched an 8-0 lead with two sparkling tries by scrum half Paul Evans one converted by Derek Jones and held on to win 8-5.

> Llanelli by employing over-vigorous methods made themselves the most unpopular team of the day and were roundly booed off the field. It is unfortunate that Llanelli's image has to suffer because of a couple of completely unnecessary acts.
>
> Still the final made us all remember the good things-and none of us will ever forget the glory of the losers on the day when Amman United shook Welsh rugby's top teams.
>
> *Ex-soccer twin stars*
>
> Twin brothers John Thomas and David Thomas played against each other in the WRU Sevens final. Scrum half John was the star of the Amman United team. David was a key man at centre for Cardiff College of Education.
>
> When they were at school John played soccer while David made his mark at rugby. In Saturday's tournament it was former soccer man John who shone with an aggregate of 17 points-David scored only one try.
>
> *Round-by-round results*
>
> First round: Glamorgan Wanderers beat Caerphilly 11-3; Neath beat Cwmavon 23-3; Bridgend beat Newport 13-8; Amman United beat Ebbw Vale 15-14; Ruthin beat Whitland 10-0; Cardiff College of Education beat Cwmllynfell 10-0; Pontypool beat Felinfoel 16-5; Llanelli beat Pontypool United 15-3.
>
> Second round: Neath beat Glamorgan Wanderers 13-0; Amman United beat Bridgend 6-3; Cardiff College of Education beat Ruthin 18-5; Llanelli beat Pontypool United 5-0.
>
> Semi-finals: Amman United beat Neath 10-8; Cardiff College of Education beat Llanelli 8-5.
>
> Final: Cardiff College of Education beat Amman United 11-10.

The 6th May 1967 provided one of the greatest days in the history of the Amman with the exploits of our great sevens team at Aberavon. Included is an excellent account of that day by Owen Jones and John Billot. I would like to record my own special memory of that day:

Towards the end of the match against a star-studded Bridgend team, Amman were leading by 6 points to 3 when Bridgend forward Colin Standing (a Barbarian) was put clear for what would have been a winning score. Hard on his heels came John Bach, who dived full-length to ankle-tap Standing, and left him beating the ground in frustration.

District F Sevens Winners 1965-66

Back row: Martin Jones, Jeff Butt, Gethin James, Ken Davies.
Front row: Phil James (Chairman), John Thomas, Hywel Evans (Capt.), Dai Thomas, Nev Anthony (Secretary).

Welsh Sevens Finalists 1967

Back row: John Pugh, Alan Arnold, Trevor Evans, Gordon Thomas, Ian Penman.
Front row: Martin Jones, John Thomas, Hywel Evans (Capt.), Colin Davies, Owen Jones.

83

SINE DIE (Life Ban) for Bobbie Hunt
By Howard Gabe Davies

A life ban was imposed that was to last 42 years and only ended as a result of the world amateur rugby game being declared open by the Chairman, Mr Vernon Pugh, of the International Rugby Board in August 1995.

It all started with James Rees, known as Jim-y-Gas, a character who received his nickname by being an employee of the Gas Board; he travelled throughout Wales with his work and was well known. Jim arranged a charity game with Cardigan RFC to help raise funds for the Cardigan club, who were then members of the Welsh Junior Union.

Jim y Gas raised an invitation team called 'Captain Mantle's XV' (gas mantle) and picked players from various sources: veteran Amman United players, young Amman Quins players and tragically some ex-rugby league players, and one of these was a renowned ex-Llanelli player. For Bobby and the Amman boys it was a charity match, a day-out in Cardigan and a bit of a fun game and they did not think much about it.

The game was played on the Cardigan Grammar School field on the 28th February, 1953: Cardigan RFC v Western Valley XV (Captain Mantle's XV)

Captain Mantle's team, with seven bus-loads of supporters, left the Amman for Cardigan Town. Bobby remembers that Cardigan pubs made a roaring trade and the Amman supporters had a great day out, but for different reason, Bobby did not! All the players had paid for an after-match meal – 'When I got there, the supporters had eaten everything and there was no more food left; the only food remaining was some chocolate fingers to eat; it still rankles today.'

However, the following week, the cat was left out of the bag when someone informed the Welsh Rugby Union that rugby league players had played with union players. It was said that an Amman committeeman had reported the transgression to the WRU. Others said that the exceptional play of the ex-Llanelli and now rugby league player had left such an impression on the crowd that everyone present had wanted to know who the player was!

The Proceedings of the Meetings of the Welsh Rugby Union Volume 4-6 1951-1954 General Purposes Committee – 9th April 1953 Minute 212 Cardigan v Western Valley XV

212. **Cardigan V Western Valley XV** The Committee considered a report on a match played at Cardigan, on 28th February 1953, between Cardigan R.F.C, and a team called Western Valleys XV, partly composed of players of the Rugby League. In a letter dated 13th March, on the matter, Mr. Geo Thomas, chairman of Cardigan R.F.C, said that neither he nor any member of his Club had any idea that there were "professional" players in the Western Valleys XV, and that if they had, the match would certainly not have been played.

The Secretary informed the Committee that he had written on 11th March to Mr. F.T. Day, asking him to get a full report on the matter, for the Committee's consideration as soon as possible. He, the Secretary, understood that this report would soon be received.

It was subsequently - RESOLVED - That a sub-committee be appointed, consisting of Messrs Daniel Jones, David Jones, Danny Davies, Vincent Griffiths, Enoch Rees and J.W. Eaull, to enquire fully into this matter, after the consideration by the Committee of Mr. F.T. Day's report.

Minute 225 Cardigan v Western Valley XV (Vol. 5. Paragraph 212)

225. **Cardigan v Western Valley XV** (Vol.5. paragraph 212).
The Secretary read a letter from Mr. F.T. Day, of the Junior Union, covering a letter of explanation of this matter from the Secretary of the Cardigan R.F.C, dated 26th March 1953, which stated that -
(1). The game was played on the Cardigan Grammar School Ground.
(2). The fixture was arranged between the Cardigan R.F.C, and Mr. Jim Rees, 2 Folland Road, Glanamman.
(3). No guarantee was given.
(4). Decision to play the game was made by Cardigan R.F.C, Committee.
In this connection it is pointed out that this Club has never been asked to submit its fixture list to the Pembrokeshire and District Junior Rugby Union, or any directive ever given that permission should be requested and given before playing any game, -

> permission, therefore, was not asked.
> (5) The referee was Mr. Ted Cole, who it was understood is in the W.R.U, and who travelled with the Western Valleys XV.
> (6) I can assure you that this Club had no inkling whatsoever that Rugby League members were included in the visiting team.
>
> The Committee – RESOLVED – That Cardigan R.F.C, be suspended pending a full enquiry into the matter by the Sub-Committee appointed for this purpose.

Minute 35 Cardigan R.F.C. (Volume. 5. Paras. 212 and 225)

> 35. **Cardigan R.F.C (Vol.5.paras.212 and 225)** Mr. David Jones, chairman of the Sub-Committee, gave a full report of the enquiry held at Neath, on the 20th June, and said that as a result of the enquiry, the Sub-Committee recommended –
> 1. That the suspension of Cardigan be removed and that they be severely censured.
> 2. That J. Rees be declared a professional and that W.R.U. Clubs be informed that he must be treated accordingly.
> 3. That B. Hunt, D. Cochran and E. Slocombe of Amman United, be declared professionals, and that Amman United be informed accordingly.
> 4. That all Clubs in the W.R.U. be warned that ignorance of the law cannot be regarded as an excuse for transgression.
> 5. That all the teams in the Junior Union and the Youth Rugby Union be supplied free of charge by the W.R.U. with a copy each of the W.R.U. By-laws and the Laws as to Professionalism.
>
> The General Purposes Committee – RESOLVED – That these recommendations be approved, and that the referee in this match – F. Cole – of Glanamman, also be "professionalised."

Bobbie, Dennie and Eddie did not appear in front of the court (WRU Disciplinary Committee); as Bobbie said, 'We never ever thought we would be banned'.

AMMAN VALLEY CHRONICLE
dated 10th September 1953

Amman United were notified by the Secretary of the Welsh Rugby Union on Saturday that four members – D Cochrane, Robert Hunt and Eddie Slocombe (former Players) and Mr James Rees a committee man had been professionalised by the W.R.U.

Th incident that led to this decision was the match played last season at Cardigan in aid of the funds of the Cardigan R.F.C.

The team from the Amman Valley was selected by Mr James Rees and contained several Rugby League Players.

Fortunately the three players, all former Amman United captains retired from playing at the end of 1952-53 season but all three played a few games last season as substitutes. Mr Rees was for the first time elected to the Amman committee at the last annual meeting.

WESTERN MAIL
Friday 4th September 1953.

Welsh Rugby Union lifts ban on Cardigan club – JBG Thomas
The general committee of the WRU meeting in Cardiff last night lifted the ban on Cardigan club imposed last April.
The club was severely censured but will be allowed to fulfil its fixtures.

Minute 78 Amman United Players' Protest.

```
78.     Amman United Players' Protest   A letter signed by D.Cochrane
E.Slocombe and B.Hunt, protesting against their having been pro-
fessionalised by the Union for their participation in the match at
Cardigan on 28th February 1953,(Vol.5.paras.225 - Vol.6.para.35),
was read by the Secretary. It was - RESOLVED - That no action
be taken.
```

To day, in 2003, Bobby bares no animosity about the life ban and his rugby career coming to an end.

Bobby has followed rugby all these years and has also helped the Amman United financially.

PROFILE OF BOBBY HUNT
By Howard Gabe Davies

Born in Garnant 17.5.1922, he started his rugby career for Cwmgorse at 17, and played for the Amman Utd RFC from 1945 – 1953. During the war years, the West Wales League was closed down due to the restrictions on travel and the war effort. Some rugby was played and Bobby turned out for the 'Frank Dallavalle' team, the Italian café owner with the now famous 'Franks Ice Cream'. Organised by Ivor Phillips; the team included rugby league players, but it was allowed during the war years of 1939/1945.

After the war, Amman Utd had very good teams and he played in two West Wales Cup Finals against Felinfoel and Tumble.

The front row was special in Denny Cochram (loose head), Iau Ward (hooker) and Bobby (tight head). In the scrums, Bobby would place the outside arm on his knee to hold up the front row and not around the opposing prop. The front row was so low that his nose touched the grass and the opposition hooker could not see the ball coming into the scrum on their put-in. The front row as a unit won so much ball that Iau Ward went on to play for Swansea (although Iau was an excellent hooker) and three other hookers also went on to play for first class rugby teams. The Amman second-row Kendrick Lewis would say that the Amman hookers had the glory, but it was Denny Cochram and Bobby Hunt who did the mischief and would always, in Welsh, say "Nage fe odd e" or "Na, ddim fe oedd wedi ennill y bel" meaning it wasn't the hooker that had won the ball but the two props.

Amman front row forward

R. Hunt, Amman United's front-row forward, ranks with the best to wear the Scarlet jersey for many years.

Always up with the ball, He has been responsible for scoring a number of tries this season. He handles the ball like a threequarter, and has a deceptive burst.

Members of the club feel that he would make an excellent centre, but Hunt is not keen to leave the forwards.

Has played a prominent part in helping to build up the splendid reputation Amman's pack has gained.

Cup Final Memories Tumble and Felinfoel

Tumble: the game was lost by a disputed drop-goal. Iau Ward had told the flankers, "You must get that outside half, he's going for the drop-kick" and the outside-half's hurried drop-kick was actually punted over – it was not a drop kick and the referee missed the error and allowed the score.

Felinfoel: the game was played without the Amman's regular outside-half Denzil Jones, who went to play for Aberavon; his father was on the Aberavon committee and wanted his son to go and play first class. Bobby and the players pleaded with Denzil to play but to no avail and Bobby is convinced that with Denzil they would have won. The front row took 5 out of 6 scrums. We had so much of the ball that our new outside-half came under tremendous pressure from the Felinfoel flankers. To relieve the pressure on the outside-half, the Amman stopped striking for the ball and left them have the ball. The referee for the game was the international referee Mr Gwyn Walters and was the only referee to pick me up on my binding; he said in that squeaky voice of his, "Do that again and I'll penalise you."

Best Kickers

Ted Ward was one of the best kickers seen.

The best kicks ever seen was by Billy Styles playing against Briton Ferry in a West Wales League Championship semi-final in Vardre; our regular kicker was Mike Rosser, a good kicker who had a tremendous rugby brain. The referee was against the Amman from the start of the game and would not award the Amman any penalties in Briton Ferry's half of the field. The Amman were awarded only three penalties in the second-half and these were 15 yards inside the Amman half on both side of the field, and Billy Styles kicked them - tremendous kicks! When Billy kicked the leather ball, you could hear the sound, "Thump"……

Players

Denzil Jones was a very good outside-half and when he played, the Amman was certain to win. Iau Ward and Denny Cochrane made the Amman Utd the best front-row in the West Wales League. Denny was a good dribbler of the ball and a strong boy at loose head. Iau Ward was an excellent hooker. Kendrick Lewis was a good second-row, Len Brown a good flanker and another good player was Bertie Bowen, a full-back from Loughor.

Payment to players

Amman paid the players ten bob for keen games (semi-final and finals). Jim Davies, the Treasurer of the Supporters Club, wanted the payment of the ten bob stopped and wanted to give blazers; the boys said, " Give us the ten bob and bugger the blazer". The Amman had good sides after the war and this continued with the foreign legionnaires. Amongst them there were the brothers Jones of Penybanc and there was some resentment with the local players having nothing at all. A meeting was called by the Chairman Bertie Davies and said that the foreign legionnaires were not being paid anything other than travelling expenses. Another meeting was called by Bertie when the subject of travelling expenses came up again. Bobby had been collecting any kind of bus tickets he could get and now had a pocketful of tickets. For a joke, he threw his bus tickets down on the table in front of the Chairman for the travelling of the shortest of journeys from his home in Garnant to the Half Moon. Bertie was not amused.

Red Card

Bobby was sent off on one Saturday and the crime committed was stopping two forwards from fighting each other; the referee thought Bobby was involved in the fisticuffs. The following Saturday, he played as a "Ferguson" and Bertie, who had not been present at this match, later asked what was the team that had played; on being told, he wanted to know who this new player Ferguson was? Bertie was told that Ferguson was an Irishman from the opencast site at Tairgwaith. Later that season, Bertie was voted off the committee for not following enough of the Amman matches.

A career-ending injury for Bobby occurred at Vardre with broken knee-ligaments. He made his own wooden splints for the leg and was in them for five months. After this, he played some games but the knee was always heavily strapped-up.

In 1953, Bobby's career came to a full stop by playing in a charity game at Cardigan, appearing in the Captain Mantle's team. In the team, there appeared some old rugby league players; this truly ended his rugby career as the WRU professionalised Bobby as a player and he was not allowed to play with union players or to participate in any form in the union game.

PROFILE OF DENNIS DAVIES
By Howard Gabe Davies

Amman Youth, Amman United, Carmarthen County, West Wales, Neath, Cwmgors and Swansea Prison Warders.

Dennis was born in Maesycware, Ammanford 27 July 1936, and spent all his years in Garnant and was employed locally as a coalminer at East Pit Colliery and Abernant Colliery.

Dennis was part of the Davies rugby family, with his first cousin, Elwyn Davies, an Amman and Swansea centre and his son Stuart Davies, a Swansea and Wales No 8 and today, a rugby pundit with BBC Wales's "Scrum Five". Dennis died at the very early age of 45 in 1981; it was a great shock to both his family and friends to lose someone who was so fit and strong. Today, his brother Pat still feels the loss deeply, not so much as a brother but rather as a father figure, due to the early death of the father Aneurin.

To describe Dennis as a giant would not be correct. He was about 5ft 10 ins in height and about the same width but he was a colossus of a man. He was all heart and, perhaps due to being a coal miner of anthracite, was very similar to the coal he mined - very hard.

He will always be remembered for having a pair of cauliflower ears that any boxer would be proud of. Dennis was not much for words but when he did speak or raise his gruff voice it was time to take notice. However, when persuaded to sing in an after-match sing-song, the gruff tone would change to a lovely tenor voice, singing the songs "Roses of Picardy" or "Rags to Riches" and one would never, ever, believe that the voice came from the same person. It was quite amazing. Ogwyn Evans recalls being with Dennis on a trip to Portugal organised by the Yorkshire Communist Party where, after a few drinks, he started to sing in a bar, clearing the adjoining establishment of its clientele as they all came to hear the marvellous Welsh tenor voice.

He was as straight as a die, honest and with left-wing, socialist ideals he was a defender of men's rights and an avid reader of The Daily Worker, the British communist newspaper. He would always tell of hearing Arthur Horner, President of the South Wales Miners Federation speak at Gwaun Cae Gurwen Hall, and of him being a marvellous orator and a true socialist. To be a friend of Dennis, you had to pass some kind of test which encompassed many of these ideals.

During his fortnight's holidays in the late 1960s he would purchase a round the world ticket and travel to far way exotic destinations, stopping in places like Rio de Janeiro, and would observe the opulence and also the abject poverty only a few streets away from the hotel. During this period most people would be spending their annual holidays at home resorts with only a few venturing to such places as Spain.

A few years later, he would go with his friend Ogwyn Evans on organised Welsh football trips to the communist countries of Eastern Europe, and would again observe the poor living conditions they had compared with the standards enjoyed in Wales. He also visited the Union of Soviet Socialist Republic (USSR) on a cruise ship calling at Russian cities, organised by the National Union of Mineworkers, and he was perhaps less left wing in his views after these visits. Ogwyn Evans relates meeting Dai Davies, the Everton and Wales goalkeeper, a Glanamman boy, at Heathrow Airport on their way to Yugoslavia in 1979 for the Wales soccer match at Zagreb. Dai Davies, on seeing Dennis, came over to them and said, " Didn't know you were a soccer fan Dennis" and he replied, "Yes, since you've been between the sticks Dai."

He was also very interested in boxing and would go to Cardiff and London to see title fights and one special fight remained in his memory, the Welterweight Championship of the World between Emile Griffith and Brian Curvis on the 22. 9.1964 in London, where Emile Griffith, one of the worlds' greatest boxers, body punched our Swansea boy Brian Curvis to a standstill. Dennis said, "He couldn't raise his gloves to defend himself at the end."

Dennis played for the Amman for 23 years and was given a gold watch by the club after his 20 years' service. A very hard rugby player, tough, fit, strong, aggressive and uncompromising and yet he was fleet-of-foot over 30 yards for a big man. He played both at second-row and prop; most of his career was played at tight-head prop but he would not play at loose-head for some unknown reason, as he would not have encountered any problems on the other side of the scrum with his strength.

Dennis's greatest asset was undoubtedly that his mere presence on the field was sufficient to make lesser team-mates giants; his toughness, strength and heart was so infectious that it spread to the other forwards to be like himself - fearless - and to give their all for the Amman. You could enter the "lion's den" with him, which it was like sometimes when going to places like Seven Sisters or Tumble. It was no longer a chore, as long as Dennis was there with you. None were afraid, and you would be happy to run through a brick wall for him; maybe some were more afraid of Dennis's wrath than they were of the opposition forwards.

When visiting Cardiff or Stradey to watch a rugby match and having conversations with fellow West Walians on the best players seen in the old West Wales League, I would raise my favourite players: Ray Clarke (Hendy), Ray Rooke (Llangennech, very much like Dennis), Ken Lang (Pontardulais), Eurfyl Williams (Brynamman) and perhaps one of the best, Meurig Williams

(Llandybie) but they would always bring up the Amman player, Dennis Davies or 'that one with the cauliflower ears from the Amman'.

His favourite team was Brynamman and if they were on the fixture list it would be the most important game of the season. Many of his fellow colliers were from Brynamman and this was the added spice for the encounter, with the bets laid on the game and the banter with Dennis telling them that he would make mince meat out of their forwards. The rugby game was now his stage on which to play the performance of his life, grandstanding to the Amman supporters, and also, more importantly, antagonising the Brynamman fans. Yet, he had two great friends from Brynamman in Eddie Rees and Glan 'Feet' Davies.

One infamous game was when Brynamman forward Eric John was winding Dennis up with insults and oaths that resulted in Eric being laid out. The referee of the day had not turned up and a Welsh Union referee, Colin Thomas, a Garnant boy, refereed the game. He was unsighted when the incident occurred and, after seeing the prone figure of Eric on the ground and Dennis near the scene, with the Brynamman crowd baying for blood and shouting insults and oaths at Dennis (which must have been music to his ears), Dennis was sent off the field to the vociferous cheering of the home crowd. As he walked, the referee was heard to say, "Sorry, Den. I've got to send you off." Dennis was not impressed and to show his displeasure, walked through the river to get to the dressing rooms.

On another occasion, again playing at Brynamman and losing by a good score to a very good team and with about 20 minutes remaining of the game, Dennis was heard to say to his fellow prop, "Howie, the game is lost." He replied, "Yes, it's down the pan, Den." His now-famous remark, "Okay then, let's win the fight" then followed that comment. He would start his antics to the fury of the Brynamman crowd and to the delight of the Amman fans; at least they would have something to talk about other than the defeat at the hands of their old rivals. He would be "in his oils" going to work for the early Monday morning shift - the name calling in the baths when changing to go underground by the Brynamman boys, and the cheers from the Amman boys; he just loved it.

Another favourite team would be Ammanford and one particular game could have been called the "Clash of the Titans". In the Ammanford pack, they had Aneurin "Coch" Williams, ex-Amman, Llandybie and Llanelli prop-forward. Aneurin had the ball in hand running at top speed and Dennis was now in his way; there was no way he was going to pass or avoid the coming clash. It seemed that time had stood still; everyone present, whether fans or players, were now anticipating what would happen next with this almighty clash of the impending two great stags. There was a loud bang, with Dennis still standing like the rock of Amman he was, but Aneurin had bounced back about 5 yards in a heap. All who were there would never forget that moment and the Amman crowd were so proud of their hero.

Dennis would go anywhere for a game of rugby. He helped Gary Phillips, the Glanamman boy who had joined the army as a youngster, and later was working for the prison service at Swansea Prison. The game was with the Swansea Prison Warders XV versus Ystradgynlais 2nd XV at Ystradgynlais with his sidekicks Talley and Howie in tow. During the game, the prison warders, amongst whom were a few old Ystradgynlais forwards, found they were playing against their old team-mates. Yet again there was this clash of who is going to be "top dog"; in the midst of the battle, Dennis wryly commented, " I thought this was a friendly, its more like World War III". I can only assume that he was unhappy at being a mere bystander.

Also another team Dennis would aid was Cwmgors. Towards the end of a season, Dai Pritchard, Secretary of Cwmgors, would be looking for players to help out the team due to shortage of players and Dennis would be called on by Dai to assist. This was the season of the Eric John affair and it also happened to be the last game of the season and Cwmgors were away to Brynamman. In the changing rooms prior to the game Dennis and Howie (again in tow) were undressing when Dai Pritchard made a head count of his players to find he now had one too many in 16 players. He turned to both Dennis and Howie and said, "I'm very sorry but one of you must drop out because I have to play the Cwmgors players first". Dennis quickly replied by saying to Howie, " Hi boy, you're not playing, put your clothes back on, I'm playing". This was a command and there was to be no discussion on the matter. What was on his mind was the comeuppance of Eric John, the Brynamman forward. Howie, now changed, was watching the Brynamman players throwing the ball about while waiting the arrival of the Cwmgors players. One of the Brynamman players who was watching the Cwmgors boys coming on to the field saw that ogre figure of "Dennis the Menace" and quickly turned to Eric John and said something to him. He then turned and saw his old adversary Dennis in Cwmgors colours; the shocked look on his face was a picture as he knew retribution was now at hand and must have surely wished he was a thousand miles away. Also playing for the Brynamman side that day was John Elgar Williams, again helping his team out and coming out of retirement to play and still showing the class player he was.

Dennis's character, I hope, is being shown in some of these stories and perhaps the last story illustrates it all. He was built like an elephant and also had a memory of one and would never forget any slight against himself or the Amman. And again his socialist ideals of fair play and equality were ever present and he would not forgive any cheating of any kind.

Amman, through their old treasurer Brian Lloyd, had a fixture against Rhiwbina Rugby Club on the morning of the Wales versus France match. The bus left the Amman very early for Cardiff on the Saturday for an 11.00 am kick off. Some players, after a Friday night with too many beers, were not in the best of "hwyl". This resulted in players not turning up but the Amman team was always a scratch side. On this occasion, the team was not playing very well and by half time was losing heavily to a team that we would have normally been able to beat without much effort. In their side, they had a brilliant wing named Gary Laycock of UWIC and Cardiff, who during the game scored a few tries and whom we all remembered from the Welsh National Sevens Final at Aberavon, when he received a suspiciously forward pass from Dai (Manora) Thomas and went on to score the winning try. Dennis, as diplomatic as could be possible in his gruff voice, told Gary Laycock "Hi! Boy, you're making mugs out of us, you better slow down a bit" but the advice was not heeded, which he must regret to this day, as after scoring another try, he found himself unable to continue to take any further part in the game. Afterwards in the showers (mixed home and away players), a Rhiwbina forward remarked, "That was a very poor show with your player stopping Gary Laycock", to be interrupted by a growl from Dennis, "Hi boy! You're talking about me," and with that the Rhiwbina forward beat a hasty retreat from the showers, unwashed.

PROFILE OF MARTIN LUTHER JONES
By Howard Gabe Davies

Born in Carmarthen 30th October 1941, Martin played wing-forward for Ammanford Secondary Modern School, Amman Youth, Amman Valley Youth, Amman Quins and Amman United during his playing career, although he played centre at times later in his career and to especially good effect in the victorious Sevens team.

His first involvement with Amman United started in 1956 with the Amman Youth. At that time, the youth only played games at the start and end of the season, due to the lack of teams in youth rugby. Players then assisted the Quins, if and when they were required.

He was chosen as captain for two seasons from 1958 to 1960, and in his last season for youth was chosen to play for both the Amman Valley Youth XV and the Valley Seven-a-Side teams. He was also chosen to play for the Amman against Ystradgynlais. A very proud moment indeed followed when, still a Youth player, he was chosen to represent the Amman United in a big match against an Invitation XV team for the opening of the Grandstand on Cwmamman Park

"This was the proudest moment of my rugby career with the official opening of the Grandstand in1959 when the club Chairman Bertie Davies took me to one side and informed me that I had been selected to play against a Select XV, a team that included many well-known players, including the Welsh International scrum-half Onllwyn Brace."

Martin played for the next 17 years in senior rugby and went on to represent both the Amman United and Quins from 1960 to 1977, and was chosen as captain of the Quins from seasons 1973 – 1976.

Martin was an excellent Sevens player, who could always be relied upon and could change from a forward to centre position without making any difference in his ability on the field of play; being so versatile was a great asset to the sevens team. This was a very successful period in the club's history; from 1966 –1970 Amman United ruled the roost in West Wales Seven-a-Side, especially in the second National Sevens Tournament Final held at Aberavon. At the final, all the first class teams played and included all the Welsh District Finalists, with the Amman representing District 'F'. It was Amman's luck to play these top class teams, beating Ebbw Vale, Bridgend and Neath, only to lose in the final to Cardiff Training College (UWIC) by 13 pts. To 12. These were exciting times for the team and supporters but most importantly for the club.

Another great occasion was the West Wales Cup semi-final against Carmarthen Quins at Ammanford in 1966. Carmarthen sides are invariably big compared to the Amman, where a big heart and lively players make up the difference. Amman matched them man for man and led by a few points with little remaining of the game, only to see the inevitable happen - a late try by Carmarthen and it was all over and out of the cup, Amman gave it their best shot and you cannot ask more of a team.

Martin's retirement from the playing side led to him becoming secretary of the Amman Quins for 12 seasons from 1978 – 1990 and this in-club tradition led to him being made the Club secretary from 1990 – 2003; this is 25 years' service as secretary.

Other honours have followed by being made a Life Member of the club in 1990 and also a Trustee in1996.

He has been Amman United for 46 years and all who have known Martin Luther know that he supports only one colour (scarlet) and that his heart must beat to the tune of "Yr Aman yw y Gore".

Martin has thoroughly enjoyed his involvement with Amman, be it as player or as an official of the club and says, "Nothing can surpass the involvement and joy of playing the game of rugby."

As club secretary, he remembers the season 1991 –1992 was quite outstanding: "The Amman team was an excellent all-round side with a pack of forwards to match any in the league and with threee-quarters that had pace to burn." It was the season that the team won the West Wales Rugby Union Welsh Brewers League Bowl, defeating Carmarthen Athletic at New Dock Stars, and in the final beating Trimsaran at Felinfoel.

Martin was especially proud to be in the right place at the right time when Shane Williams, after playing against France, received his first international cap from the President of the Welsh Rugby Union, Sir Tasker Watkins, at the after-match function at the Millennium Stadium.

" It was a fairy tale story; only 18 months previously, Shane had played his last game for the Amman United against Swansea RFC in the SWALEC cup, and now was playing international rugby against France, and I was extremely proud to see a local boy doing well."

In 2003, Martin feels "that declaring the game open was most damaging for the club without adequate planning on how the game should be organised. The game has deteriorated from the grass roots to the Welsh team, yet the first class clubs and the Welsh Rugby Union are at loggerheads on the way forward. Agreement must be reached, so that the national side becomes its first priority."

Clubman of the year 1971 Martin Luther Jones at the Afan Lido, Amman Dinner Dance

Ammanfaord Secondary School Team v Llandeilo Grammar School 1956

Martin Luther Jones Front: 5th, and of interest there are three other players shown you should recognise?

99

AMMAN UNITED 1971 - 2003
By Lyn Roberts

Season 1971-1980

It is reputed that "Woodstock" changed a generation; this may well be the case but recognition for the change in fortune at the Amman United must be given to the organisational skill and expertise of Coach Alan Thomas and the inspirational leadership of Captain Hywel Evans.

Hywel, better known these days as the much acclaimed actor Dafydd Hywel, led by example a team packed with individual talent and flair, that became the best supported side in West Wales due to the standard of rugby they produced.

Although there was no question that the individuals concerned, a mixture of youth and experience, had talent in abundance, teamwork was the key to their success.

The exuberance and flair of young players such as Peter Griffiths, Adrian Jones, Alan Rogerson, Colin Davies, Alan James, Graham George and others were complemented by the more experienced Cen "Glynmoch" Davies, Ryan Bartlett, John Thomas and Gordon Thomas, to name but a few.

John Thomas holding the Bill Everson Award for the best player of the Snelling Sevens tournament

With now well-established officials and a host of former players on the committee, the Amman were looking forward to much overdue success on the field.

Having started the season 1971-72 with a number of warm up games, including wins at Brecon and home to Briton Ferry, the league programme commenced with a 50-0 demolition of Llandeilo away from home.

Away wins at Felinfoel and Cwmllynfell followed before the first home win against arch-rivals Brynamman 18-4. Another thumping win away at Ystalyfera 42-4 preceded home wins over New Dock Stars and Penygroes. A resounding 52-6 victory at Llangennech and 18-0 win at Pontyberem ensured a clean sweep of victories against all our league opponents.

As a young supporter following this team, it was quite an adventure travelling to such faraway places as Pontyberem, Llangennech and Felinfoel. Many an hour was spent enjoying my pop and crisps with Will the driver as the after match de-brief and statistical analysis was thoroughly debated.

The opposition always seemed to be a distance away and the journeys home would take several hours, with frequent stops en-route to cool the engine. Inevitably this would coincide with a visit to a pub or club and harmonious renditions of "Bullet in My Shoulder" and "Roll Along Amman United".

The team spirit and camaraderie that existed at this time, to my own thoughts, has not since been replicated.

On the field Amman were supreme; home wins over a much improved Llandeilo and Cwmllynfell plus away wins at Felinfoel, before the closest result of the season a 6-4 victory at Brynamman were rounded off with an emphatic 54-0 home drubbing of Ystalyfera to round off the year in style.

Amman went into the New Year with the same gusto and quickly completed a full set of 18 league wins from 18 league games. In the process, the Amman scored 457 points for and conceded only 86. This resulted in Amman United winning the Eurof Davies Memorial Cup for being the team with highest points scored in the West Wales League - an excellent performance not to be replicated by an Amman United side for 20 years. They even eluded the photographers!

The championship would be decided by a play-off between the four section winners, the Amman United being drawn against old enemies Llandybie, with the tie being played at Ammanford.

The crowd at Ammanford Recreation ground was large and vociferous, the atmosphere more akin to a Wembley Cup final than any rugby match previously seen at that ground.

The game itself was a tight affair, with no quarter being asked or given by either side, as would be expected. One of my most vivid memories was when Amman's Ian Wagstaff lost his boot and played on through rucks and mauls for what seemed an eternity in his stocking feet without any stoppage in play.

A solitary penalty from Gwyn Ashby broke the stalemate, Llandybie winning 3-0. The Championship, however, went to Penclawdd who beat Llandybie 4-3 after a replay.

During the season, Ryan Bartlett set a new club scoring record with 240 points, completing the achievement during the 30-0 victory over Chepstow. The Amman also won the Bertie Davies 7s during the season.

The following season 1972-73 saw Gordon Thomas, "Butch", regaining the captaincy for the second time. Success for the senior side was a much tougher proposition, with the league providing a difficult challenge. The cup was a different story.

An unfortunate early exit in the Welsh Rugby Union Challenge cup, losing 32-12 at home to Taff's Well, proved even more disappointing when the winners drew Swansea at home in the next round.

Relaxed looking Amman at Brynamman 1973-74

Back row l-r Harry Davies, B Jones, M Davies, I Wagstaff, J Jones, A James, G George, A Jones, Russ Dunn. Front l-r R John, K Davies, P Griffiths, G Thomas Capt., A Davies, M Rogerson.

The West Wales cup brought an entirely different story and the Amman reached the semi-final stages playing Seven Sisters at Ystalyfera. The match was drawn 3-3 and had to be replayed, this time at Ystradgynlais. The Amman built up a 12-0 interval lead through a Baden Jones try, Cen Davies providing a conversion and 2 penalties.

The second half saw Seven Sisters reply with a Tom James penalty but, after having forward Watts sent off, they could not recover and the Amman sealed victory with a further Cen Davies penalty and a drop goal from Colin Davies to win 18-3.

The final at Stradey Park on the 17th April against Felinfoel proved another tough encounter. The large crowd of travelling supporters were loyal to the end as the Amman were eventually outdone by Mike Francis, who added a last minute try to his 3 penalties to seal the 13-3 victory.

The Welsh Rugby Union Challenge cup, introduced in season 1971-72, was to provide many interesting challenges for the Amman over the years. Those who witnessed one of the early encounters with Cardiff College of Education will recall seeing two of the longest kicks ever converted at Cwmamman Park by College full-back Robin Williams. In the College squad was future Wales and British Lion wing John Bevan, one of many celebrity players that the Amman United would encounter through the magic of the cup.

It was a cup match played at Amman Valley Comprehensive School ground, due to a waterlogged Cwmamman Park, that saw Rowland John become the first substitute used by the Amman United.

In November 1973, Trevor Evans and Gerwyn Jones, both ex-Amman players, played for a Swansea side coached by Ieuan Evans (ex-Amman), against the touring Australians, the match being drawn 9-9.

Amman United team for 1973-74 WWRU Cup Final.

Back row l-r N.Anthony (Sec), G George, I Wagstaff, D Jones, J Jones, M Davies, B Jones, R Dunn, E Walters, M Williams
Back row l-r E Jones, M Rogerson, C Davies, R John, G Thomas, P Griffiths, A Jones, C Davies

Amman United and Llanelli forwards get to grips in the mud.

104

Vast crowds on the Bank enjoy the action as Amman takes on Llanelli.

Alan Dvies presents Eurof Walters with Claude Davey's jersey

Gordon Butch retained the captaincy for the 1974-75 season and in so doing became the first player to captain the club on three occasions.

The highlight of the season without doubt was the third round WRU cup-tie against Llanelli at Cwmamman Park. The tie was played on 25th January 1975, exactly a week after Trevor Evans had made his Wales debut against France in Paris.

Also making his Wales debut that day was Ray Gravelle of Llanelli, whose work in recent years as TV personality and commentator has raised the profile of "Roll along Amman United" in Welsh rugby folklore.

Indeed, in respect of the Amman's reputation, Llanelli paid tribute by fielding a nearly full-strength team despite playing Newport at Rodney Parade the same afternoon. The gate receipts for the day were recorded as £604.80, a substantial total considering the entrance fee was only 20p, but there appeared to be far in excess of 3,000 people at the ground.

Much to the relief of Llanelli's coach, former Amman player Carwyn James, they won comfortably by the handsome score of 51-0, going on once again to win the cup. This was no consolation, however, to former Scarlets John Thomas and Cen Davies amidst the Amman ranks.

In season 1975-76, under the captaincy of Jeff Thomas, another who had first class experience with Swansea, and new coach Huw Harries, the Amman made the trip to Gwent to take on the famous Pontypool front row in the Welsh Cup. The Amman once again gave a good account of themselves with the versatile Mike Mackay, who had previously played second row against Llanelli, now lining up in the centre alongside John (Bach) Thomas.

Ray Prosser's uncompromising team, with five internationals in the pack and superbly led by Welsh player of the year Terry Cobner, eventually proved too strong for the Amman, running out winners by 37-6 but not before we had led 6-0.

League positions in the West Wales Rugby Union at this time became a bit of a lottery with the 10 team section, 4 up, 4 down format, resulting in continuous changes to the league structure and the club's status. Amman ended season 1975-76, being restored to Section 'A'.

Jeff Thomas continued as captain for his second season 1976-77 but success was to elude us. In a very tough section victories were hard to come by. The situation was made even more difficult with the retirement of a number of key players.

In one bizarre incident at a home match with Crynant the game was a stalemate, without any score, and the ball had gone over the dead ball line. Dai "Clough" Evans, leapt over the old rope fence to retrieve the ball and kicked it back over towards the Amman player Arwyn Roberts so that he could prepare for a drop-out to restart the game. A Crynant player picked up the ball and strode over the try line and putting it down underneath the posts. The referee amazingly awarded a try as he deemed the ball to be in play. The decision sparked frantic protestations from Amman players and supporters alike but to no avail. We eventually lost 12-9.

Although this defeat was avenged with a 9-3 away victory inspired by Arwyn Roberts at full back the Amman finished bottom of the league and were relegated along with Penclawdd, Crynant and Ystradgynlais.

Although the team were relatively unsuccessful, individuals were continuing to be recognised, Graham George for one, regularly anchoring the Carmarthenshire County pack at a time when first class players made up the bulk of the team. Adrian Jones was another.

The most significant moment in the Amman's history came at the end of March 1977, when Trevor Evans was chosen to tour New Zealand with the British Lions - a fantastic achievement for the player and great honour for club, community and the Amman Valley.

Presentation of a British Lions Jersey by Trevor Evans to the Club Secretary Nevin Anthony, with Chairman Phil James in the background 1977.

Amman United hosted a touring side that Easter 1977, Sandford, running out easy winners 48-6. Then Sandford scored a consolation try being neatly converted by star guest player, Noir Thomas.

Graham George, who seemed to have been around forever, took over the captaincy in season 1977-78 with a new club coach in Colin Thomas, ex-Brynamman scrum-half. These were to prove difficult times for the Amman, with experienced players diminishing in numbers through retirement and injuries. A number of youngsters came through to take their places, perhaps before they were ready.

One such youngster was Clive Williams, who made his debut as a centre against Ystalyfera at the age of 18. Chico (Alan Davies), who took the liberty of dropping a number of players after the previous week's performance, was selecting the team that week..

Not expecting a call-up, Clive was busy putting in a load of coal when Chico called to get him for training. So excited was he about being selected, he managed to persuade Chico to fill sacks with him (a feat in itself) and rushing, ripped his hand open against the dashing. Quite typically of this individual, he bandaged himself up and went on to play the match.

Clive "Bruiser" Williams in typical pose - Oops, the ball's gone

Graham George was clearly the elder statesman of the team and respected by all. He kept going and, with Adrian Jones, looked after the youngsters around him who lacked experience rather than ability.

Young forwards such as Peter Cole, Andrew Evans, John Thomas, Phil Davies and Lyn Roberts would be indebted to Graham and the occasional cameo appearance from Rowland Booty.

The Amman United's 75th Anniversary was celebrated in season 1978-79 with a Dinner Dance at the Top Rank, Swansea and Ian Penman making the trek down from Scotland for the occasion with Stan Stennett providing the cabaret.

This was a start of lean times for the Amman with the process of re-building and development of players for the future. Keith Griffiths, the flame-haired open-side from Betws, took over the captaincy in season 1979-80 and led by example, becoming the Amman's player of the year.

However, the slide down the sections was to continue and the 1970s gave way to the 1980s without too many fireworks on the pitch.

The club itself provided a warm welcome to visitors, amongst them Coventry RFC in 1978.

Amman officials with guest from Coventry RFC 1978.

Regularly found visiting the clubhouse around the early to mid-seventies would be England and Lions prop Fran Cotton, with his friend the England scrum-half Steve Smith.

Indeed, Fran Cotton, who became British Isles Manager will be one of our guest speakers at the Amman United Centenary Dinner on the 14th May 2004.

Fran Cotton receives a tankard from Club President Marcus Roberts, Phil James holds England jersey presented by Fran as Edward Thomas looks on.

109

British Lion Trevor Evans with School's Internationals Rhys Harries left and Jeff Price.

1982/83 Season

Back row l-r Eurfyl Williams referee, M Evans, C Williams, R Morgan, P Davies, R Herdman, W Llewellyn, R Hartnell, A Davies.
Mid-row l-r K Lewis, A Jones, D Campbell, J Gwyn Jones Capt., A Robinson, M Howells.
Front B Davies, H Williams, D Evans, and S Phillips.

1985/86

Back row B Howells, N Bundock, C Williams, M Evans, S Mackay, W Williams, R Morgan, G George, A Davies, S Phillips, and H Davies.
Front row K Roberts, S Hopkin, K Lewis, D Evans, Jeff Price Capt., D Campbell, A Robinson, B Davies, G Bundock.

Seasons 1981-1990

Malcolm Davies took over the captaincy for the seasons1980-81 and 1981-82. Dobbin, as he is known to many, was an extremely talented back-row forward whose ability deserved greater recognition.

I recall one particular team talk, prior to playing Bryncoch at home, that was inspirational and full of passion. At the time, both teams were unbeaten and we went out and won convincingly. Unfortunately we couldn't keep this form going and eventually slipped down the table before being relegated again.

It was around this time that three players in particular established themselves as regulars in the Amman side: Clive "Bruiser" Williams, nicknamed by a rather sore Mike Taylor after a training session tackle. Darrel Campbell, undoubtedly the finest hooker ever to play for the Amman and described by former WRU President, the late Ieuan Evans, as the best hooker in West Wales, including Swansea, Llanelli and Neath. Few would disagree. The third, of course, is Mike "Mole" Evans, the tall curly-haired boy who started as a wing but went on to be another excellent back-row forward and played for the Amman over four decades, starting in the late 1970s and finishing in 2000.

The trio was never far apart and formed the nucleus of the side during the 1980s, helping to rebuild the team and develop other players along the way. Each in their turn was rewarded with the captaincy.

Amman United v Nantymoel 20/10/1990 M Evans & C Williams chase a loose ball watched closely by D Campbell far left

Players who featured regularly in the early 1980s included Martin Howells, Kevin Lewis, Anthony Jones, Brian Davies and the evergreen Graham George, who has given this club such great service.

John Gwyn Jones took up the captaincy in season 1982-83 (from a place north-east of here we are not allowed to mention). John led a bit of a social revival at the club, reminding players that this was a game to be enjoyed. The touring guitar resulting in a singsong - win, lose or draw.

Social activities revolving around the club remained buoyant throughout, despite indifferent performances on the field. Particularly successful were the Club carnivals and Carnival Weeks. These drew large crowds to the park for a variety of entertaining events, including It's a knockout, tug-of-war, boxing and wrestling.

No it's not the Ladies Committee. It is Klondike Kate v Mitzi Muller, Ladies wrestling bout

Although a rugby club, the Amman recognised other sporting achievements by individuals from the community, Wales and Everton goalkeeper Dai Davies being a typical example.

President Marcus Roberts presents Dai Davies with a memento to mark his record number of Welsh caps

The Amman ended the season 1982-83 as runners-up in Section 'E' to Skewen and were promoted. Unfortunately, Clive Williams picked up a back injury that was to keep him out of the game for the next two seasons.

First-aid man Alan Jones restrains a normally placid Graham Bundock as Roy Morgan is laid low by a stray boot

Club awards that year recognised Clive Williams as Player of the Year, Roger Hartnell deservedly as Clubman of the Year and another character, Mad Martin Evans or Taff, as he was known to his Hell's Angels colleagues, as Quins Player of the year. Martin, a tenacious forward, was sadly taken from this life early through illness in 1993. The many friends that attended will never forget his funeral procession and service. "Ride free brother, wherever you may be".

Darrel Campbell ascended to the captaincy for the first time in season 1983-84 as one would expect from this great club servant, leading by example, with another of the club's loyal servants, Clive Brooks, taking up the coaching duties.

The next few years were barren in terms of trophy success, with only the Dewi Phillips cup won in the season 1985-86, a 15-a-side competition, to show for our efforts. This was won after a hard fought tournament at Ammanford, only to find that there was no water to shower, the boys having to use Betws mine as a last ditch alternative.

These years though proved to be a huge success in terms of player development, with a number of quality players coming through to stake their claims for key positions. The captaincy passed to Mike Mole then Jeff Price and eventually Clive Williams in season 1986-87.

This proved to be a highly successful season, winning the West Wales Section 'D' Title. Kev Lewis was so delighted after the presentation of the trophy that he took it home and slept with it.

Clive Williams receives the West Wales R U Section D Champion's Trophy

Also that season, we won the C.C. Evans Cup defeating Llandovery in the semi-final and Llandybie in the final and ended as runners-up in the Bertie Davies Memorial 7s.

One of our most exiting new talents, fullback Alan Davies, broke the club's points scoring record with 246 points.

Much of this improvement could be credited to the coach, Colin Mathews. When Clive Williams expressed concerns over poor turn-out for training (something not unusual for this club) Colin replied philosophically. *"It is not the people who are not here that you have to worry about, it's the ones who have turned up, so always do your best for them."* He certainly did, and this approach produced a winning team and improved attitudes to training.

Unfortunately, the next season was not so good; work commitments limited Colin's availability and much unrest and infighting amongst players resulted in a poor season and relegation.

We did, however, win the Dewi Phillips cup yet again, with the majority of players away on tour, thanks to Clive Williams and the outstanding Rhys Harries.

Clive Williams was selected Captain for the third consecutive season, the only person in the Amman's history to have this honour.

Mike "Mole" Evans in pursuit of Malcolm Dacey. Cardiff v Amman United 17/12/1988

Roy Morgan, Mike Evans, Adrian Phillips, Paul Rees, Clive Williams and Darrel Campbell keep Cardiff at Bay as Neil Bundock clears

This season saw the Amman have a particularly good run in the Welsh cup. Their reward for a titanic victory 27-26 away at Blaenau Gwent, with Nick Griffiths' magnificent match winning drop-goal, was a fourth round tie with Cardiff at the Arm's Park. A wonderful day out for the whole club but the team were eventually overwhelmed 54-0.

The young Amman side were developing a reputation for their style of play, with a powerful front-row combination of Adrian Phillips, Darrel Campbell and Graham Bundock the platform was there for Justin Power and Nick Griffiths to release the backs.

Captain Steve Phillips at centre guided them through to another big cup-tie in December 1990 at home to Newport. As described in the Sunday Mirror 23/12/90 in Chris Smart's rugby round up." Newport booked their place in next round... but it took all their skill and stamina to win 22-0 against the stubborn lads from Amman united. United defended heroically with Alan Davies and Clive Williams outstanding."

The game is well remembered by the vast crowd who will never forgive referee Derek Bevan for not awarding a penalty try for the Amman. He has been reminded on several subsequent visits. Coach Peter Griffiths could be proud of his players' efforts.

They were rewarded to some extent by winning the C.C.Evans Cup.

Amman United season 1986/87

Clive Williams, R Hartnell, Ieuan Evans, Martin Evans 1983

Amman United Squad v Cardiff 17/12/1988

Richard Williams, Alan Davies and Darrel Campbell representing Carmarthenshire with Welsh Counties Cup

Amman United v Newport 22/12/1990

Back row M Jones, P Griffiths, C Williams, G Watkins, P Williams, A Phillips, R Morgan, A Price, L Clancy, G Bundock, N Bundock, B Howells.
Front A Davies, S Lyles, C Morgan, A Davies, D Calow, S Phillips Capt., D Campbell, A Bartlett, J Power, C Thomas.
Mascot Ryan Williams.

119

Ryan Williams in action for Welsh Schools

Amman United season 1990/91

Back L/R L Clancy, P Rees, S Mackay, M Evans, A Price, G Watkins, A Phillips, A Bartlett, G Bundock, and P Williams.
Front C Williams, D Campbell, J Power, S James, S Phillips Capt., N Griffiths, S Lyles, and M Howells.

Season 1991-2000

Clive Williams with Darrel Campbell as Captain joined Peter Griffiths as coach for the 1991-92 season. This was to prove an epic season for the club.

Firstly a good cup run brought another home tie with Newport. The Amman having gained in experience and confidence with the pack in superb form took the game to Newport.

Roy Morgan and Kev Morris adding height and pace to support the powerful front row, the Amman were extremely unlucky to be beaten 8-6. They deserved a victory for their efforts.

The league was of greatest importance and the Amman swept to a record of 18 wins from 18 games, emulating their counterparts of 20 years previously. Nick Griffiths had achieved the same fete as his father Peter had done at outside-half.

Defeating Resolven away to clinch the clean sweep brought bittersweet memories for Clive Williams whose last appearance at this ground ended with a broken leg.

This time the Amman went on to defeat Carmarthen Athletic in the semi-final and Trimsaran in the final at Felinfoel to win the West Wales Championship Bowl.

A night to remember followed for all involved but particularly so for Captain Darrel Campbell, man of the match Adrian Phillips and full-back Alan Davies who again set a new club points record for a season with 304.

Liam Clancy dances past Newport's David Llewelllyn

Duncan Calow gets to grips with Newport and Wales lock David Waters

Four players Steve James, Graham Watkins, Adrian Phillips and Nick Griffiths played in all 18-league games.

Darrel Campbell retained the captaincy for season 1992-93 and in so doing became only the third player to captain the club for three seasons. The West Wales league was again reorganised for this season, which brought little success for the Amman.

Huw Marshall, Welsh schools cap at second-row was elected Captain for 1993-94 season but left to join Llangennech leaving Nick Griffiths to take over the captaincy duties.

Nick himself was elected captain for the season 1994-95 which saw the introduction of the Welsh National League system. A significant change with the scrapping of the West Wales league structure and seeing a number of Pembrokeshire teams becoming regular visitors on our fixture lists.

It was also a time that saw a number of players leaving to try their luck in "higher" divisions. As a result lean times were once again upon us as we struggled to compete and survive in the league structure.

North Walian Dyfed Llewellyn, who had joined from Penarth, was elected captain for season 1995-96 a strong running and tough-tackling centre. Some indifferent performances did not help the cause and the Amman were to find themselves stuck in Division 5 West for a number of years.

Performances did improve and we narrowly missed out on promotion in consecutive years.

Seasons 1996-97 with Graham Watkins as captain.

Season 1997-98 with Karl Worsfold.

Season 1998-99 with Steve Mackay offered much hope and encouragement, but good performances often gave way to a New Year slump on each occasion.

Unfortunately, professionalism had arrived in Welsh rugby, openly. Many mediocre clubs jumping on the bandwagon in an effort to buy success. This resulted in a merry-go-round of journeymen players leaving loyalty behind as they followed the gold rush.

The season 1998-99 saw a rebellion amongst the senior ranks, with both Swansea and Cardiff attempting to join the English league structure. As a result both lost their seeding status for the Welsh Cup and the Amman were fortunate to draw Swansea at home.

This would be Swansea's first game against Welsh opposition for the season and the Amman was assured of a bumper crowd and big pay-day.

Due to adverse weather conditions the match was postponed on the scheduled Saturday but with a concerted effort of players, committee and volunteers, the match was played the next day Sunday 25th October 1998.

Swansea did us the honour of bringing along a number of Internationals, Paul Arnold, Colin Charvis, Garin Jenkins, Paul Moriarty, Andy Moore and Chris Anthony included. The game was set fair for a shock result when Steve Lyles scored under the posts almost from the kick-off. Amman was up 7-0 with less than a minute gone. Swansea's full time professionals eventually swamped us by 100-7. A great day was marred by some unnecessary comments by then Swansea coach, John Plumtree, long since departed back to the Southern Hemisphere.

Coaches at this time were former Wales and Neath winger Alan Edmunds, and the ever popular Owain Lloyd. They worked hard together to overcome the obvious difficulties producing some splendid performances but promotion and trophy success eluded them.

One player made his Amman debut during this period and stood out. In a mid-week rearranged fixture with Laugharne, Shane Williams, a second-half substitute at scrum half entered the fray. He scored four tries in a space of 10 minutes with hardly a hand laid on him.

Veteran prop Graham Bundock took up the captaincy for season 1999-2000 with a new coaching team of Adrian Phillips and Nick Griffiths. Again performances were promising but success eluded us. One young man who did find success was flanker Alwyn Davies, playing the occasional game for the Amman on his way up the first class ranks, who went on to captain Wales at Under- 21 level.

The name of Amman United was to feature strongly in rugby circles with the arrival on the International stage of the wonderfully talented Shane Williams whose performances and try scoring records with Neath led to a Welsh squad call-up.

I will never forget that moment on 4th February 2000 when Shane won his first cap as a replacement against France in the Six Nations. On holiday at the time in Copenhagen (not a known rugby stronghold) the whole pub looked on in amazement as my wife and I celebrated the achievement. Amman United had now arrived in Denmark!

The arrival of the new millennium did not bring the club success on the field but we again retained our position in Division 5 West.

Amman United season 1991/92

Amman United celebrates at Resolven after clinching clean sweep of league wins

Back D Davies, S Lyles, N Bundock, A Price, C Williams, A Phillips, A Bateman, S Phillips, G Bundock, P Williams, G Watkins, and R Phillips.
Front M Jones, C Templeton, P Griffiths, D Campbell, N Griffiths, A Davies, S Mackay, and S James.

Amman United v Newport 19/12/1992

Amman United and Swansea 25/10/1998

Amman United season 2001/2002

Back C Phillips, S Herbert, S Rees, S Morris, A Thomas, P George, C James, J Williams, T Davies, C Rees, S Griffiths, P Nolan, J James, Lyn Roberts Team Manager.
Front C Thomas, S James, A Davies, Shaun Davies Capt., J Herbert sponsor, M Jones Sec, L Thomas, G Lewis.

Pat Nolan with headgear and Shaun Davies competing for the ball against Glais 19/4/2003

The Amman Eight on the charge against Ammanford 26/4/03

C James, A Rees, S Davies, T Davies, C Rees, K Nottingham, S Morris, K Worsfold with ball, R Williams.

Amman United Season 2002/2003

Back M Jones Sec, Angharad Rees First Aid, J James, S Rees, J Davies, H Jenkins, T Davies, C Rees, S Davies, P Nolan, G Davies, S Duncan, K Worsfold, S Morris, D Williams, Phil John Coach, Lyn Roberts Team Manager.
Front Rhodri Williams, L Thomas, S James, K Nottingham, Alun Rees Captain, P George, A Thomas, Carl James, Ryan Williams.

Season 2000-2003

When Shaun Davies was elected captain for the season 2000-2001 he became the first player to have been elected as captain of the Youth, Quins and Amman United. An unique achievement. More so for a man whose career had been in jeopardy following a serious eye injury a few years previous.

The start of the season saw a mass exodus of 16 players to local rivals, all left for various reasons. A sad result of the mercenary attitude of players and clubs alike and only one could honestly say he was going to play at a higher standard.

This was an unfortunate start to the season and triggered a fight for survival in the league. Early setbacks in the Principality cup, losing away to Abercarn and also in the West Wales cup losing to Abercrave, set the alarm bells ringing.

The league started much better claiming three wins on the trot, but reality was about to set in. Defeat after defeat followed but of most concern was the non-availability of players. Regularly having to take the field with few or no substitute players and on occasions struggling to maintain a full XV on the field of play. It was an exceptionally bad autumn in terms of weather and numerous games were postponed due to waterlogged pitches, home and away. This turned out to be a blessing in disguise.

We managed to rescue one particular fixture after the goalposts fell down overnight. A quick call to Mono Scaffolding and a temporary upright saw us through the rest of the season.

Heavy defeats followed at Gorseinon and Hendy that were particularly painful before we picked ourselves up, turning in a series of good results, including beating Hendy at home to ensure our survival in the league, Tycroes being the relegated team.

We were indebted to a number of Youth players who answered the call for help throughout the season including Adrian Thomas, Tristan Manning and Nick Davies.

Season 2001-2002 continued in a similar vein, with another tough campaign to hold on to our status in Division 5. Brynamman relegated the previous season being the form team in the league made matters more difficult to bear.

Pat Nolan, who had played a few games in the mid-1980s for the Amman returned to bolster the pack and provide a ball-winning second-row partner for Shaun Davies. Along with the return of Phil John as coach this brought much needed experience to the side.

Although our fortunes had not been good there was an air of optimism. We recorded our first away win at Fishguard 11-10 and having won convincingly at Ammanford looked forward to facing league leaders Brynamman.

The Amman played them off the park and led for almost 90 minutes of the game before disaster struck. None other than Nick Griffiths (ex-Amman) deprived us of a deserved win when he converted a very late try wide out. Never have the players been seen so disappointed.

But by far the bleakest day was April 27th when we faced Llandeilo away.

Despite the Quins not having a game we could only muster 10 players. This was a disaster and to try and contact players as Team Manager was to no avail, the players were conveniently unavailable and their mobile phones were switched off. Steve "Big Bird" Phillips answered the call and with two borrowed Llandeilo players we took the field eventually with 14 men to play rugby. Roy Morgan later joined the match to make up our contingent to 15 but the fixture was played and officials and supporters were proud of the effort of those Amman players who represented the club on the rugby field.

This was not the first time for such a dilemma; hopefully it will be the last. Mrs M Bowen of Loughor recalled an occasion whereby her father in law, James Bertie Bowen, a former Amman player went along to see the Amman play at Pontardulais in a cup match back in 1956. The Amman surprisingly was struggling and took the field with 14 men. Bertie borrowed togs and took to the field. He was 54 years of age and the Amman won.

This spirit is what represents the Amman as a club, unfortunately it is not present in sufficient number of individuals.

Alun Rees took up the captaincy for season 2002-2003 and we have once again struggled. Winning only two games before the turn of the year. Our performances have been naïve rather than poor, losing several games by a single score, often in injury time.

We eventually won 21-20 at home to Llandybie only to lose to Llandeilo, the eventual league champions the following week. There was however a better spirit in the camp and with the return of experienced campaigners Karl Worsfold and Kevin Morris, together with Ryan Williams things took a sudden turn for the better.

A run of six consecutive wins pulled us clear of the bottom two relegation places. Another restructure in Welsh rugby with the senior clubs accepting a provincial set up was to cause us further difficulties.

The proposed new structure would mean that six teams would effectively be relegated. Our current position would leave us with five Pembrokeshire teams on our fixture list and a very expensive travel bill, as the least of our problems.

A home win over Bynea 85 - 10 was followed by victory at Llandybie in the C. C. Evans cup. Then a narrow 17-15 defeat in an ill-tempered game at Lampeter left us in a precarious position. Victories home against Glais and very pleasingly away at Ammanford left us eventually needing to beat Loughor, who had beaten us by a 40 point margin the previous week to clinch the final promotion spot.

Having narrowly lost out to Cwmllynfell 24-18 in the cup semi-final, the Amman kept the best for last.

In one of the most entertaining games seen on the park for some time Amman United defeated Loughor by 61-11 with Dean Williams in spectacular form claiming two tries as did Karl Nottingham and Karl Worsfold.

Performances in 2003 have been much improved and the Amman can look forward to the Centenary season in Division 4 South West. Unfortunately the

WRU have now confirmed after much speculation that the Amman United will be playing in Division 4 South West and playing many teams to our east in Pyle, Maesteg Celtic Rhigos and Cefn Cribbwr.

Alun Rees is captain for the second season and has the double honour of being captain in the Centenary season along with coaches Pat Nolan and Phil John, and with Team Manager Lyn Roberts ensuring a stable environment for this young side.

The future once again looks bright for the Amman United.

Roll along Amman United.

PROFILE GRAHAM GEORGE
By John Vince Williams

Amman Valley Grammar School, Pantyffynnon Youth, Amman United, Carmarthen County and Amman Quins.

Graham started playing rugby on the tip behind the Garnant Club and owned his own rugby ball. He wasn't the type of boy when things didn't go his way to then leave with his ball.

He started playing organised rugby at Amman Valley Grammar School in 1960. During this period he would watch the Amman United or Quins whichever was at home on the Saturday.

On leaving school in 1966 he played youth rugby with Pantyffynnon Youth team and although they never won anything, he enjoyed his rugby at Pantyffynnon and had plenty of fun with the boys.

In season 1968-69, he had a permit from Pantyffynnon to play three games for the Amman United and eventually had a transfer to the Amman and played for the 1st XV for the rest of the season.

In season 1971-72 was the greatest achievement of his career in winning 18 championship matches out of a total of 18 and in doing so also won the Eurof Davies Memorial Cup for the highest points scored by any team in the West Wales league with 457 points. Our captain that season was Hywel Evans.

His most memorable game was on January 22nd 1975, a day Llanelli RFC fielded two teams one to play the Amman United in the Welsh Cup and the other against Newport. Llanelli had 15 International players in their team and they brought the famous forward Delme Thomas a Wales and British Lion out of retirement to play and its little wonder that we lost 51-0.

In season 1975-76 we played Pontypool in the Welsh Cup at Pontypool and eventually lost 36-6.

In season 1973-74 was his biggest disappointment in losing in the final of the West Wales Challenge Cup to Felinfoel at Stradey Park, Llanelli.

In season 1977-78, he had the honour of being selected captain and also at the end of the season was awarded the trophy of Clubman of the Year.

Season 1978-79 was the 75th Anniversary of the club and was again elected captain for a second term and led the team to victory over Llanelli.

In season 1979-80 he was called upon to captain the side after captain Keith Griffiths returned to his village club Betws.

He represented Carmarthen County on three occasions.

At the end of a long career in the Amman United team, he continued playing for the Quins for a number of seasons until his retirement in season 1989-90.

In recognition of his long and distinguished career the Amman United awarded Graham an Amman Cap and an inscribed watch for his loyal services to the club.

PROFILE - DARREL CAMPBELL
By Lyn Roberts

Darrel made his senior bow for the Amman Quins in 1978 before going on to represent the Amman United for the first time at Burry Port and then Carmarthen Quins in 1979.

The regular hooker at this time was Andrew Evans and he and Darrel went on to share appearances as they fought hard for a permanent place in the team.

Moving on to College did not deter Darrel and he returned home regularly on weekends to represent the Amman.

"Jim" or "Sir" as he is often called represented the Amman with some distinction and established for himself an excellent reputation in West Wales rugby.

He captained the club on three occasions, most notably 1991-92 season when the club won the West Wales Bowl, winning all 18-league games.

Individual honours during his playing career included 23 games for Carmarthen County, whom he now represents as Team Manager. Darrel was awarded with his County cap for his 10th game after defeating North Wales at Bangor.

He also played 26 matches for the West Wales Rugby Union representative team, including a tour of North Wales and a representative match against Spain at Stradey Park in 1985.

Recognition from the first class clubs saw him play occasional games for Llanelli, Swansea, Neath and Aberavon, but a regular place eluded him. Their loss, our gain.

Darrel also enjoyed playing sevens and was rewarded with some fine performances by being selected to tour the West Country of England with Public Schools Wanderers.

His rugby travels also took him to the United States where he played for California State University, Long Beach.

He recalls playing with many fine Amman players. In the early days Graham George, Colin "Talley" Davies and Peter Griffiths left a lasting impression. Towards the latter end of his career front row colleagues Adrian Phillips and Graham Bundock provided the foundation of an awesome Amman pack, which released the ball to the flair of three-quarters such as Nick Griffiths and Alan Davies.

Two players that will always be associated with Darrel are Mike "Mole" Evans and Clive "Bruiser" Williams. A trio that were very rarely separated on or off the field.

There were also many fine coaches who left lasting impressions but none more so than Clive "Bruiser".

Highlights of his Amman career were undoubtedly winning the West Wales

Bowl. Playing against Newport twice and Cardiff in the Welsh Cup. But typically of his modesty Darrel identifies beating a high flying Dunvant team, home and away in season 1983-84, with Martin Evans and Lyn Roberts as his props as equal to any other achievement.

After his playing days were curtailed by a niggling back injury Darrel joined the club committee and has been an ever present and faithful member since 1993. He is now the Vice-Chairman of the club.

Despite all his achievements Darrel maintains that playing for the Amman is what he enjoyed the most-"Yma maen' nghalon i."

THE AMMAN HARLEQUINS RFC 1947 – 2003
THE MIGHTY QUINS
By Lyn Roberts

The current generation of players all recognise the Amman Quins as the club's second team. Indeed, this has been so since their formation in 1947, but second XV sides have existed throughout the whole history of Amman United.

It is known that a number of teams played in the villages of Glanamman and Garnant during the early years of Amman United and, if not intentionally, acted as nursery teams for the senior side.

Early references indicate that two of those sides namely Garnant Rangers and Amman Rovers RFC were extremely successful in their own rights.

Garnant Rangers could boast of five seasons when they remained unbeaten, whilst the Amman Rovers went through their entire seven year existence without defeat before replacing the senior Amman United side in the Llanelli and District league around 1911.

The Garnant Rangers unfortunately disbanded and after finding themselves idle for a whole season they reformed as Garnant Juniors. Starting off with specially arranged training facilities at the Raven Hotel stables before moving shortly afterwards to what was described as the "more sumptuous quarters" at the Colliers Arms.

After two successful seasons, during which several mammoth Glanamman v Garnant encounters took place, they lost use of the Hendre field and, being made homeless, they amalgamated with Amman United.

After the First World War two further sides appeared. Prospect Stars, acknowledged as one of the best junior sides, who supplied many players to the Amman United and Grenig Rovers.

Grenig Rovers were formed in 1924 after a meeting in the long room of the Amman Hotel. They went on to be a valuable nursery side and keen rivals of the Prospect Stars.

The Amman Juniors followed some years later, formed in 1933. They remained unbeaten for four years from seasons1933-1938 and in the season 1935-36 they won the Swansea and District League and Amman Valley Challenge Cup. Each of the 24 players being rewarded with a pullover in the club's colours courtesy of the president, Mr Dudley Folland.

In 1939 the side ceased to play on the outbreak of Second World War..

At the end of the war in 1945, 16 out of the 24 players moved up to the senior team Amman United.

In 1947, Amman Harlequins as it is to this day were formed as a separate entity with their own set of officials and accounts. The first recorded officials were Arthur Evans, secretary, Moelwyn Rees, chairman, and Freddie Schofield, treasurer. Mr Schofield was tragically killed in the Llandough air disaster during his term of office.

In seasons 1948-49-50 the Quins were winners of the Swansea and District Challenge Cup, under the captaincy of Gareth John who was captain for three successive seasons. The Quins were unfortunate not to win a third successive title the following year after being pipped at the semi-final stage with a team badly depleted by injuries.

In 1951 the Amman Quins ceased to operate as a separate entity and came under the wing of the main Amman United Club. The role of Harlequins secretary as an official of the club continued for the next 50 years.

Amman Harlequins RFC winners of the Swansea and District Rugby League Championship Challenge Cup 1948-49 and 1949-50

Several of the Quins secretaries have gone on to hold the office of secretary of the Amman United including Egwad Rees, Wally Bowen, Sid Davies, Nevin Anthony and Martin Luther Jones.

In season 1957-58, the Quins joined the Llanelli and District league following a proposal by the secretary Nevin Anthony.

The viability of the Quins has long been a bone of contention in recent years as it was in the late 1950s and early 1960s. Then, as now, the problem the team faces is a lack of players, due on many occasions to supporting the 1st team the Amman, often leaving the Quins struggling to find a team on a Saturday.

On many occasions games have consequently had to be cancelled. The continued survival of the Quins is always a hot topic in many a committee meeting.

But the Quins continue to survive, and rightly so. The concept of the second team side is to allow rugby players in Cwmamman the opportunity to play rugby football, a nursery side that provides a stepping stone between youth rugby and senior rugby with youngsters having more time to mature and develop. And most importantly it provides an opportunity for those rugby players who may not be blessed with the talent and ability to play at a higher level. It affords them the opportunity to play rugby, enjoy the game and the social activities associated with being part of the team. Both Amman teams are the breeding ground for future officials, committee and members of our club.

During the mid-1960s the Quins had an abundance of good players and performances and spirits improved. Many of the talented players who were to impress for the Amman United in latter years were to gain valuable experience as they first learned their craft with the Quins. This of course remains so, to the current day.

Seasons would rarely pass incident free, tales are often recalled of the bizarre and comical events on and off the field. Not surprising when teams often included many characters of note.

A story of one particular occasion in the late-1960s: The Quins returned home to the Amman clubhouse after playing Laugharne away. Well, not all of them returned, as several were hospitalised after a brutal encounter, with the walking wounded resembling a scene from a hospital Accident & Emergency Unit. There was much discontent over the opposition's approach to the game retribution would be sought!

The following week the Quins were to play Laugharne at home in the 1st round of the Llanelli & District cup. The teams for the Saturday were posted and to the horror and disbelief of the opposition, the side included the legendary Dennis Davies, an Amman hero, and several other Amman United regular players dropped from the 1st team and were now being chosen for the Quins as part of a cunning plan for retribution.

The game took place in early January, a particularly cold period of the year. There was indeed doubt as to whether the fixture would be played due to a hard frost. The pitch was declared playable and the wounded warriors with the help of Dennis and company were set to exact revenge. The Quins' captain was instructed that if he won the toss-up, he was to choose to kick-off. Luckily, for the Amman, they won the toss and kicked-off. No attempt was made by the Quins forwards to catch the ball and the bodies of Laugharne players were strewn everywhere on the ground as the rampant Quins forwards unleashed their pent up anger from the previous week's events. Their efforts to gain full retribution however remained frustrated, as a very nervous official decided after witnessing the events from the kick-off, that he was not refereeing a war, and soon declared that the ground was too hard and promptly abandoned the match. Laugharne however, were sent home with their tails between their legs and hopefully with the message "you don't mess with the Amman boys."

Seasons 1966 – 1974, proved to be a highly successful era for the Quins.

In 1966-67 they won the Llanelli and District League Champions Challenge Shield and the Welsh Junior Union 7s Championship.

Amman Quins 7s team 1967 Welsh Districts Juniors Champions

Back Row: Huw Joshua, John Pugh, Hywel Evans.
Seated: John Thomas, Owen Jones (captain), Martin Jones, David Thomas.

Amman Quins v Penybanc 1966-67 final at Betws

Back Row L-R: Alun West (Referee), Hywel Evans, John Davies, Gareth Jenkins, Raymond Evans, New Anthony, Clive Brooks, Rowland Davies, Malvern Evans, Alan Jones.
Seated L-R: Owen Jones, Hywel Williams, Colin Davies, Ken 'Iki' Davies (Captain), Martin Jones, Mike Williams.

Amman Quins - Celebrations in the clubhouse

Past v Present Boxing Day 1971-72

Back Row L-R: Alan Thomas, David Jones, Rowland Davies, Jeff Butt, Eurof Walters, Brian Davies, Glan James, Winston James, Jeff Thomas, Gordon Thomas, Vyron Thomas, Lennie Jones, Ieuan Davies, Ray Edwards, Edgar Llewelyn, Carwyn Thomas, Huw Harries, Dennis Davies, Ryan Bartlett.

In season 1968-69 they won the Llanelli and District Sevens and the Doreen Rogers Cup. The Doreen Rogers Cup was won on a further three occasions in seasons 1969-70, 1972-73, and 1973-74.

The secretary for the season 1974-1975 was Hywel Williams. Hywel had the luxury not enjoyed by the majority of future secretaries the availability of a large pool of players.

Both Glan James and Keith Morgan followed before retiring to the greens at Glynhir Golf Club, where they regularly reminisce over the great days they had with the Quins, whilst antagonising old adversaries, in particular those coming from the Brynamman and Llandybie clubs.

Martin Luther Jones followed and was to hold office as secretary for a full 12 years, becoming the longest serving Quins secretary before taking up the same role with the Amman United. Denver Jones regularly supported him with the first-aid duties.

Martin Howells took up the chalice for the next four years before moving on to refereeing and he was followed as Quins Secretary by Alan Arnold.

In 1995, the Quins legend Ken "Ike" Davies took office and after eight years remains the Quins Secretary in 2003.

Ken "Ike", the karaoke king, and eloquent public speaker, has had a long and successful association with the Quins. His three terms, as captain 1966-

1969 was the most successful in the Quins history. His popularity off the field is also echoed by his wizardry on the field, in both Sevens and XV a-side.

Despite the passing of time he remains an ever present figure at all Quins games. There is some truth in that the dodgy knees are curtailing his involvement and restricting his active participation (Paul Paddock reckons Mary doesn't agree with this prognosis).

As is customary the one-man bands, who run the line, do the first aid and occasionally drive the bus, are far too often taken for granted. The club is indebted for the contribution of Ken 'Ike', Martin Luther, and so many others over the years.

Clive Brooks follows Ike in the long serving captaincy list, he gave excellent service to the Quins and Amman over the years as a player, coach and committeeman.

These elder statesmen fully embraced the ethos of developing the younger players; both have encouraged and helped many along the way and those who benefited have learnt a great deal about the social aspects of the game (how to get a hangover).

The Quins over the years have been blessed with characters, Chris Preston being a star of recent seasons. The rugby ability of some may have been limited but their commitment and dedication to this rugby club was never in doubt. Many such characters accidentally embarked on their rugby careers after being "Shanghaied" out of the local pubs on a Saturday afternoon to make-up the numbers. Others, loyal to the core, would turn up week-in- week-out despite regularly being overlooked by selection.

From the early days the Quins have been indebted to the likes of Gareth John, Viv "Coch" Williams, Kendrick Lewis, Norman Bevan and Alban Morgan to name but a few. Gareth "Buck" Jenkins and Pat Brosnan were loyal characters who like Wally Bowen, Nev Anthony and Martin Luther Jones, gave their all to the cause on and off the rugby field.

Youngsters on their way up the ladder and senior players in the twilight years of their career have flowed through in abundance in David Williams (Dai Baker), Harold Jones (Haggis), Keith Hughes, Keith Morgan, Terry "Bach "Thomas and Dr. Alan Jones.

The late 1970s and early 1980s saw the likes of Roger Hartnell, Wyn and Brian Hogarth, Stuart Duncan, Noir Thomas, Lyn Roberts, Viv Madge, Cefin Campbell and Lance Williams amongst a bunch of players coming through the ranks.

The late 1980s and 1990s saw Shaun Davies being selected as captain on several occasions as a reward for his loyalty.

Rugby families have also been strong throughout with the Quins from Gareth and Glyn John in the formative years and also now Richard and Stuart Davies; many sets of brothers have represented the Quins, along with a couple of father and son combinations. The brothers Clive and Keith Williams, Shaun and Phil Davies, Thomas and Stuart Davies, Darrel and Cefin Campbell, Lance

Amman Quins XV 1983-84

and Clive Williams and of course the Morris brothers. Graham George played alongside son Mike, who did likewise with brother Paul, and Kevin Lewis and son Gavin. Ken "Ike" will be a proud man as he sees the family connection extend further with his son James being elected captain of the Quins for our Centenary season.

The fortunes of the Quins seem to have improved in recent seasons. Although it remains a struggle at times to round-up sufficient players, we have managed to fulfil our fixtures. Competitively we have held our position in the league and cup competitions. There have been many sides of high repute that have folded due to today's shortages of players, this indeed is a good sign for the future of the Quins.

In season 2001-2002, the Quins ended up runners-up in their league section and reached the semi-final of the Llanelli and District cup, being defeated by Newcastle Emlyn in a close fought encounter at Carmarthen.

Season 2002-2003, saw a sound performance in the league and we reached the final of the C.C.Evans cup, unfortunately losing to local rivals Brynamman 2nd XV at Cwmllynfell.

The centenary season will once again demand much of the committee and loyal helpers to ensure that our commitments are met in full. The players, the unsung heroes who can be relied upon for every game such as Simon "Slug

"Duncan, Wyn Thomas, Charles Weller, Jeremy Buchanan, James "Ike", Adrian Brown, Justin "Boxer" James, Richard and Steaming Stu Davies, will work hard to improve further on recent performances and bring home a long overdue trophy success.

I am sure that Ken and James "Ike" will rouse several renditions of "The Mighty Quins" throughout the season.

C.C. Evans Cup Final at Cwmllynfell RFC 2003
Amman Quins v Brynamman, Lost 0-8

AMMAN YOUTH RUGBY FOOTBALL CLUB
1949 - 2003
By John Vince Williams

The Welsh Youth Rugby Union was formed by the Welsh Rugby Union in 1949 in order to foster and organise games for youths under eighteen years of age who were not in secondary, grammar or public schools. It was formally constituted at a General Meeting held at Neath on May 11th 1949.

In season1949-50, the first active season for Amman United who were founder members of the Amman Valley District Youth along with 11 other clubs, the District Youth was second in size only to Cardiff District with13 teams. The chairman of the District was Mr W. Lang, Gorseinon RFC, the Secretary Mr A. Walters, Brynamman RFC and the Treasurer Mr W.J. Adams, Tumble RFC. The Secretary was Mr D.P. Thomas, who was also secretary of the Amman RFC.

Seasons 1949-1960

A local newspaper was to mention the Amman Youth in its game played on Monday, 10 September 1950 at Cwmamman Park played against Ammanford and lost11-0 against a more experienced Ammanford team. In those days, the Youth played at the start of the season and at the end of the season; they could not play in the middle of the season, when the clocks were turned back for the winter months, because the absence of floodlights in that era meant insufficient light. Added to this was the fact that there was only one field available on a Saturday for either the Amman or the Quins and, as a result, the youth usually played in the week.

Early success came in the season 1952-53, when the Youth went to the final of the Amman Valley and District League play-off against Gorseinon and drew 6-6. Each side shared the shield for six months. In the same year, the Amman Valley won the Captain Crawshay Cup for the first time, beating Mid Glamorgan Youth; in the team there were eight players from the Amman United, Dennis Davies, Winston James, Lyn Jones, Dai Price, Jarvis Styles, Raymond Walters, Eurof Walters and John Williams.

More success followed in season 1954-55 when the Youth shared the 7s competition with Cefneithin. Season 1954-55 saw the first Youth International from the club, when Peter Gerrard was selected to represent the Welsh Youth against France in Cardiff, winning 9-0, and Germany in Hanover, again winning by 25-5.

Season 1955-56 saw the youth successful again in the District 7s competition, this time winning the title and sharing the league title with Gorseinon Youth. This was the season that Malvern Evans had his Youth Cap.

Amman United Youth Team Season 1952-53

Back Row L-R: - Bertie Davies (Chairman), Islwyn Arnold, Peter Gerrard, Dennis Davies, John Jones, Jarvis Styles, Gareth Llewellyn, Winston James, E.B.Davies (Secretary), Tom Watkins (Trainer).
Middle Row L-R: - Roy Evans, Raymond Walters, Ryan Jones (Capt.), Dai Price, Eurof Walters, John Edwards.
Seated: - John Williams, William Ceidrich Davies.

Amman United Youth Team Season 1955-56

Back Row L-R: - Huw Harris, Terry Ward, Brian Thomas, Randall Williams, Glyn Jenkins, Glan James, Ieuan Thomas, Joe Edwards, Ieuan Evans (Coach).
Middle Row L-R: - Tom Ellis Howells (Treasurer), Elwyn Owen, John Morgan, John Williams, Ritchie Bundock, Eirian Jenkins, Ieuan Bevan, Viv Williams (Secretary).
Front Row L-R: - Danny Price, Glyn James (Capt.), Keith Hughes.

He represented Wales against Germany at Swansea, winning 32-0; he was also selected for the game against France at Bourg and lost 20-11. Scrum-half Glyn James was selected as a reserve for this game.

The Youth went to the final of the league competition again in season 1956-57, playing Gorseinon again, but this time the title was shared as the result was a draw, with each club keeping the shield for six months.

From the successful 1955-56 and 1956-57 teams, the district selectors picked Huw Harris to play in the district team. The team was successful in winning the Crawshay Cup in 1957-58, a Welsh Youth inter-district competition, beating Cardiff in the final. Huw, together with Morton Howells (Tumble) and Roy Evans (Cwmllynfell), won their Welsh Youth caps against France in Chambery but unfortunately they lost 6-0.

In the following two seasons, prior to the 1960s, the Youth ran teams but were unsuccessful.

Amman United Youth 7s Team Season 1955-56

Back Row L-R: - Doug Jones (First Aid), Glyn Jenkins, Randall Williams, Viv Williams (Secretary).
Middle Row L-R: - Elwyn Owen, John Morgan, John Williams, Ritchie Bundock, Brian Thomas.
Front Row L-R: - Glyn James, Huw Harris, Eirian Jenkins.

147

Seasons 1960-1970

The Youth ran teams for each season from 1960-61 to 1963-64. Season 1964-65 saw the team struggling for the lack of players. The team started to play but later disbanded after a number of cancelled games. The players who were available to play then went to other teams in the district to play their rugby, as they were too young to play for the Amman United or the Quins. Some went to play for Llandybie Youth but most went to Pantyffynnon Youth.

It was whilst playing for these teams that Trevor Evans (Pantyffynnon) won his Youth cap in 1966 and Jeff Thomas (Llandybie) won his cap in 1967

The popularity of Pantyffynnon Youth with players from Cwmamman can be seen in the photograph of Pantyffynnon Youth in season 1967-68, with no less than fourteen players being from Cwmamman.

Season 1968-69 saw the Amman Youth re-start; most of the players down at Pantyffynnon returned to the Amman Youth. The previous summer, the Amman Committee negotiated with the local education authority the lease of the field next to the Twyn Primary School, known locally as Cae Polly. Work was carried out to erect posts and mark out a rugby pitch and this was where the Youth would play their home games. This meant that the Youth could play on a Saturday at home, and it didn't matter if the Quins or the Amman were also home as the club now had two pitches, which benefited the club with extra revenue on a Saturday as there were two home games. The first home game played by The Youth on Cae Polly was against Pyle Youth on September 7th.

The Youth in 1969-70 had a reasonably good season, losing to Tumble in the Cup and League but they won the annual Sevens competition, beating Cwmllynfell in sevens the final.

The first team photograph of the 1970s is this one of the 1971-72 team.

The Youth played their first foreign opponents in season 1972-73, when they played Conostoga University, an American touring team. The game was won by the Youth. The highlight of the game was watching the opposing hooker throwing a long ball, American Football style, from the lineout straight out to the outside-centre. People watched in amazement as nothing like this had previously been seen on Cwmamman Park.

The last photograph taken of a youth team in the 1970s is the one of the 1973-74 team with Brian Knight as captain.

Phil Davies went on to have a final Youth Trial the following season 1974-75.

Season 1977-78 was a season when the Youth were reasonably successful and reached the District cup final at Brynamman against Cwmllynfell Youth but lost 15-3.

During the Amman's 75th anniversary season 1978-79, the Youth went to the final of the cup competition but lost again to Cwmllynfell 11-0. Due to the number of teams in the district, it was decided to split the league into two sections, something similar to the old West Wales Rugby Union format, and the winners of each section would play each other in the League Cup Final.

Pantyffynon Youth Team Season 1967-68

Back Row L-R: - Barry Jones, Mike Hughes, Huw Jenkins, Jeff Zschieschenek, Roger Lewis, David Bartlett, Rhydian Davies, Trevor Hopkin, Graham George, Referee.
Middle Row: - Phillip Hartnell, Glyn Rees, Roger Hewitt, Adrian Jones (Capt.), Harry Davies, Charles Timothy, Rowland John.
Front Row L-R: - Richard Rees, Peter Griffiths, Brian Davies, Alun Morris, Malcolm Davies, Russell Dunn.

Amman United Youth Team Season 1969-70

Back Row L-R: - Eric Jones, Dorian Jones, Malcolm Davies, Alan Cochran, Haydn James.
Middle Row L-R: - Martin Thomas, Hywel Roberts, Jeff Jones, Richard Remington, Mike Mckay.
Front Row: - L-R: - Martin Rogerson, Terry Thomas, Glyn Rees (Capt.), Rowland John, Malcolm James.

Cwmllynfell Youth won one section and the Amman Youth the other. The final was played in Brynamman and Cwmllynfell Youth won. After these hard matches, the Youth went on tour for the first time during Easter 1979 and played Rhyl and District Youth. It was the first time that the Youth had played in North Wales. The team met on Saturday morning and travelled up to Rhyl, booking into their hotel prior to the game. Despite all the rush, the youth won their game 26-6.

The following year 1979-80 saw the Youth go to the final of the Amman Valley Youth 7s at Llandybie but they lost 14-10 to Pontyberem Youth after extra time. It was also the season that Mike Francis had a final trial for the Welsh Youth in Llangennech.

During Easter, the Youth ventured over the border for their tour of Bournemouth, winning their game 15-12. They also entered a 7s tournament on the Sunday at nearby Swanage and lost in the final. This was the most adventurous tour undertaken as they left on a Friday and returned on the Monday.

Amman United Youth Team Season 1971-72

Back Row L-R: - Dai Worsfold, Haydn Timothy, Noel Evans, Carl Sheligah, Stephen Samuel, Justin Rees, John Gwyn Jones, Winston James (Secretary).
Front Row L-R: - David Williams, Neil Killbane, Viv Madge, Wayne Davies, Eric Jones (Capt.), Colin Hughes, Keith Davies, Iwan Williams.

Amman United Youth Team v Constoga High School 1973

Back Row L-R: - Phil Johnson, Noel Evans, Kevin Mckay, Phil Davies, Warren Harris, Jeff Morgan, Neil Killbane.
Front Row L-R: - David Williams, Brian Knight, Wayne Davies, John Phillips, John Gwyn Jones (Capt.), Colin Hughes, Viv Madge, Huw Morgan.

Amman United Youth Team Season 1973-74

Back Row L-R: - Phil Davies, Linden Evans, Peter Cole, Brian Rees, Wyn James.
Middle Row L-R: - Martin Mathews, Rheinallt Lewis, Phil John, Viv Madge.
Front Row L-R: - Meurig Roberts, John Looney, Brian Knight (Capt.), Martin Howells, James Davies.

Seasons 1980-90

The 1980-81 season started well with the Youth again going to the final of the Amman Valley Youth Sevens but this time losing to a very good Lampeter side 30-6. In the Cup competition, the Youth lost in the semi-final to Ammanford 3-0. At the end of season, a tour went to Halifax. The Youth played Halifax Vandals on the Saturday and won 48-0, and on the Monday played Halifax and won again 28-4.

The highlight of the 1981-82 season was the Easter tour to Whitley Bay, Newcastle, playing two games, winning against Seghill Colts 40-12 and losing to Blaydon Racers 16-12. The youth lost to Llandovery 12-6 in the semi-final of the cup.

Season 1982-83 saw the Youth losing to Tumble Youth in the cup, 18-9. In season 1983-84, the youth struggled to field a side and by Christmas, after cancelling five games on the trot, it was decided to cancel all the remaining games for the season.

A new start for the season 1984-85 saw the Youth winning more games than losing. In the cup, the youth played Cwmllynfell Youth in the first round and drew 10-10 on Cae Polly. The replay in Cwmllynfell was played four weeks later due to the weather and the result was another draw, this time 12-12. The third match was played at Llandybie and the Youth won 18-3. In the next round, the youth played Llandovery Youth and drew 3-3; the replay on Cwmamman Park saw the Youth win 6-0. The semi-final saw the Youth playing Brynamman Youth at Cwmgors. The Youth lost 12-3 and Brynamman Youth went on to win the cup, beating Llandybie Youth 6-4 in the final on Cwmamman Park.

Amman United Youth Team Season 1984-85

Back Row L-R: - David Power, Shaun Davies, Graham Bundock, Adrian Phillips, Kevin Morris, Kieron Ferry, Brian Jones, Steve Mckay (Capt.).
Front Row L-R: - Richard Davies, Anthony Jones, Richard Williams, Alan Davies, Carwyn Thomas, Stephen Mathews, Stephen Rogers, Paul Jones.
Photograph taken by Mark James Prior to semi-final in Cwmgors.

Amman United Youth v Halifax Vandals - Easter 1985

Back Row L-R: - John Francis, Phil Owen, Clive Brooks, John V. Williams, Shaun Davies, Roger Hartnell, Kevin Morris, Alan Davies, Kieron Ferry, Dai John James, Paul Jones, Stephen Mathews, Brian Jones, Dai Worsfold.
Front Row L-R: - David Power, Anthony Jones, Richard Williams, Carwyn Thomas, Steve Mckay (Capt.), Richard Davies, Nick Griffiths, Referee.

In between these replays, the Youth went on tour to Halifax and again played Halifax Vandals winning 21-7, and Halifax, this time losing 6-0.

Season 1985-86 saw the youth playing Lampeter Youth in the semi-final of the cup at Llandovery and losing 18-9.

In season 1986-87 the Amman Youth had a young side that played up until Christmas and then had to disband due to the lack of front row players.

Season 1987-88 saw the youth reaching the semi-final, again losing to Llandybie Youth 26-6 at Ammanford. On the way to the semi-final they beat Cwmllynfell Youth 23-9 on Cae Polly and Cwmgors Youth 19-4, also at Cae Polly. The name of Cae Polly for the rugby pitch was taken from the horse that used to graze in the field.

During seasons 1988-89 and 1989-90, the Amman Youth struggled to carry on due to the lack of players. They started the season but could not continue to the end.

Seasons 1990-2000

The first team of the 1990s didn't play a game until January 1991, as there were insufficient numbers of player eligible to play for the youth. They played Betws Youth at Cae Polly and won 32-14. This was a good start and they played a further seven games before the end of the season.

Season 1991-92 saw the Youth play a full season and lose to Brynamman in the first round of the cup 13-9. The following season 1992-93, the Youth again played a full season but lost to Lampeter away in the cup 15-3. The only team photograph of the 1990s is the one of season 1992-93, taken at Glanamman Community Centre.

Amman United Youth Team Season 1992-93

Back Row L-R: - Aled Rees, Thomos Williams, Andrew Lewis, Jonathan Morgan, Karl Nottingham, Owen Madge, Scott Fairburn.
Middle Row L-R: - Mark Jones, Paul George, Alwyn Davies, Shane Fairburn, Ross Smith, Stephen Morris.
Front Row L-R: - Stuart Davies, Alun Rees, John Williams (Sec), Karl Worsfold (Capt.), Carl James, Stuart Clark, Stephen Owen.
Photograph Mark James.

In the following two seasons 1993-94, 1994-95, the Youth played full seasons of rugby and reached the semi-final of the cup in 1994-95, losing to Tumble 15-12 On the way to the semi final the Youth beat Lampeter 6-3. The end of the season also saw the Youth going on tour, this time to Bethesda in North Wales and, in a close match, the Youth eventually won 12-13.

Season 1995-96 was a bad year as the Youth again could not field a team.

Season 1996-97 saw the Youth reconstituted and play a full season of rugby. They lost to Tumble Youth in the cup 27-35 and returned to North Wales for the annual tour, this time playing at Pwllheli and staying in the Pontins holiday camp. The Youth won the game against Pwllheli by 64-5, with Darrell

Buchanan scoring a hat trick of tries.

Season 1997-98 saw the first game being played on the new Golwg yr Amman pitch, across the river from the main stand. It was against Llandovery Youth and the Youth lost 20-0. Due to the number of cuts sustained by players on both sides, it was decided not to use the pitch again, as the field was in an unplayable state.

Season 1998-99 saw the Youth enter into a new venture by entering the Welsh Youth Knockout Cup for the first time, playing Newport Youth, who were the holders of the cup, at Newport. The Youth eventually lost 48-0 but the score did not reflect the game as the Youth gave a good account of themselves, even though Newport Youth boasted 15 internationals in their team and six on the substitutes bench. Newport Youth went on to the final of the competition and lost to Pontypridd Youth. This was also the season that the club had their first youth internationals for 40 years when Mathew Brayley and Stephen Phillips both played in the Welsh Youth teams in the Four Nations Tournament in Scotland. Mathew played against England (17-9) and Stephen played against Scotland (16-11). Both Mathew and Stephen played against Ireland and won 15-10. They also played in the Tri-Nations tournament in Portugal. At the end of the season The Amman Youth lost in the cup to Ammanford by 20-6 and went on tour to Llandudno, losing the game 24-21.

Season 1999-2000, the Youth played a full season of fixtures and played Llandovery away in the cup, losing 10-8. As this was the first round, they then went on to play in the plate competition and played Cwmgors Youth away, winning 23-3. In the final, the youth played Brynamman and lost 7-5, with Brynamman Youth scoring and converting a try in the last moments of the game.

Season 2000-03

Season 2000-01 was a season when the Youth again entered the Welsh Youth Knockout Cup. The Youth progressed further than on the previous occasion they entered the cup. The first match was against Penclawdd Youth at home and they won 37-3. The next round saw the Youth play against Tumble Youth at home; the Youth had not beaten Tumble for a number of years but on this occasion they were successful, winning 12-8. They were now into the last eight of the competition and the draw was a home game against London Welsh. The game was played in late February on Cwmamman Park. London Welsh went in at half time leading 14-0, having scored two converted tries. In the second half, playing down the park in front of a large crowd, the Youth gave a tremendous performance, scoring two tries but failing to convert either. Emyr Lewis and Geraint Davies scored the tries; another try was scored by the Youth but this was disallowed because of a forward pass. The final score was 14-10 to London Welsh.

In the East Carmarthenshire Cup, the Youth were drawn again against Tumble Youth. They were all out to win this game and won 36-7. In all, the

Youth played them four times during the season, winning one and losing three. In the three games that the Youth lost, Tumble scored 118 points; it shows what the win in the Welsh Youth Cup had meant to the Youth team.

The annual tour saw the Youth travel down to Penzance. In a physical game against Penzance Youth, they eventually won 22-13

Amman United Youth v London Welsh Youth

Back Row L-R: - Wayne Crocker, Clive Bale, Roy Morgans, Viv Madge, Rhys Jones, Geraint Davies, Stuart Davies, Chris Rees, Emyr Lewis, Peter Evans, Thomas Davies, Gareth Evans, Arwel Roberts, Stuart Griffiths, Brian Davies, Darrell Campbell.
Front Row L-R: - John V. Williams (Secretary), Darren Dunning, Rhys Thomas, Rhys Richards, Mathew Jones, Rhodri Williams, Nick Davies (Capt.), Cellan Phillips, Tristian Manning, Gareth Evans, Andrew Lacey, Paul Davies, Rhodri Williams.
Photograph Mark James

Men of Amman who have influenced Welsh Youth Rugby

E.B.Davies

Eirwyn Davies played for the Club after the Second World War and was instrumental in setting up a youth team in the club. He became the first assistant secretary of the Amman Valley District, moving on to become the secretary of the district in the early 1950s. He became a member of the Welsh Youth Executive Committee during this time. It was in 1960 that he became the secretary of the Welsh Youth Rugby Union, a post he held until he finished in 1983. His greatest achievement was the post of Welsh Rugby Union President in season 1983-84. He was chairman of the Welsh Youth for a two-year period from 1985-87. He then retired from rugby administration.

Ieuan Evans

Ieuan played for the Amman after the war and he became the secretary of the club from 1953-57. He was also the secretary of he Youth XV from 1961-63. Ieuan became the secretary of the Amman Valley District in 1963, a post he held until 1972. During this time he was also a member of the Welsh Youth Executive Committee. Ieuan is better remembered for his coaching abilities. He was the coach of the Amman Youth from 1950-53. He then progressed to coach the Amman senior side from 1953-57 and from 1958-62. Throughout this time, Ieuan also coached the Amman Valley and District Youth XV. In 1962-63, he created history as he became the first coach of an International Rugby side anywhere in the World, when he became the coach of the Welsh Youth XV, It was he who introduced the squad system to youth and indeed British Rugby. It would be a post that he held until 1979. In 1967-69, he was the coach of Llanelli. He then crossed the Loughor Bridge and went to coach Swansea, strengthening the side with players who had represented the Welsh Youth and players he had coached through the Amman Valley Youth. Ieuan was selected as a W.R.U. National Representative from 1976-92 and became President of the Welsh Rugby Union in season 1991-92.

Ivor Phillips

Ivor Phillips was born in Garnant but did not play for the Amman. He was left handicapped following an accident when he was a child. He got knocked down by a car, which left him with a damaged arm. As a young man, Ivor moved to Newport to work and he became the Magistrates' Clerk for the county of Monmouthshire. Ivor was involved with Youth rugby from the onset and attended the first meeting at the Castle Hotel Neath in 1949. He was the first secretary of the Newport District and, as such, a member of the Welsh Youth Executive Committee. When the Youth District boundaries changed, Ivor became the secretary and treasurer of the new South Monmouthshire District. Ivor served as Treasurer to the Welsh Youth Rugby Union from 1960-63, and was the Chairman of the Union from 1972-74.

AMMAN UNITED JUNIORS RFC
Under 8s to Under 16s
By Hywel Roberts

AMMAN UNITED JUNIORS
1972 - 2003

Through the years there have been many attempts to establish Junior Rugby sides and foster rugby in the area of Cwmamman, giving youngsters the chance to represent their village. The organisers and volunteers have met with mixed fortunes and some were more successful than others.

Season 1972-73 saw the introduction of Junior Rugby to clubs for the first time with the East Carmarthenshire U-15s League.

The South Wales Guardian reported - *September 1972 saw the formation of the East Carmarthenshire Under 15s League – where Amman United Under-15s prospered. Indeed, they exceeded all expectations and went on to win the championship, beating Furnace 4-3 in a hard fought encounter at Penygroes.*

Our first caption shows the photograph of David Bevan, raising a trophy as Captain of the successful Amman United Juniors Under-15s in 1972.

Since then Junior teams have come and gone, until the current Juniors were formed in 1987 and have had an unbroken run since. The second caption we have is that of the Amman United Under-14 squad that went to a tournament at Bournemouth in 1990, under the guidance Alan (Chico) Davies, and Alan King. This picture shows several boys who not only represented the Amman United but also went on to play 1st Class rugby and represent Wales.

The following photograph is of the entire squad of boys who played in that 1972 season

Back Row L-R: - D Bevan, G Evans, A Morgan, R Hartner, A Evans, R Anderson, D Pugh, A Lewis, P Coles
Middle Row L-R: - C Cambell, Lyn Roberts, M Williams, D Richards, R Bush
Front Row L-R: - J McRobert, H Owen, (A Thomas, P Rogers, mascots) S Richards, I Dodd, N Thomas

Note the young Shane Williams, Neath and Wales, kneeling bottom left

160

The second caption we have is that of the Amman United Under-14 squad that went to a tournament at Bournemouth in 1990, under the guidance Alan (Chico) Davies, and Alan King. This picture shows several boys who not only represented the Amman United but also went on to play 1st Class rugby and represent Wales.

This team formed the backbone of the current Amman Juniors and started playing friendly games against established Swansea and District teams.

Although they were playing against well-organised sides, the boys proved that they could compete with the best of them, and the Amman United have benefited since then by having players come up from the Junior Section through to youth and Quins and to the 1st XV team. Adults that came forward during this initial period, as well as the above mentioned, were Kathleen (Hartnell) Jones, Reene Evans, and Tegwyn Davies; they worked hard with the boys and the Amman committee to ensure that the team succeeded. Though they have now finished with the Juniors, they laid the foundations that other members have followed ensuring the Juniors have a future.

During the 1990s, following this initial success the Junior Section went from strength to strength, as the various age groups were formed and as more and more boys joined the Amman Juniors. At their peak, there were five teams boasting squads of twenty-plus boys of various ages playing for the Amman Juniors. This was from primary school age through to under-sixteen age group; over a 100 boys and some girls in the lower age groups from Cwmamman area were turning out on Sunday mornings to play rugby for the Amman United Juniors.

Nantgaredig Tournament.

Photograph shows the Amman United Juniors in competition at Nantgaredig. The four fine figures standing at the rear row are Russell Dunn, Steve Simmons, Hywel Roberts and, sadly, the deceased Calvin Phillips.

The following are newspaper cuttings from The South Wales Guardian and events involving the Amman United Juniors.

NEW COMPETITION A GREAT SUCCESS

THE AMMAN United Juniors were on of 10 teams invited to participate in the first indoor under-12 mini-rugby tournament hosted by Nantgaredig RFC — and what a day it turned out to be for the Cwmaman side.

The Amman's qualifying group consisted of teams from Trimsaran, Narberth, Llandovery and Ferryside, each proving to be worthy tournament contenders.

However, the Amman squad put together an excellent display of committed rugby to qualify undefeated for the semi-finals, with Trimsaran through as runners-up.

From the second group, Tumble also qualified undefeated with Carmarthen Athletic taking second place.

This paired the Amman with Athletic in a stirring semi-final, and again the Amman delivered the goods to run out 10-0 winners.

Trimsaran put an end to Tumble's undefeated run in their semi-final, setting the scene for an exciting finish to the competition.

In the earlier stages the Amman had just edged out Trimsaran by a single score in the final minute.

But at the end of a full day of rugby, the Amman were able to move up a gear to achieve a convincing 22-0 win to take the tournament and become the first name on the perpetual shield.

It was a remarkable tournament fact that the Amman scored a total of 78 points in six games, and conceded none.

The squad consisted of: Richard Dunn (capt); Arwel Davies; Stuart Killick; Gareth Lewis; Stephen Phillips; Andrew Thomas; Lee Thomas; Carwyn James; James Simmons; Emyr Timothy; David Evans and Christopher Preston. Reserves were Alun Jones, Richard Evans and Robert Griffiths.

The victory put the icing on the cake in what has been an enjoyable and encouraging season for the juniors and their loyal fans.

Juniors entertain

AMMAN United Under-11s hosted Felinfoel on Sunday and both teams contributed to an exciting game of junior rugby.

For the home side, forward Jonathan James had another outstanding match, and with Thomas Davies and Emyr Lewis in support, the solid platform up front provided the quality second-phase ball that the backs used so well.

Andrew Lacey, enjoying the good possession at scrum-half, crossed for the Amman's first score, converted by Ian Killick.

Christopher Davies made some penetrating runs, but the score was restricted to 7-0 at the interval.

In the second-half, the Amman stretched their lead with a fine try from Ian Killick, which he also converted.

However, Felinfoel were in no mood to surrender, and a spirited display saw them crossing for a try that went unconverted.

At this point the Amman were forced on the defensive with Geraint Davies and Alex Harries putting in some telling tackles.

The visitors were kept at bay until the final minutes when their efforts were rewarded with a converted score, which wasn't quite enough as the Amman held on to a slender, but deserved two point victory.

The Under-12s hosted Llangadog, who took the field with three Amman guests to make up the numbers.

The Amman started strongly with Andrew Roberts and Nicholas Davies putting in some excellent work up front.

The second phase ball was put to good use and one excellent move saw the ball spread out to Gareth Evans, who crossed for a fine try converted by Ryan Williams.

Within minutes Robert Harlow was rewarded for his efforts with a good score in the corner following some excellent support work, Williams was again successful with the kick.

The Amman play was now flowing, with good work coming from Clive Bale and Neil Roberts up front, while Ryan Williams and Adrian Thomas marshalling the three-quarters.

However, Llangadog were to strike back, ironically through 'guests' Steven Phillips and Stuart Davies, who grabbed a try apiece. Davies was successful with both conversions.

With the scores tied, Stuart Davies again broke through and looked to be in for another score.

However, centre Adrian Thomas appeared from nowhere to bring off a match saving tackle, earning a deserved 14-14 draw.

Promising start to new season

THE AMMAN Under-14s kicked off this season's campaign by entertaining Swansea and District side Morriston.

Despite the unavailability of a number of regulars, they took the lead.

Good second phase ball was won and spread along the three-quarter line to Darrel Buchanan, who put his head back and raced 40 metres to score in the corner.

This first period saw the Amman pinning down the visitors for much of the time.

Robert Griffiths having an excellent match at full-back, and forwards Steven Phillips, Christopher Anthony and Andrew Thomas working well.

However Morriston replied with a converted score just before the interval.

This seemed to lift their heads for the second half, and Amman paid the price, falling victim to three successive scores.

However, a short penalty, quickly taken by Richard Dunn found Emyr Timothy out wide, and the powerful centre outran the visitors defence for a good score.

But the comeback wasn't to be, as Morriston replied with a further score to run out winners at 28-10.

The previous day, the Amman Under-11s had the honour of playing against Llandovery, in the curtain raiser to the Drovers Heineken League match with Mountain Ash.

The youngsters showed a vast improvement after the previous week's heavy defeat, and contained a lively Llandovery side to a final score 25-10 in favour of the home side.

The Amman's scorers were Thomas Davies and Jonathan James.

The visitors were also grateful for the exceptional hospitality they received from Llandovery.

Photograph action shot of Andrew Roberts going past a tackler from Camberslang when the Amman Juniors hosted the Scottish side at Cwmamman Park

Next picture is of John Vince Williams, a loyal supporter of the Junior Section since its inception; some of his photographs have been used in this Junior Section of the Centenary Book.

The next photograph shows the Amman United Juniors Under-16 age group on tour in Ireland in 1996; Eric Jones, Russell Dunn, Noir Thomas, and John Vince Williams managed the team. During this period with the Juniors, the team took some notable scalps, proving to be one of the most difficult sides to play against in West Wales; beating not only local opposition, they also beat teams from Ireland, England, and Scotland, winning several tournaments along the way. Again, a few of these players went on to play for 1st class rugby teams and to represent Wales.

They say that success follows success, and this was to be proven correct over and over again as the Juniors, who had been with the club from Under-9 age group, flourished. They followed in the footsteps of their elders, cumulating in a number of representations at Schools, Districts, County and International level.

One such side is shown as before and after in the next two photographs

This was the 11-age group playing at Penclawdd in 1993; the next picture shows mostly the same boys at under-16 age group, having won a tournament at Tumble.

Everyone of the above represented the District Schools, District 'F', Carmarthen County and Wales; four went on to play 1st Class rugby, three represented Wales at various age levels; they also were part of the County relay champions and represented their school and county at various athletic field and track events.

165

The success of this side is unparalleled due to the collective ability of the players and between the ages of Under-15 and Under-16, they went unbeaten for thirty out of thirty-two games, being the highest points scorers in both District 'F' Carmarthenshire and District 'E' Swansea.

With success comes awards, and the Junior Section has been unequalled in giving generously to the children of Cwmamman during their Annual Presentation evenings. To go with these evenings, there have had to be guests to make presentations and we have been fortunate in obtaining the services of some of the best Welsh players of recent years in Robert Jones, Paul Thorburn, Gwyn Jones, Anthony Clement, Rupert Moon, our own British Lion, Trevor Evans, and several others who have played their part in ensuring a successful evening. Following are some photographs of Junior presentation nights.

First Picture Robert Jones presenting Andrew Roberts
Second Picture Paul Thorburn presenting Ryan Williams

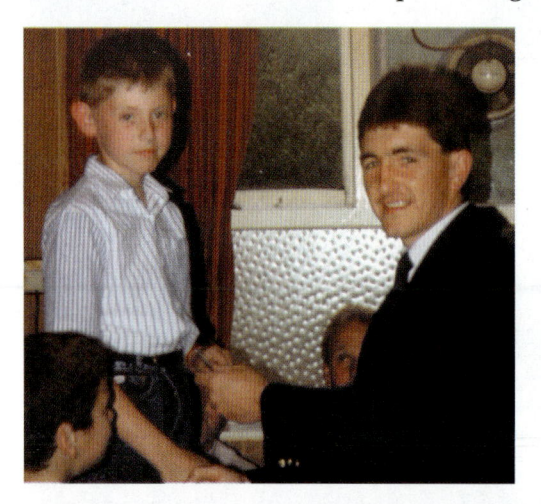

Anthony Clement presenting Arwel Roberts; in the background County Councillor and Cwmamman Town, Mayor Kevin Madge, and John Schropfer of the W.R.U.

Here we have Trevor Evans, Amman United, Swansea, Wales, & British Lions presenting Matthew Brayley, Amman United Juniors, Swansea, Wales U19 Captain

Clive Williams, Chairman of the Junior Section, presenting Ioan Cunningham, Amman Juniors, who captained Wales at all school age groups, now with Llanelli, with a framed photograph of Ioan representing West Wales against East Wales

Not to be outdone by the boys, here is a picture of one of the Junior girls being presented by Trevor Evans

The photo shows Sian Rees being presented by Trevor Evans. Sian played for Dinefwr District Schools on the wing.

Martin Jones, Amman United Secretary, and a staunch supporter of the Junior Section, presenting Ryan Williams with a trophy in recognition of Ryan winning his Welsh cap at Under- 15 age group.

To finish off this section, we can show why the rugby stars of Wales and the British Lions enjoyed being with us on our presentation evenings - the ladies section of the Juniors, who have assisted and supported the youngsters through the years from their early beginnings and still continuing to do so to this very day.

A very special thanks is due to Trevor Evans, who has given so much to the Juniors over the years, and also to the Amman United for sponsoring our presentation evenings.

There are many people who need to be thanked and congratulated for the success of the Junior Section, those that have already been mentioned and the others who have remained in the background but have worked hard to ensure that the name of Amman United will live on and be respected by all.

The Juniors have been proud ambassadors of the club and have been made welcome at other clubs throughout Wales, as well as the places they have visited in Ireland and England. We have also shown our hospitality to those who have visited us from England and as far away as Scotland.

We have played against and beaten, among others, teams such as Llanelli, Narberth, Llandovery, Dunvant, Glamorgan Wanderers, Camberslang of Scotland, and Lydney from Gloucester. To this end, the boys who have gone through the ranks of the Juniors and those to follow, owe the following people a special mention and a great debt : many people who have given their time and patience to the boys and girls, and who have gone on the WRU coaching courses and first aid courses, attended various meetings to ensure that the Amman Juniors were looked after to the best of their ability.

Special gratitude goes to our referees Terry Thomas, Moelwyn Jones and Doug Thomas; all are Welsh Rugby Union referees who have given their time freely on Sunday morning, taking control of games from Under-8 up to Under-16.

The following is a list of those who have ensured the success of the Amman United Juniors: -

Edgar Morris, Chairman Amman United
Martin Luther Jones, Secretary Amman United
The Amman United Committee

Alan (Chico) Davies	Darrel Campbell
Alan King	Tegwyn Davies
Calvin Phillips	Steve (Amman Fruits) Simmons
Malcolm (Dobbin) Davies.	Russell Dunn
Mair Dunn	Rachel Madge
Viv Madge	Clive Williams
Eric Jones	Karl Worsfold
Mike Davies	Yvonne (Jones) Roberts
June Roberts	Noir Thomas
Hywel Roberts	John Vince Williams

It is always difficult to start naming people for fear of offending others who have worked just as hard but have not been named; to these our sincerest apology.

Rachel Madge is the longest serving member of the Juniors, having been involved with them for the last thirteen years and continues to be so today and with always a smile on her face. Rachel is one of many who have passed courses in both coaching and first aid. She has taken on all the roles imaginable running the Juniors and special thanks is owed to her.

During his period with the Juniors, Hywel Roberts became Chairman of the Junior Section, then became Secretary; he went on to become Chairman of District 'F' and was on the W.R.U, working party on the development of Junior Rugby in Wales, attending monthly meetings at Cardiff. He was also appointed Team Manager of the District Under-16s age group.

Through the hard work and dedication of everyone involved, the Junior Section have given the youth of Cwmamman the opportunity to learn the game, to be part of the Amman United RFC, and given the youngsters belief and confidence in themselves.

The Amman, though, have had to pay a price for this success with players that have come up through the various age groups being targeted by the higher division teams and also first class clubs taking the most talented boys away from the Amman United. Due to this, many ex-Amman Junior players can be seen gracing first class grounds across Wales week in, week out.

Amman United RFC Under 10s Season 2002-03

Back Row L-R: - Dylan James, Keiron Tommey, Nicholas Jones, Jordan Rees, Liam Wooley, Joshua Harries, Gerwyn John (Coach).
Front Row L-R: - Richard Card, Daniel James, Corey Robins (Capt), Sean Llewellyn, Sam Rees, Johnathon Lewis.

Amman United RFC Under 12s Season 2002-03

Back Row L-R: - Simon Card (Coach), Shaun Davies, Joshua Rees, Patrick Stephenson, Thomas Watson, Adam Morris, Christopher Price, Dylan Bates, Gareth John.
Front Row L-R: - Johnathon Williams, Ryan Card, Keiron Rees (Capt), Calvin Robins, Micheal Fuller, James Scutt.

Amman United RFC Under 14s Season 2002-03

Back Row L-R: - Shaun Daves (Coach), James Davies, Damian Davies, Iwan Davies, Andrew Jones, Christian Gregory, Darell Campbell (Coach).
Front Row L-R: - Christian Madge, Cellan Jones, Joel Foster (Capt), Mathew Madge, Sion Mangan

Amman United RFC Under 15s Season 2002-03

Back Row L-R: - Gerwyn John (Sec), Dale Calow, Mathew Cayton, Lee Fletcher, Santino DeAngelo, Nicholas Hadley, Johnathon James, Lloyd Griffiths, Kevin Jones (Coach), Thomas Davies (Coach).
Front Row L-R: - Darrel John, David Fisher, Joshua Rees, Thomas Mathews, Robert Thomas (Capt), Ross Knight, Glyndwr Thomas, Robert James, Gavin Madge, Ademola Adebola.

Below is the list of Amman United Junior players who have achieved honours; we must apologise in advance if there are any players names that we may have omitted.

Honours

Matthew Brayley, Amman Juniors, Amman Youth, Swansea and Wales Under-19 and 21

Ioan Cunningham, Amman Juniors, Llanelli and Wales all Levels

Steffan Edwards, Amman Juniors, Amman Youth, Swansea and Welsh Schools

Alwyn Davies, Amman Juniors, Amman Youth, Aberavon

Gareth King, Amman Juniors, Llanelli, Newport and Wales

Nathan Brew, Amman Juniors, Welsh Schools, Welsh Youth and Newport

Ryan Williams, Amman Juniors, Llanelli and Welsh Schools.

Steve Phillips, Amman Juniors, Amman Youth, Neath and Wales Youth

Shane Williams, Amman Juniors, Neath and Wales

Chris Hughes, Amman Juniors, Llanelli, Pontypool and Welsh Schools

Gavin Elliot, Amman Juniors, Welsh Schools, District & County Honours

Steven Thomas, Amman Juniors, Carmarthen County, District 'F', District Schools, Welsh Development Squad

Richard Dunn, Amman Juniors, West Wales, Carmarthen County, District 'F', District Schools, Swansea

Arwel Davies, Amman Juniors, District Schools, District 'F', Carmarthen County.

Emyr Timothy, Amman Juniors, District Schools, District 'F', Carmarthen County

Nick Davies, Amman Juniors, District Schools, District 'F', Carmarthen County, Welsh Development Squad

Adrian Thomas, Amman Juniors, District Schools, District 'F', Carmarthen County.

District Honours

Clive Bale, Amman Juniors, District 'F' Juniors and Amman Valley Youth

Rhodri Williams, Amman Juniors, District 'F' Juniors, Amman Valley Youth and Welsh Youth Trial

Gareth Evans, Amman Juniors, Dinefwr Schools, District Schools, District 'F'

Mike Maddocks, Amman Juniors, District Schools and District 'F'

Tristan Manning, Amman Juniors, Dinefwr Schools, District Schools and District 'F'

Wayne Crocker, Amman Juniors, District Schools and District 'F'

Andrew Roberts, Amman Juniors, Dinefwr Schools, District Schools and District 'F'

Gavin Lewis, Amman Juniors, Dinefwr Schools, District Schools, District 'F', Swansea Academy and British Army

Thomas Davies, Amman Juniors, District 'F' and Swansea Academy
Geraint Davies, Amman Juniors, District 'F', District Schools and District Youth
Kristian Williams, Amman Juniors, District 'F' and Swansea Academy
Gerwyn Roberts, Amman Juniors and District 'F
Emyr Lewis, Amman Juniors, District Schools, District 'F' and Gloucester Academy
Ross Coughlin, Amman Juniors and District 'F'

The success of the Amman United Juniors continues to grow, through the late 1990s to the current season of 2002-2003.

The following are our latest crop of young players who are starting on their rugby career with the Amman United and have already brought honours to both themselves and the Amman United Rugby Club and are players to look out for in the near future.

1998-2003
Gareth John, Amman Juniors and Dinefwr Schools
David Mathews, Amman Juniors and Dinefwr Schools
Daryl John, Amman Juniors, Dinefwr Schools and District 'F'
Gavin Madge, Amman Juniors and Dinefwr Schools
Ross Knight, Amman Juniors and Dinefwr Schools
Justin James, Amman Juniors, Dinefwr Schools and District 'F'
Chris Eady, Amman Juniors, Swansea Valley Schools, District 'F' and West Wales
Stuart Dunn, Amman Juniors, Dinefwr Schools, District Schools, District 'F' and West Wales trials
Christian Madge, Amman Juniors, Dinefwr Schools, District Schools, District 'F' and West Wales Trials
Sean Mangam, Amman Juniors, Dinefwr Schools, District Schools and District 'F'
Joel Foster, Amman Juniors, Dinefwr Schools, District Schools and District 'F'
Robert Thomas, Amman Juniors, District Schools, District F
Nathan Jenkins, Amman Juniors, Dinefwr Schools, District schools, District 'F'
Lloyd Griffiths, Amman Juniors, Dinefwr Schools, District Schools and District 'F'
Dylan Bates, Amman Juniors, Dinefwr Schools and West Wales Trials
Kael Ace, Amman Juniors and Dinefwr Schools
Kieran Rees, Amman Juniors and Dinefwr Schools

We should look to the future beyond our Centenary Year, and I am very pleased that we now have a very strong Junior Rugby Section.

The future of the club is in the hands of these young players.

AMMAN VALLEY JUNIOR SCHOOLS
By John Vince Williams

Seasons 1970-80
Season 1970-71 saw an important development in the Valley with the Amman Valley Junior Schools League coming into being. This provided rugby for boys in Standards 3 & 4 who would otherwise have had to wait until they were in secondary education before starting to play rugby. Both Garnant Primary School and Glanamman Primary School played on Cwmamman Park. The games were played on a Friday afternoon after school. Garnant were reasonably successful during the course of the first season and there was always keen rivalry between the two sides. Apart from allowing the teams to play on the Park, the Amman United also provided jerseys for both teams, Garnant School in red and Glanamman School in white.

These teams hopefully would benefit the Amman United in future years, as these players were to become the future Youth and Amman players team members. The earliest photograph of Garnant Junior School is season 1971-72.

Garnant Primary School Team Season 1971-72

Back Row L-R: - Mr Alan Thomas, Carl Jeremiah, Alun Thomas, Carl Evans, Steven Davies, Jeff Price, Mr Trevor Davies.
Middle Row L-R: - Darrel Campbell, Michael Thomas, Tony Scullion, Roy Morgans, Meirion Griffiths.
Front Row L-R: - Huw Davies, Jeff Rees, Michael Evans, Keith Williams (Capt.), Jimmy Looney, Kevin Jones, Ashley Thomas.

Garnant Primary School 'A' Team

Back Row L-R: - Carl Evans, Stephen Price, Mike Evans, Keith Williams, David Herdman.
Front Row L-R: - Stephen Hunt, Christopher Griffiths (Capt.), Tony Lock.

Glanamman Primary School 'A' Team

Back Row L-R: - Russell Mathews, David Richards, Paul Davies, Philip Williams, Peter Day.
Front Row L-R: - Roger Jones, Terence Roberts (Capt.), Emlyn Llewellyn.

Both Garnant and Glanamman were successful in Sevens rugby, playing each other in the final of the tournament held at Llandovery in April 1971.

Glanamman 'A' reached the final by having a bye in their first round, winning Ammanford 'A' 12-0 in the second round, winning Coedmor 6-3 in the third round, and winning Betws 9-3 in the semi-final.

Garnant 'A' reached the final, by winning Talley/Llansawel 12-0 in the first round, winning Llandeilo 'A' 9-0 in the second round, winning Brynamman 3-0 in the third round and winning Parcyrhun 'A' 3-0 in the semi-final. Both of their last two matches went to extra time.

In the final, Glanamman beat Garnant 6-3 in extra time with Terence Roberts and Philip Williams scoring for the winners and David Herdman scoring for Garnant.

Photographs of both teams are shown.

As there were no trophies provided by the tournament organizers for both winners and runners up, Amman United R.F.C. decided to provide trophies for both teams, as they were both local schools to the club. The presentation was made at the Community Centre in Glanamman, in what was the first official occasion held at the centre. The gesture proved fruitful as there were three future Captains of the club in the two teams, one for the Amman United and two for the Amman Quins, namely Mike Evans, Keith Williams and Phil Williams respectively.

THE RUGBY LEAGUE CONNECTION
By Eurof Walters

The importance of the Amman Valley as a breeding ground for Rugby League players had been appreciated by Northern Union Clubs even before the formation of Amman United but increased in importance when all the talent was harnessed under one banner.

Jack Evans

The first export from the valley was Jack Evans, a three-quarter who played for Penybont Rovers prior to joining Llanelli. He joined Swinton RLFC in 1896 and made his debut against Leigh in October 1897. Jack represented Swinton until 1907, playing 252 games and scoring 28 tries and 33 goals. He won one Lancashire County Cap and gained a Rugby League Cup Winner's Medal when Swinton beat Salford 16-8 at Fallowfield. He returned briefly to coach the Mid-Rhondda Northern Union team on retirement.

He fathered three sons, Jack, Bryn and Harold, all of whom won Lancashire County Caps. Jack Junior represented Wales and Great Britain, and Bryn played for England and Great Britain. Both accompanied Billo Rees and the Great Britain team to Australia in 1928. All three brothers played for Swinton and Bryn was Billo's half-back partner for club and Great Britain.

D J Rees

Amman United's outside-half and captain in 1904/05 joined Llanelli in 1905/06 season, scored 10 tries and was selected as Welsh Reserve during that season. He joined in 1908 Aberdare Northern Union Rugby Club for a substantial fee of £50. Aberdare were members of the Monmouthshire and Glamorganshire Northern Rugby League Clubs, who regularly played against Lancashire, Yorkshire, Wales and England.

Joe Rees

Joe played for the Amman in 1913 as a 16-year-old. When serving in the armed forces during the 1st World War, he represented Wales in a services international. In 1919, he went to Swinton for a trial but was thought too frail for league - probably Swinton's biggest mistake.

Rees Rees

Rees, brother of Joe and Billo, played centre or outside-half for the Amman from 1919 to 1921, joined Hull Kingston Rovers in 1921 and made his debut against Wakefield Trinity on 21st January 1922. He quickly became a favourite at Craven Park and was known as the 'Lion of Hull'. He played 41 games in 1922/23 season and scored a try in the 15-5 championship final win at Headingley. He transferred to Warrington in 1924 and finished playing in 1927.

Billo Rees

Billo, brother of Joe, Rees and Nathan, played scrum-half and outside-half for the Amman from 1919 to 1921 and joined Swinton Rugby League in November 1921, after playing with Llanelli and Swansea; he made his first appearance as scrum-half against St Helens on 3rd November. Disillusioned with life in the reserves, Billo returned home for the summer and was chosen for the Amman in September 1922 but was sent off by the referee before kick-off as being an 'UNDESIRABLE'.

255. *Billo Rees, a Welshman in English colours.*

Billo returned to Swinton and swiftly settled as first choice outside-half and remained so until 1934. In the Xmas period 1924, Swinton (and Billo) played three championship games on Xmas Day, Boxing Day and the following day the 27th. They won all three due to an immaculate display by Billo but lost the championship final against Hull KR 9-5, with brother Rees playing for Hull KR. Billo won a Hospitals Cup Final Winner's Medal in the competition's inaugural season against Salford. He won a Lancashire Cup Final Winner's medal against Wigan in 1925/26 and received his first Welsh Cap against England at Pontypridd in April 1926. Four days later, Billo was a member of the Swinton team which won the Rugby League Cup Final for the first time against Oldham at Rochdale; this was the first time that BBC Radio had made a live commentary of a rugby league game.

Swinton RLFC 1925-26

Swinton RLFC 1926-27

Billo was capped for Great Britain against New Zealand in October 1926 and in January 1927. Both Billo and Bryn Evans played together for the first time for Great Britain against New Zealand. He won a Championship Winner's Medal when Swinton beat Warrington in the Championship Final 1927. In season 1927/28 Billo was a member of the Swinton team that won the Lancashire Cup, Lancashire League, Rugby League Championship and the

Swinton RLFC 1927-28

Winners of the Rugby League Challenge Cup, Rugby League Championship Cup, Lancashire Cup, Lancashire League Cup

After the match the Australians were entertained at Swinton Conservative Club where their tour manager, the legendary Harry Sunderland, paid an unlikely but gracious tribute to the behaviour of the Swinton crowd earlier in the day. He said, *"It did my heart good to hear the cheers of the crowd when Hodgson kicked his third penalty"*, and he also went on to congratulate the play of Billo Rees and Bryn Evans, adding that, *"No player had ever left Australia with a bigger reputation than Billo Rees."* Finally, Sunderland commented that he hoped that the success of the Swinton club would continue, and that in Australia the name of Swinton was a household word. It was all very cordial, but the Rugby League authorities were less impressed and due to the nasty flavour of the game full written reports were requested from each of the three match officials.

Billo Rees, scurge of the Australians, outside Chorley Road.

Further honour followed with his selection for the Great Britain tour of Australia. There were three Swinton players selected to tour, the other two being the brothers Jack and Bryn Evans, the first brothers selected to tour with Great Britain. Born in Swinton they were the sons of Jack Evans from the Amman Valley.

On the 1928 tour of Australia, Billo had the magnificent record of representing Great Britain on nineteen occasions (which included six tests), both as scrum-half (5 times) and as outside-half (16 times). The Australian Team Manager said, *"No player has ever left Australia with a bigger reputation than Billo Rees."*

Billo Rees represented Great Britain on 11 occasions, five of these in the U.K.

Other honours were 6 Welsh Caps and 3 England Caps. He was one of only 5 Welshmen to play for England (the others were Jim Sullivan, Gus Risman, Jack Morley, Norman Fender). He also won two Monmouth and Glamorgan Northern Union Caps, two Rugby League Final Winners Medals and two runners-up medals, two Championship Final winner medals, two runners-up medals and two Lancashire Cup Winner's Medals, plus one Welsh Rugby Union reserves cap.

Billo retired at the end of season 1932/33 and became steward of Swinton Social Club.

RL Cup Final Programme 1931

Dai Davies

Dai, a scrum-half, played for the Amman Juniors 1920/1923 and Amman United 1921/1923, left to join Neath and represented the club for three years before joining Broughton Rangers in 1926. A magnificent scrum-half, he must be placed on record as the unluckiest rugby league player ever. Dai played in three Wembley finals for three different clubs and was on the losing side each time.

Dai played for Warrington in the final in 1933 and scored two tries as a wing. In 1935, having transferred to Huddersfield, he lost in the final 11-8. Again, playing as Keighley's captain in 1937, the club reached the final for the only time in their history and lost to Widnes 18-5. This was Dai's last game, having played 335 first class rugby league games in an 11-year career. Dai seemed to make a habit of losing at Wembley, having played for Wales against Australia in 1930 and 1933 and was on the losing side both times.

Four Welsh caps seems little reward for a player recognised as one of the great rugby league half-back players of his era.

DM Davies

DM Davies and his brother Jack Davies

DM Davies Sprint Training from Greyhound Traps

Evan Phillips

Evan joined the Amman United on cessation of hostilities in 1919 and was an outstanding loose-forward who later joined Llanelli as a flanker in 1922/3 season. The following season, Evan was a member of the Llanelli team who played the Amman on the Cwmamman Park, the result being a draw game at 6-6. The game was stopped for twenty minutes while committeemen herded cows from the pitch Evan was awarded the All Blacks Captain Porter's Jersey as the best loose-forward that Porter had seen on tour after his game for Llanelli. He was selected as travelling Welsh reserve to Ireland and the following season joined Broughton Rangers in 1926.

Evan played loose-forward; centre, wing and stand-off before injuries put paid to his career at the end of 1928.

Evan returned home to take up an important post as a union representative in the mining industry.

Jack Elwyn Evans

Jack played wing for the Amman for the seasons 1920/23 and was capped from Llanelli as a wing for Wales in 1924. He signed for Broughton Rangers in January 1926 and made his debut against Widnes. He represented Broughton for two seasons and scored 10 tries until retirement in 1928.

Garfield Phillips

Garfield played on the wing and was the youngest player to play for the Amman as a 15-year-old in 1913. He joined Keighley from Neath in 1926 and was a regular member of the team for two years, playing 34 games and scoring 7 tries.

JACK ELWYN EVANS
Amman, Llanelli and Wales

Jack Davies

Jack was the brother of Dai Davies and from a well-known Cwmamman footballing family. Jack, a steady, reliable full-back, failed to consolidate his place with the Amman and joined Ammanford RFC, from whom he was later lured north to Keighley for £250 in 1926. Jack stayed as a regular team member until September 1928, when he joined Dewsbury and made his debut in October 1928 against Bradford Northern.

Jack was full-back for Dewsbury when they reached the first Wembley Cup Final in 1928 and was the first player to drop a goal at this venue. However, Jack followed brother Dai as a losing finalist with Wigan victorious at 13-2. Co-incidentally, Jack's last game for Dewsbury was once more against Bradford Northern.

Wally Watkins

Wally, a full-back, played for the Amman United from 1929 to 1938, went to Broughton Rangers in 1929 but failed to agree terms with the club and returned to the Amman to give many years' service as a steady and reliable full-back.

William David Evans

Dai 'Gwen' played centre for the Amman in 1930 and represented Llanelli for a season before joining Halifax. Dai was also an ex-Weston-super-Mare and Somerset County player. He made his rugby league debut for Halifax against Bradford Northern in September 1933 and played there until 1935, then transferred to Dewsbury until the end of 1936. Dai took up refereeing and refereed top-class games before eventually coaching a French Rugby League Club team when the game took off in that country.

Emrys Evans

Emrys, a wing-forward, played for Amman United from 1933 to 1936, left to join Llanelli and was capped for Wales in 1937/8 as a wing-forward. He joined Salford in September 1939 and scored 2 tries on his debut. The Second World War interrupted his career. He joined Wigan in 1947 for two seasons. He was capped for Wales Rugby League in 1945 against England at Wigan.

Ted Ward

Ted played for the Amman Juniors 1933, Ammanford in 1936 and Amman United in 1937 and signed for Wigan from Llanelli in January 1938 after a very successful Welsh Final Trial and served Wigan for over a decade. A well-balanced centre with a deadly accurate boot, he was the rugby league top scorer in 1947-48 with 139 goals and 302 points. He topped this in the following season with 155 goals and 361 points.

Ted was a member of the 1946 League Lions to Australia and New Zealand and appeared in 12 matches including two tests. He was selected as captain of Great Britain against New Zealand and also of Wales against the tourists.

A member of the Wigan Lancashire Cup winning team in 1938/39, he missed the Wembley Final in 1946 due to being in Australia with the Lions League team.

Ted won a Challenge Cup Winner's medal in 1948 against Bradford Northern and won a further two Lancashire Cup Winner's medals

In 1951/52, at 33 years of age, Ted joined the ill-fated Cardiff Rugby League Club. He returned to Central Park, Wigan as coach and was instrumental in signing Billy Boston for the club.

Ted Ward being presented to King Edward with Wigan at Wembley

Ted Ward place kicking

Ted Ward as Captain of Great Britain with the Duke of Gloucester.

Wales Team v England at Central Park, Wigan.
September 20th 1947.

Amman Valley Rugby League Team v Llanelli Rugby League Team

The early 1950s saw the formation of a rugby league team in Ammanford, Llanelli and Ystradgynlais which created a great deal of interest but was short lived. However, Iau Ward, Mock Ward and Gwilym Ward made appearances for the Llanelli RL team.

Captain Mantle XV

Several Amman United players played in a game arranged by Jim Rees (Y Gas) in an invitation team called Captain Mantle's XV at Cardigan RFC. Unknown to them, the team contained several rugby league players, and they later found themselves professionalised by the Welsh Rugby Union. Referee Ted Cole, Committeeman James Rees and Amman players Denny Cochran, Bobby Hunt and Eddie Slocombe were suspended Sine die but the other participants escaped punishment.

John Williams

A 15-year old Amman Valley schoolboy made the news with an article in The Western Mail & South Wales News on Friday March 27, 1953. It read: *'NEVER TOO YOUNG - They are never too young seems to be the slogan of Northern Rugby League clubs when seeking Welsh Rugby Union players for this week the parents of 15-year old John Williams, Amman United Youth inside-half were approached by a Northern club for the signature of their son. They offered to pay John's way through college after he had completed his county school education, but the offer was turned down'.*

Glyn James

A hard, durable scrum-half, Glyn James was approached by Wigan to turn professional and was offered an apprenticeship with the National Coal Board in Lancashire, but loathe to leave Cwmamman, he turned the offer down.

Secret Rugby League Trials

Amman United players Gordon Thomas and John Thomas, both star players of the Amman teams of the 1970s, went to Huddersfield for trials and were offered terms that were unacceptable to them and thankfully returned to represent Amman for many years.

RUGBY FAMILY CONNECTIONS

DYNASTY (Dinasti) – A succession of people from the same family who play a prominent role in business, politics or another field.

Most rugby clubs and indeed many organisations have family connections, which spread over a period of time. However, very few organisations, and fewer still rugby clubs have family connections extending over decades or even more.

Amman United RFC are exceptional in that they have three families or dynasties, who have extended their influences and talent to sport in general, and rugby in particular, and have made the name of Amman United synonymous with sporting talent world-wide.

The three families referred to are:
(1) The Bevans
(2) The Reeses (Plough)
(3) The Wards

Bevan Rugby Family by Norman Bevan

The Bevan family became involved with the Amman United within a year of its formation and the family connection was still ongoing in the 1970s.

The Bevan family has the record of three generations with unbroken service to the club.

For the first 50 years of the centenary, a Bevan had been in the Amman United ranks. Evan Bevan, a member of the first team in 1903, had 50 years service, his brother Joe 40 years to his credit, while Willie, their youngest brother, had 5 years service, making a combined total of 95 years service to the club.

Evan, who played for the Amman before and after the First World War, captained the side on three occasions, the first being in 1910. He was also captain of the team that played the first game on their new ground at Cwmamman Park; under him the team kept a ground record. After his playing days, he was made a Life Member of the club.

Joe played for the side for years but retired to become a referee. In 1953, he celebrated 40 years connection with the club as player and committeeman, and in 1922 he was appointed Treasurer of Amman United Rugby Football Club, holding the post for 23 years. He was also a Life Member like his brother Evan.

Poor health prevented the younger brother Willie from extending his club involvement after 5 years. Both Evan and Joe were alive to attend the fiftieth anniversary celebrations of the club.

His three sons followed Evan into the team. Mal (outside half or centre), played for the Amman for 23 years. After this time, he carried on playing for the Quins at the age of 50 (he said it was to encourage and teach the younger members of the team). Eddie played for the side for 12 years. Both joined the club in the late 1920s. Harold finished playing after a short term of service. Both Mal and Eddie followed in their father's footsteps and captained the side in the 1930s. After his playing days, Eddie left to serve on the committee of Cwmgorse RFC.

Willie's son Freddie also joined the club in the late 1920s and played for the team with Mal and Eddie during the 1930's. Like his cousins, he also captained the side. After his retirement from playing, he became a successful W.R.U. referee.

After the Second World War, Norman and Reggie (grandsons of Willie) carried on the family traditions. At the beginning, their careers proceeded in tandem. In 1943-1945 they played for the Amman Valley County School 1st XV (Reggie at full back and Norman at scrum half) and during holidays played for Amman Quins. In 1946, they both entered Trinity College; Carmarthen and both played for the 1st XV during 1946 and 1947. Norman was Vice-Captain of the team in 1947. They then joined the Royal Air Force to do their National Service, during which Norman was captain of his station team. On demobilisation, they returned to Trinity College to complete their studies. Norman was again the college scrum-half. Both played for Amman United during vacations. On leaving college in 1950, they re-joined Amman United, Reggie playing full back and Norman half-back or centre three-quarter. Reggie finished playing in 1952, when he took up a teaching post in Huddersfield. Norman was appointed Vice-Captain of Amman United during the 50th Anniversary of 1953.

When Norman finished playing for the club in 1955, it appeared to be the end of the Bevan association.

The only family member to have played for the Amman since has been Ieuan (Mal's son) who played during the 1960's before he left to join Cwmgorse. Huw (Norman's son), made one or two appearances for the Amman in the 1980s but played mainly for the Quins. David (Reggie's son), played for the Amman Youth team in the 1970s and was a member of their cup-winning side of 1973/1974.

Rees Rugby Family by Eurof Walters

The second dynasty was the Rees family, more familiarly known as the 'Plough' family. Their involvement with Amman United began in 1910 and has continued with gaps until the 1970s. Indeed, the family connection to sporting excellence is still being carried into the second century of Amman United's history.

The family consisted of seven brothers and two sisters. All seven brothers played for the Amman club over a period of time with two members making their mark at the highest level of Rugby Union and Rugby League. Two sisters married two second-row forwards who both represented the Amman club.

During the 1920s, it was a known fact that Joe Rees could select a family team (including in-laws and cousins) which was capable of taking on and beating the best in West Wales.

The team is noted below:

Joe Rees, Jack Elwyn Evans, Rees Rees, John Griffiths, David Rees, Billo Rees, Joseph Henry Griffiths, H. Joshua, David Griffiths, Sid Griffiths, Nathan Rees, Jim Richards, Charles Rees, Frank Griffiths and W.L. Llewellyn.

Joe Rees

Joe Rees started playing for the Amman at 16 years of age in 1909 and joined Swansea RFC in 1914, after playing for the Amman United versus Aberavon in the Hospitals Cup semi-final.

Joe served in the Army during the First World War and was capped for his country in wartime international in France. Returning to Swansea after active service, he soon made his mark in Welsh Rugby and was officially capped in 1919. He retained his Welsh Team place until 1924, when a recurring knee injury forced him to retire. He captained Wales in 1922 and Swansea in the season 1922-23.

Judge Rowe Harding wrote in 1930 that 'Joe Rees was undoubtedly the finest fullback I have seen. His kicking was accurate, his defence miraculous. His tackling for a man of his stature was magnificent. During the years I played with Joe, I never saw him beaten more than once a season'.

Praise indeed for a man from Amman United. Joe continued to play cricket for Swansea for many years and was a familiar figure in Swansea, carrying out his duties as a school attendance officer.

Rees Rees

Rees played for Amman, Llanelli, Swansea and Neath before throwing in his lot with Hull Kingston Rovers in 1922. He proved to be a good signing for Hull KR and played for them until 1925, appearing in their championship final team in 1923. He then transferred to Warrington where he became a valued team regular. Injuries caused him to retire from playing at the end of the season 1924-25.

Billo Rees

Billo's career is noted in other sections of this book. Suffice to say, he was the outstanding half-back in rugby league from 1921 to 1933 and can rightly be classed as the finest half-back to play rugby league between the wars.

He and brother Rees Rees met in a championship play-off in 1924-25 when Swinton were for once on the losing side.

A member of the 1928 Rugby League Touring side to Australia, he played more games than any one else on tour – 19 games out of 24.

Nathan Rees

Nathan was not the youngest but was the pillar and mainstay of the Plough family – the brother who looked after the rest and was always there when needed.

A hard and uncompromising forward, he led by example and was honoured with the captaincy of the club in 1926-27. He became the forth brother to wear the white jersey of Swansea following the footsteps of Joe Rees and Billo but had no hesitation in returning to play for Amman. A hard hitting batsman he played cricket for Ravenswood for many years. A more than competent tennis player he was singles champion of the Amman Valley from 1923-1926. No mean feat in an area extending from Cwmllynfell to Llandeilo. Also known as the best miner in the Amman Valley, his talent for mining was recognised by the National Coal Board by being named as the Best Collier in Wales in 1950.

Charles Rees

Charles was a wing-forward of exceptional talent, who played for the Amman intermittently for 10 years but was more interested in four-legged sporting activities

Glyn Rees

Glyn, who played only a few games but who had the co-ordination and perfect eyesight of the rest of the family, was a more-than-competent tennis player as well as a snooker and billiards player of note.

David Rees

David, a wing three-quarter with an exceptional side step, represented Amman for four seasons. He transferred to Brynamman on moving there at the time of his marriage and is well known as the father-in-law of Amman, Llanelli and Harlequins scrum-half Howard Jones.

John Rees

The son of Nathan, had all the attributes of the Plough family – ball-playing skills, complete co-ordination, a competitive spirit and belief in his own ability.

His sporting career started with Ammanford Bears Soccer Team but soon changed to the more physical sport of rugby, initially with Amman Quins but then he progressed to being a regular member of Amman United, playing with distinction as a wing-forward, No. 8 and wing three-quarter with equal efficiency.

His sporting prowess was further enhanced by appearances with Ammanford Cricket Club as an all-rounder and with the Carmarthenshire County Bowls Team.

He also served the Amman club as committeeman and Treasurer for many years.

David Charles Rees, son of Charles, represented Great Britain in the Winter Olympics as a member of the Cross-Country Skiing Team, further proof of the ability of this sporting family.

Rowland Phillips, younger son of Charles, started his rugby carer with Amman Youth, then the Quins and finally Amman United. He transferred to Llandybie RFC, which he captained. Rowland was a hard, uncompromising back-row-forward typical of the Plough family.

Huw Joshua was a typical English type of centre a seven-a-side expert and a member of Amman's successful side of the seventies. Possessing a side step off either foot and an eye for an opening, he was a valued member of the club in the 1970s.

Leah Evans and Daniel Evans

The beginning of the second century of Amman United and sport in the Amman Valley has seen the emergence of two members of the 'Plough' family, which extends the contribution of this family to over 80 years.

Great-grandchildren of Nathan Rees, they have ensured that the Rees family contribution to the sporting heritage of the Amman Valley will be extended into the second century.

Leah has already represented Wales in athletics and has represented Dinefwr, Carmarthenshire and West Wales in netball and hockey.

Daniel has already represented West Wales, Carmarthenshire and Dinefwr at rugby at three different age groups. He plays fullback, which raises visions of a new Joe Rees. A footballer of note, he plays soccer for Ammanford in his age group. An all-round sportsman, he has already played for Ammanford Cricket second X1 at 13 years of age. He has represented West Wales at cricket for the past three years and scored his maiden century on tour in Somerset in 2002. He is currently Welsh and British Junior Schoolboys hurdles champion.

Ward Rugby Family by Howard Gabe Davies

Ward Family 1930s, Back: - WD Ward, M Ward, E Ward
Front: - G Ward, William Ward, Miriam Ward, Olwen Ward, E Ward

The third dynasty, the Ward family, began its association with Amman United with the father playing for the club prior to 1920. The five sons followed him into Amman colours, and with three of them being elected club captains, this family's contribution to rugby in Cwmamman must be recognised as being exceptional.

The Ward family originated from a family of cattle dealers in Co Kerry, Ireland. Edward Ward emigrated to Australia as a young man and for many years worked on the infamous Nullabore plain railways where thousands died from the harsh conditions, disease and snake-bites. Edward returned to Wales to work in the Rhondda coal mines and found his future wife, who was a Jones from a farming family in Llandysul. The custom then was for girls to go out to work and the boys to remain at home on the farm. Edward Ward married and settled in Tylorstown and their son William Henry left home for the new anthracite collieries in Ammanford. He started playing rugby for Ammanford and was later coaxed to play for the Amman United with a promise of a job at a local colliery with an increase in wages.

William Henry married Olwen Griffiths, the sister of Myfanwy, who was the mother of the Bevan boys, so the Wards and Bevans were first cousins, who later were to dominate the Amman teams of the future years. William and Olwen had six children, five boys and a girl. William Henry Ward brought up his children very strictly and no one would dare to argue or answer back their father. William Henry's five boys went on to play for the Amman United and in first class rugby.

Edwin, known as Eddie - Amman Utd and Neath.

Eddie was a very classy centre three-quarter, a good attacking and creative player, and a good passer of the ball. He was at his strongest as a defensive player and was compared with the great Claude Davey. Many regarded Eddie as a more polished player than his illustrious brother Ted.

William David (W. D.), known as Iau - Amman Utd, Neath, Aberavon and Swansea

Iau was nicknamed as a child by Eddie, who had difficulty-saying David and it sounded as Iau, and the rest of the family picked this nickname up.

Iau was a hooker and the only forward of the five brothers. Before the war, Iau played for Neath and Aberavon and was paid more in expenses by Aberavon than a week's wages in the colliery; he later played two seasons after the war for Swansea. During the war, Iau played for charity teams to raise funds, and was always selected for the Claude Davey XV by Claude, as they were big friends on and off the field. Also during the war, Arthur Rees, the old Welsh international, asked Iau at short notice to bring a team to a Sevens Tournament at Llangadog, and all four brothers Iau, Mock, Gwilym and Ted played together in the team. They lost narrowly in the final to a team captained by Bleddyn Williams. They were all young men in college and university and the Amman boys were mostly coal miners. After the war, Iau played for the Amman and was the best hooker in the West Wales League. Swansea wanted a hooker due to injury and were informed that Iau Ward of the Amman was the best. Iau was picked for Swansea to play with their international front row. Iau said "this was a mistake as the All Whites front row scrummaged high and I liked going low and we were not suited to each other." Iau played after the war with very good Amman sides who went to play in two West Wales Championship Finals at Stradey. At his funeral in 1977, none other than Cliff Jones, the Old Welsh international outside-half and member of the Big Five attended his funeral and Iau was highly regarded among many rugby pundits. Ivor David, the famous referee, said "The war robbed the Ward boys of international honours, especially Iau"

Roll of Honour
1939—1947

William Fishwick Antell
Charles Norris Clay
Cyril Davies
James Glyndwr Davies
Dd. Kenneth Vincent Edwards
David Emlyn Evans
John Vernon Evans
Edgar Hopkin
Gwyn Hopkin
T. A. Cyril Jenkins
David Winston Jenkins
James Douglas Jones
Gerwyn Jones
Ernest Phillip Lewis
Wm. George Robert Marsh
Walter Graham Matthews
Albert Thomas
Emrys Thomas
David Meurig Thomas
Arthur Emlyn Watkins
William Ogwyn Williams
William Gruffydd Williams

Thomas William Cledwyn Jones-Hopkin

"The names of those who in their lives fought for life,
Who wore at their hearts the fire's centre.
Born of the sun they travelled a short while towards the sun,
And left the vivid air signed with their honour."

(Stephen Spender).

"South Wales Voice," Ystalyfera

Memorial Rugby Match
Wednesday, April 21st, 1948

"Nid da lle gellir gwell"

Claude Davey's XV
versus
Ivor Jones' XV

County Grammar School
Sports Ground, Ystalyfera

KICK OFF — 6.30 p.m.

Kick off by Mr. Howell Lewis, Delfryn, Ystalyfera
(the School's first Welsh International)

The Ystalyfera Town Band
(Conductor, Mr. R. C. Davies), will be in attendance

Proceeds in aid of the Ystalyfera County School Old Pupils' Memorial Fund

---

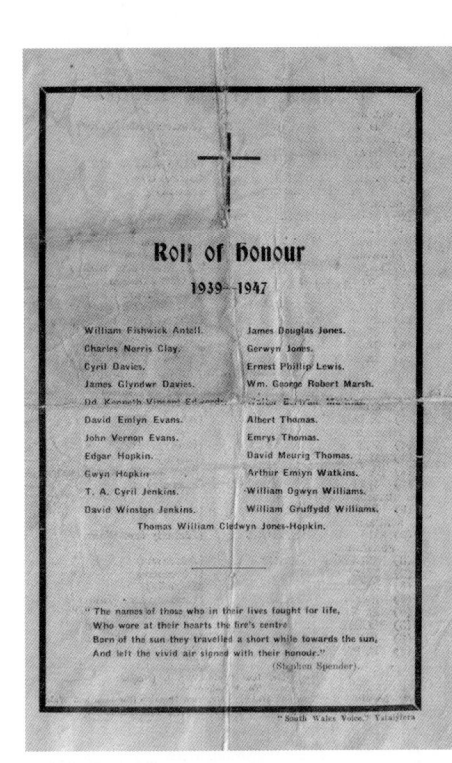

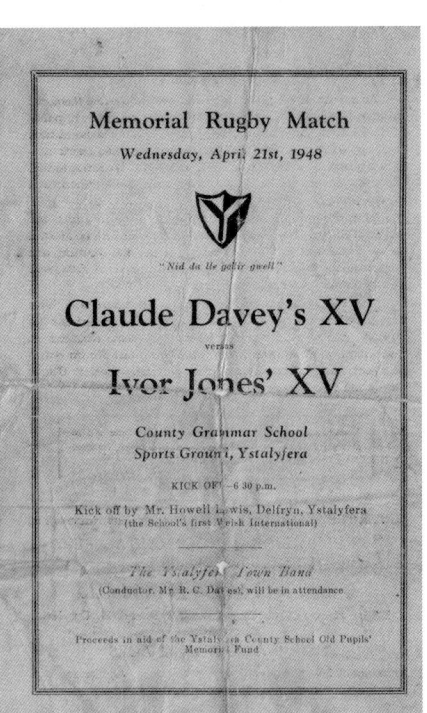

To Our Patrons:

As a result of the great success of the Jubilee and Memorial matches held here during the last two years, the general public of the Swansea and Amman Valleys have certainly demonstrated their appreciation of the high standard of play and sportsmanship displayed by the teams on those occasions. We are sure that the sides on view this evening will maintain the high standard of the past.

With the proceeds of this match, we hope to attain our target of £1,000. Next term, a part of this sum will be allotted to the erection of a Tablet to commemorate the sacrifice, and perpetuate the names of the twenty-three old pupils of Ystalyfera County School, who died in the Second World War.

The Old Pupils' Association thank all those who have contributed to the success of the match: the public for its support; the players, many of whom have come distances at much inconvenience; the Ystalyfera Town Band for its entertainment; and the sponsors of the two teams, Messrs. Claude Davey and Ivor Jones.

Immediately before the kick-off, a one-minute silence will be observed followed by the "Last Post" and Welsh National Anthem.

AFTER THE MATCH, complete your evening's entertainment at
THE PREMIER BALLROOM, YSTALYFERA

FLANNEL DANCE
M.C's: Messrs Claude Davey, D. Glyn Davies, H. Greville, Emlyn Davies.
Music by the RHYTHM ACES
Dancing: 7.30—12.0 p.m.   Admission: 2/6
LATE BUSES TO GWAUNCAEGURWEN.

CLAUDE DAVEY'S XV. (Red)
FULL BACK:
(1) *D. GLYN DAVIES (Swansea and Wales)
THREE-QUARTERS:
(2) W. D. WILLIAMS (Maesteg)
(3) R. GRAVELLE (Aberavon)
(4) ALUN THOMAS (Swansea)
(5) K. MADDOCKS (Neath)
OUTSIDE-HALF:
(6) DENZIL JONES (Swansea)
SCRUM-HALF:
(7) LEN OATES (Aberavon)
FORWARDS:
(8) *EMLYN DAVIES (Aberavon and Wales)
(9) W. D. WARD (Amman United)
(10) *DAI JONES (Swansea and Wales)
(11) CONRAD JENKINS (Swansea University)
(12) *E. L. BEVAN (British Army and Wales)
(13) W. D. JOHNSON (Swansea)
(14) *DESMOND JONES (Llanelly and Wales)
(15) D. T. MEREDITH (Neath)

IVOR JONES' XV. (Green)
FULL BACK:
(15) J. DREW (Aberavon)
THREE-QUARTERS:
(14) R. MICHAEL (Pontypridd)
(13) D. P. JONES (Neath)
(12) †S. T. J. WALTER (Blackheath and Aberavon)
(11) WYN LLOYD (Llanelly)
OUTSIDE-HALF:
(10) DAN E. LEWIS (Swansea)
SCRUM-HALF:
(9) *HANDEL GREVILLE (Llanelly and Wales)
FORWARDS:
(8) TREVOR GEORGE (Aberavon)
(7) W. THOMAS (Aberavon)
(6) JESS COLE (Llanelly)
(5) STAN WILLIAMS (Llanelly and Wales)
(4) D. G. SWAIN (Swansea)
(3) *OSSIE WILLIAMS (Llanelly and Wales)
(2) BRYN EVANS (Swansea)
(1) D. M. JAMES (Aberavon)

Referee: Mr. Ivor David, W.R.U. (Neath).
Touch Judges:
*Mr. Tom Day, (Swansea and Wales); *Mr. Tom Hopkins (Swansea and Wales).
*International.   †British Services International.

*7 a Side Tournament 1943
Llandovery
W.H. Morgan. M. Ward, W.D. Ward. T.?
Iuean Edwards. Ted Ward - Gwilym Ward*

Evan Morgan, known as Mock - Amman Utd and Llanelli

Mock was a scrum-half and bit of a clown and would play outside-half, centre and wing, and couldn't stick to the one position. Mock would go on the field with a fag in his mouth and was not really interested in playing; nevertheless, he was a talented player. On one occasion Amman played at Abercrave and there had been some bad feeling between the two clubs in their previous games with fighting. Iau had warned Mock before the game to behave himself. During the game Mock was about to put the ball into the scrum when he said 'What's this awful smell of onions?' This led to an enormous eruption in the scrum as the Abercrave players took this as an insult to their parentage. A derogative name for the people of Abercrave is the 'Spaniards', following the immigration of Spanish workers to the village.

Edward Harold, known as Ted - Amman Juniors, Ammanford, Amman United, Neath, Llanelli, Wigan Rugby League, Wales Rugby League and Great Britain Rugby League

Ted was a centre and had a very distinguished rugby career on the rugby field but did not, in the union game, do justice to himself as he went north to Wigan Rugby League.

Ted was not allowed to play rugby by his father as having caught tuberculosis when a young boy and had been hospitalized in Talgarth for 18 months; he also later had a nasty accident on a motor bike. Ted, despite all this, did play for the Amman Juniors but always in away games to avoid his father finding out. Ewart Davies, the Ammanford dentist and a WRU District 'F' representative, had recognized Ted's talent and showed a keen interest. Ted was to become his protege and he invited Ted to play for Ammanford and later for Neath as a 17-year-old. Ted later transferred to Llanelli with a promise of a job as a policeman, which was not kept.

Ted played in a Final Welsh trial at Newport in the Possibles team and The Western Mail report on the Monday 6th December, 1937 of the trial by the 'Old Stager' stated: *E. H. Ward (Llanelly) filled the vacancy with such sprightliness that he became an outstanding figure'*. Ted signed for Wigan before the Welsh team was announced and a distinguished rugby league career followed.

Bittersweet weekend as Ward stars then signs!

By J. R. JONES

SINCE he could perform with equal aplomb at either centre, fly-half or full-back, E. H. (Ted) Ward, might well have been a power in the Welsh XVs of those transitionary seasons immediately after World War II.

But alas, by then Ted was irrevocably lost to the union game, for like so many of the rising young stars of those last war haunted seasons before Hitler finally unleashed his Stukas and Panzers over Europe, he had taken his budding talent to the rugby league.

He did so in January, 1938, and in deference to — or possibly in revolt against — his chapel up-bringing in the God-fearing Amman Valley had chosen the Sabbath on which to sign on for Wigan for a £350 fee, which was certainly no pittance by the standards of those penny-pinching times.

Down at Stradey the news was greeted with wailing and gnashing of teeth. And understandably, for only the previous afternoon they had watched Ted turn in a performance marvellous enough to suggest that those who had been acclaiming him as the new Albert Jenkins were

opened by back-row forward Stan Williams, who bullocked over from a line-out.

Cheers

But no-one could steal the show from Ted on what was to be his last appearance at Stradey, and fittingly it was the cheers for the soaring drop goal with which he put the issue beyond doubt which were ringing in his ears as he

departed the arena, alas for ever.

History records how Ted Ward went on to become one of the greatest of rugby league players, obtaining almost every honour the professional players, obtaining almost every honour the professional game had to offer, touring Australia and New Zealand with the British side and captaining his club Wigan, to cup final and championship triumphs.

But what is not generally recorded is the triumph over adversity which made the later triumphs possible. Stricken by a lung illness soon after his arrival at Wigan in 1938, he spent almost the whole of the war years in a sanitorium, surely often despairing of ever kicking a ball again.

LLANELLI: G. Thomas; G. Rees, G. Trehearne, E. H. Ward, E. Jones; D. L. Thomas,

J. H. T. Evans; W. H. Williams, B. Evans, E. Evans, H. Matthews, P. Moxey, J. Bowen, S. Williams, J. L. G. Morgan.
CARDIFF: E. Jones; A. H. Jones, H. Edwards, T. J. Roberts, G. Porter; L. Williams, W. H. Pugh; G. Williams, J. Regan, R. Bale, L. G. Thomas, I. Heatley, L. Spence, S. Davies, R. Roberts.
Scorers: Llanelli — Stan Williams, try; Ted Ward, drop goal.

Ted Ward, a Great Britain tourist in 1946, was a classy Welsh centre three-quarter who came from Llanelli in 1938 and played 213 games for Wigan. Effectively taking over the kicking duties from Jim Sullivan, he accumulated 480 goals to add to his 57 tries. After missing the 1946 championship final win, due to being on board the Indomitable as it headed Down Under for the first post-war tour, he was in the successful line-ups of 1947 and 1950 and was a winner at Wembley in 1948. He played for Great Britain 3 times and Wales 13.

After joining the short-lived Cardiff venture in 1951, he returned to Central Park in 1953 as coach for a three-year period.

Ted was the Rugby League highest points scorer in the season 1947/48 with 312 points (141 goals) and in 1948/49 with 361 points (155 goals); a Great Britain test player in two tests in Australia in 1946 and one in New Zealand in 1947 and Challenge Cup winner in 1947/48.

Ted was the first Captain of Great Britain Rugby League, as the previous league teams had been called England, and the Welsh, Scottish and Irish players were unhappy about playing for England.

Whilst on tour in Australia and New Zealand in 1946, Ted played in every position in the team other than hooker, which showed what a versatile player and a great asset to the team Ted was. During the tour, Ted was captain for a mid-week game against Newcastle and Districts and the captain of their team was another Garnant boy Kerry Madge. Both boys went to the same school in Garnant prior to the Madge family emigrating to Australia and both spoke to each other in Welsh, to the amazement of the other players.

During his period as Wigan coach, Ted signed some young players who became Rugby League Hall of Fame Greats in Billy Boston, Eric Ashton, Brian McTigue and David Bolton; they were part of the Ted Ward Academy.

In the early 1950s, Ted sent down to the Amman secretary and coach, Ieuan Evans, a set of 30 jerseys, shorts and socks with the red and white hoops of Wigan rugby league; after the war, rugby kit was in short supply due to rationing. (If only the WRU had found out that the kit had come from Wigan).

THURSDAY, May 19th, 1988

Ex-rugby star dies

• Ted Ward, top-scoring Rugby League star.

Ted Ward, the Glanaman-born Rugby League star who captained Wales and Great Britain in the forties, has died at Llandeilo, aged 71.

Mr. Ward Bevan his playing career before the war in the union code. He played with Amman United, Ammanford, Neath and Llanelli, before earning a Welsh trial at Newport. He had an outstanding game, playing at centre, was promoted to the Probables in the second half, and scored several tries and goals. Another member of the side was the legendary Cliff Jones.

Before the Welsh team was announced, however, he signed pro-

When his playing days ended he carried on as Wigan's coach and signed up some of the side's top stars, like Cardiff's Billy Boston, Eric Ashton and Brian McTigue.

He retired in 1956 and returned home to work for many years as a welder for Crompton Parkinson. His last job was with British Coal at Betws. A bachelor, Mr. Ward left no family. His funeral was held at Swansea Crematorium on May 11.

Gwilym - Amman Utd, Llanelli and Aberavon

Gwilym was a wing who also played outside-half and hated the position. During the war years (rugby was suspended during the war years and travelling was restricted to 7 miles) he played for the Frank Dallavalle team, the Garnant Italian café owner, now famous as ice-cream maker 'Franks'. While at Llanelli, Gwilym found the travelling to the games very difficult, finishing work in the colliery on a Saturday, rushing to Llanelli by kick-off. Away games were even harder; a game at Northampton would entail leaving Northampton on a Saturday night at 8 p.m. and getting back into Llanelli at 5 a.m. in the morning, then another wait of about 5 hours for a bus home leaving at around 10 a.m. on a Sunday morning. Gwilym was getting more for playing with the Amman at 30 bob a game showing that better money was to be had playing for the Amman than going to play first class.

Playing in the West Wales Cup Final against Tumble, Gwilym ran 70 yards to score a try and Amman were now 1 point behind with the kick remaining. Normally, Gwilym took the short-range kicks. Captain W.H. Thomas asked Watt Jones to take the kick as he thought that Gwilym was too exhausted after the 70 yard run. The kick was missed and that was the closest the Amman came to winning the West Wales Cup.

Gwilym only recalls the three brothers playing together for the Amman.

When Gwilym and Iau finished playing for the Amman, they both took part in the ill-fated attempt to start rugby league in South Wales and played for Llanelli RL team that played at Stebonheath.

SOUTHEND TOUR 1967
By Peter Williams

Not many towns can claim fame whilst stuttering the name of a rugby club. However, Southend can do so as it hosted Amman United tours on three occasions. The last one, in 1968, proved to be the most successful, both result-wise and enjoyment-wise.

Nev Anthony, secretary, and Al Thomas, captain, were invited to a function to collect a plaque presented to the Amman for being the most outstanding team of the tournament. They played two and won two.

On the eve of the game against Old West Cliffians, both OWC and AURFC were present in the clubhouse. OWC departed early for bed in order to be at their very best for the following day's game against the Amman. On the other hand, the Amman team continued with their serious training techniques.

The following day, the Amman proved too strong for their opposition. Hugh Harris ran rings round the opposing open side loose forward and, after a try scored by Hugh, the forward remarked, "I'll get you!" Hugh's reply was, "When you get me, you'll be too old!"

Many comical instances occurred during the tour, which must be mentioned. Nevertheless, names of individuals will not be divulged. It will be interesting to note how many members of the tour party can remember the following flashbacks.

Starting point of the tour, as usual, was the Half Moon. Everybody was present including one supporter who was on his way to work. On the spur of the moment, he blurted out, "Give me fifteen minutes and call for me on the way!"

The bus driver was a local lad and a keen supporter of the Amman. Whilst driving along, the bus spluttered to a halt and could not be restarted. Surprise, surprise, surprise! What do you think was perched on top of the high embankment running alongside the road? You've guessed correctly. A pub! The bus was soon empty and the pub was soon full. We were told that the landlady was Sandie Shaw's mother and we were gullible enough to believe it. A replacement bus arrived after a couple of hours had elapsed and we were asked by Mrs.Shaw to empty our glasses. Very seriously, the driver remarked," You cannot hurry these boys, you know; they are very highly trained athletes and cannot be hurried!"

On arrival at our destination, the pier in Southend was soon accommodating grown-ups sliding down the helter-skelter and displaying oysters, which had slid off their shells onto the floor, being swallowed, sawdust and all. Waste not, want not!

The lizard-faced bouncer, in one of the pubs, brought terror to our hearts when he looked at us. What a massive, ugly, evil-looking person he was. One small-built player was standing on the seat to have a good view of the proceedings when 'lizard face' snarled at him, "Get down!" He slid down into the seating position in a flash.

The "borrower" of an air stewardess's hat resulted in the "borrower" cadging a lift on the pillion of a passing moped with the stewardess and her colleagues in hot pursuit. He made a clean breakaway and he still has the hat!

Two of the lads were walking back to the hotel; both worse for wear. One muttered quite unintelligible words, to which the other said, "Mae e'n dweud bod e'n moyn bwyd."

What about the second row forward who went to hospital suffering from concussion? At the hospital, an accompanying committeeman complained of not feeling well. What happened? The player was discharged and the committeeman was kept in overnight!

How do you cure a hangover? One player's remedy for another player was to take him to a restaurant and order the following meal...

First Course   Tomato soup.
Second course   Tomato soup.
Dessert   Tomato soup.
It worked!

Have you heard of the game "Loopy-loo"? It's quite simple to play. A party of about six, down glasses of vodka and orange and smash the empty glasses in the fireplace. The owner was watching but did not pass one comment. He reserved judgement until a later date.

The last morning saw a frightened looking committeeman running from the toilet with a deluge of water in hot pursuit. Luckily, one of the players was a builder and performed temporary repairs to the water system.

There were many silent, sleeping, survivors on the long return journey to Cwmaman who were woken up outside the Half Moon to witness a presentation, to the landlord, of a large wooden carving of a large animal!

Two weeks later, the club received an invoice for the following...
(i)   Broken glasses
(ii) Repairs to toilet
(iii) Repairs to bedroom wall

The chairman was not at all pleased but the players sold tote tickets to cover the invoice.

FALLINGBOSTEL 1971
by Peter Williams

Quoting the immortal words of Max Boyce, "We saved our weekly shillings for Fallingbostel trip", had prepared us well for the long-awaited tour of Germany. On the day of departure, all forty of us met in the Amman H.Q. and, immediately commenced training! The coach trip to Harwich went quite well but the North Sea voyage went even better! Mind you, nobody felt quite one hundred per cent the following day on the coach journey to Fallingbostel.

Tommy met us in Bremen Haven and informed us, quite proudly with a stuck-out chest, that he had received delivery of extra stock of liquid refreshments for his cellar that, in normal circumstances, would last the Sergeants' Mess for a whole week! Huh! How wrong he was! On the morrow, he was frantically phoning the Brewery for extra supplies of Draught Double Diamond! However, after that slight miscalculation, he made sure that his stock never dwindled below the quarter mark!

As some food for thought, (please excuse the cliché), the cooks in the Sergeants' Mess ensured that only the best was served to these highly trained athletes of ours.

The Regimental Team on the campsite was good but no match for the Amman boys. We won every game. The last game had been arranged against an unbeaten Army team from another camp, which included south Pacific forwards who resembled a solid concrete wall. We were well supported by Fallingbostel soldiers and the encounter proved to be hard, close battle. Our lads survived the onslaught and, to the delight of their supporters, proved to be valiant victors. The Amman United's record remained intact.

On the social side, who can forget Belsen and glimpses of Big Bertha, Reeper Bahn, Winklestrasse and, of course, Snow White and the Seven Dwarfs. As one very famous politician once said, "They went as boys but returned as men."

Many comical instances were encountered, such as the two un-named committeemen who found great difficulty eating their breakfasts one morning because their gums were hurting them. I wonder who, during the night, changed their false teeth around!!!

The return sea crossing was a complete disaster because of the adverse weather conditions. Not one member of the party could be seen anywhere on the ferry and the anticipated birthday celebrations of one committee member were postponed until a later date.

During a coach stop on the M4, we had a party photograph taken with the giant bottle of brandy occupying a prime position in the front.

In conclusion, Phil James our chairman was most grateful that the tour party had incurred no costs for misdemeanours which could have been passed on to the club.

MEMORIES ARE MADE OF THIS.

Fallingbostal Tour 1971

German Tour: - L-R Eurof Walters, Clive Brooks, Alan Davies, Raymond Evans, Peter Williams, Front: - Adrian Jones

Alan Arnold and other players in lineout

'YR AMAN YW Y GORE'
gan Hywel Evans

Pan ofynwyd i mi ysgrifennu ychydig eiriau am y clwb anhygoel hwn, roedd hi'n anodd gwybod ble i ddechrau. Mae'r Aman wedi bod yn rhan bwysig iawn o'm plentyndod a'm magwraeth. Yr Aman yw'n dîm i wedi bod erioed, felly anghofiwch Llanelli, Castell Nedd, Abertawe – yr Aman yw y gore.

Dwi'n cofio fy anrheg pwysicaf pan oeddwn yn fachgen ifanc – pêl rygbi wrth Santa! Roeddwn yn byw ar y pryd ym Mhenybont a drws nesaf roedd y cawr o ganolwr John Cisco Francis yn byw. Dwi'n cofio'r Nadolig hynny fel ddoe, eira fel carped ar y cae a John yn mynd a finnau, crwtyn wyth mlwydd oed allan i chwarae gyda'r bêl rygbi newydd. Gwaetha'r modd mae rhagor o dai wedi cael eu hadeiladu ar fy Mharc yr Arfau personol i erbyn hyn. Dyddiau difyr!

Doedd Prynhawn Sadwrn ddim yn gyflawn heb fynd i weld yr Aman ar y parc, pob penwythnos, yn gwylio fy arwyr yn chwarae. Mae'r atgofion yn felys wrth gofio fy nhad yn adrodd storiau am y cewri aeth lan i ogledd Lloegr i ennill eu bywoliaeth trwy chwarae yn rygbi'r gynghrair. Bois fel Bilo Rees, Ted Ward, Dai Cefnder Davies a chwaraeodd mewn chwe 'cup final' a cholli pob un. Un o'r rhaglenni mwyaf pleserus nes i fwynhau yn fy ngyrfa oedd gwneud cynhyrchiad am fois o bentrefi Cymraeg aeth i fyny i chwarae rygbi'r gynghrair blynyddoedd yn ôl. Braint oedd cael eu cyfweld a gwrando ar eu storiau difyr – a llawer o'r cewri yma a ddechreuodd eu gyrfa yn chwarae i'r clwb unigryw hwn.

Y gêm gyntaf ges i i'r Aman oedd yn erbyn Gorseinon – Dai Lloyd oedd capten yr ymwelwyr a ddaeth yn y blynyddoedd i ddod yn gapten ei hunan ar yr Aman. Roeddwn i wedi blino shwd gymaint nes i fi gripian bant o'r cae (wedi blino'n lan). Atgofion hefyd am y gêm oherwydd cael rhoi mreichiau o gwmpas un o 'legends' y clwb sef Dennis Davies – cawr o ddyn ym mhob ystyr or gair! Un o'r atgofion sy'n aros yn y cof yw clywed y dyn hynaws yma ar adegau yn canu ar ôl rhai gemau. Heb anghofio wrth gwrs Nev, Frankie Laine, Anthony ' Bullet in my shoulder' – dyddiau da.

Cael y fraint wedyn i fod yn gapten ar yr Aman ddwywaith. Dyna beth oedd gwireddu breuddwyd crwtyn bach o Benybont, Glanaman. Yn y flwyddyn gyntaf fel capten, y clwb yn mynd twy'r tymor heb golli un gêm yn hen gynghrair Gorllewin Cymru- chwarae un deg chwech o gemau – ennill undeg chwech o gemau – y tîm cyntaf i wneud hynny erioed yn hanes y gem yn y gorllewin.

Wrth gwrs, un o f' atgofion personol melysaf oedd bod yn gapten ar y tîm saith bob ochr a gyrhaeddodd y rownd derfynol yn Aberafan. Yna, yn syfrdanol, yn curo Glyn Ebwy, Pen-y- Bont a Chastell Nedd cyn colli i dîm Coleg Caerdydd, a oedd yn llawn o chwaraewyr dosbarth cyntaf, o un pwynt yn y rownd olaf. Mae'r cof yn dal yn fyw. Gweld wyneb fy nhad yn llawn balchder, cannoedd ar gannoedd o gefnogwyr o gartref, ac ugeiniau o faneri yn chwifio yn yr awyr, a chlywed " Yr Aman yw y gore" yn atseinio trwy cae y Talbot Athletic yn Aberafon.

Ble bynnag yr wyf yn y byd, a ble bynnag mae rygbi'n rhan or sgwrs, mae hanes Clwb yr Aman wastad yn cael ei drafod rhywbryd. Mae hyd yn oed rhai o ddramau Cymraeg y theatr yn cynnwys y gân anfarwol "Roll along Amman United, roll along !" a chredwch chi fi mae wedi cael ei chanu gan 'Yours Truly' ym mhedwar ban y byd

Felly i orffen, gyda'r holl atgofion yn llifo nôl yn fy mhen a'm calon, llongyfarchiadau i glwb yr Aman. Ymlaen bois bach – yr Aman yw y gore !

Thanks for the MEMORIES
by Eurof Walters

Wednesday March 22nd 1948 is the first vivid recollection I have of Amman United. It was the third time that Amman had met Briton Ferry in the third round of the West Wales Cup. On the neutral Vardre ground, Will Styles, a Kenfig Hill policeman and back row forward, kicked three beautiful penalty goals to beat Briton Ferry by 9 points to 6.

Amman proceeded to the semi-final, drew with Abercrave 0–0 at Ystradgynlais, drew the replay at Cwmllynfell 9–9 and eventually beat Abercrave at Brynamman 5-0 to reach the West Wales Cup Final played at Stradey on 1st May 1948. Amman lost by 11 points to 6. So began a love affair which has lasted over half a century, and little did I think then that I would be involved in writing the history of Amman United during their centenary year.

Having an involvement with an organisation for over 50 years as player and administrator has given thousands of unforgettable memories and whilst many cannot be made public there are a great many which can be recounted without fear of recrimination.

Bertie Davies entered my life one September evening in 1951 when he asked me to play for the Youth side, which was short of players. He and the youth secretary, EB Davies, got together a team which was good enough to win the Amman Valley and Loughor Valley Shield and we were rewarded by having a presentation night in Garnant Club, when twenty players who had represented the Youth during the season were presented with a blazer badge. This was identical to the 1st XV badge except for two things: - it was blue, the youth colours, not red, and instead of AURFC was the letters AYRFC.

This badge has never been awarded since to any other Amman side.

Moving on to play for both Quins and 1st XV the following season, together with six other players from the youth, the difference in standards and hardness soon became apparent. The rules governing 'stayaways' were strict and everyone knew that the bus would not be returning on five occasions during the season but as youngsters we were well looked after by the elder players and friendships forged then have lasted 50 years. It was a source of wonderment to me how Bertie could always find a public house that was open – wherever we were - and this in the time of strict licensing hours! It was only to eat the sandwiches and pickles of course, but he always seemed on very good terms with the landlady.

On one such stayaway in Swansea with the Quins there occurred an event that very few people believe to be true. I have a vivid recollection of Jarvis Styles and Dennis Davies drinking Crème de Menthe in the No.10 pub - small glasses in large hands with little fingers sticking out like "toffs", both with large grins on their faces – they really liked the colour. I don't think either of them touched

211

it ever again.

Bertie Davies, at first sight, was an unlikely character to be club chairman but he had what it takes to be a good chairman, a certain charisma. Well respected throughout Welsh Rugby, he would speak to anyone on equal terms and was probably one of the most persuasive people I have ever met. Despite his harmless appearance, he had a stubborn streak and was known to have taken committeemen outside the meeting, punched them into submission and returned to the chair for the rest of the meeting.

During this period, the privilege of playing and becoming friends with such players as Perris James, brothers Gwyn, Vince and Hubert Jones, Ieuan Evans and others were, and are, memories to treasure.

Ieuan Evans was one of the longest kickers of a rugby ball I have ever seen and also had the shortest fuse. He had no patience at all with anyone who made a mistake (not including himself) and would shout and scream at anybody who took his fancy.

However, his brother in law Gwyn Jones and another Amman wing, Ellis Williams, were able to keep him quiet without any problems.

Ieuan later coached Llanelli, Swansea and the Welsh Youth before becoming a Welsh Rugby Union member and ultimately President of the Welsh Rugby Union.

A rugby man through and through, not afraid to speak his mind he was a friend over a number of years.

Over the years Amman have had, or seemed to have had, bus drivers out of the ordinary.

Firstly Jack Davies, always immaculately dressed with collar, tie and hat, a friend to every player and a drinking partner for Bertie.

Then Noel Davies, who convinced a landlord outside Abergavenny that the bus contained a body of highly trained and superb athletes who only wished a soft drink whilst the bus was being repaired – a fact he tended to disagree with when they drank the pub dry before opening time.

Will (of Rees and Williams) was never in any hurry to go home and would cheerfully enjoy the company at whatever hostelry the bus stopped.

Derrick Williams hated motorways so much that he drove the youth team to Halifax without touching any until he was 10 miles from his destination. The bus arrived at a roundabout above a motorway and he immediately hit a fire engine.

No one can swear that he did not feel slightly nervous when Chicken George was the driver, with buses going around corners while George rolled a cigarette and argued with whoever sat behind him.

Phil James, who succeeded Bertie as Chairman, was a caring and possibly tight-fisted man who had Amman United in his blood. A prolific fundraiser for the club, he loved and served the Amman well in excess of 40 years.

His good lady Agnes was Chairwoman and leader of a Ladies' Committee which raised money, organised food and functions and looked after all and sundry for many years.

During latter years, the number of people prepared to serve as committeemen has dropped off alarmingly but the 1950s and early1960s were quite different. Annual General Meetings were held in the Institute in Glanamman, upstairs in Garnant Club or in the Cadet Hut with well in excess of 150 members attending and over 35 members trying for 20 seats on the committee. Bertie Davies in the chair, ballot papers distributed, counters and checkers delegated and results announced before the conclusion of the chairman's report.

Harold Davies was Bertie's brother and father of the infamous Rowland. Over the years, Harold proved to be a good friend and was a life member of the club. Amman were playing in Porthcawl near the end of the one season. Only 14 players turned up and before reaching Porthcawl, Harold had agreed to play – on the wing at 56 years of age! Trying to save his legs and stop him collapsing, the plan was not to give him the ball at all. Unfortunately, three times Harold could have been set clear but the pass was never given for him to score. He never forgave me for denying him the opportunity of scoring three tries.

Baggage men are an integral part of rugby clubs and no one could ever have had a more sincere and hardworking baggage master than the Amman had in Max Williams. Severely disabled, he never let his disability interfere with his commitment to the club, and as a committeeman was always to be relied on. No one who ever attended a meeting when Max was present will ever forget his immortal phrase 'Now hold the f------- boat Mr Chairman' and then would follow pearls of wisdom or otherwise.

During their formative years, Amman quickly gained a reputation for having good singers within their ranks. This continued well into the sixties and seventies. Who can ever forget Colin Davies and John Gwyn singing "Sweet Caroline", John Thomas with "Carlo", brother David with "My Way", Nev Anthony's famous rendering of "Bullet in my Shoulder", Al Thomas with "Yankee Sailor", Gordon Thomas with "San Francisco" and Hywel Williams as choirmaster.

Amman supporters remember different things about different games but all Amman supporters will never forget the decade of success which the Seven-a-Side Team gave them, culminating in that glorious day at the Talbot Ground, Aberavon.

There are instances, which stand out in the memory for different reasons: -

Watching probably the best Amman backrow ever in Jeff Thomas, Gordon Thomas and Trevor Evans demolishing a very strong Waunarlwydd team, John Bach Thomas tackling forwards twice his weight, Dennis Davies laying out Eric John in front of the stand at Brynamman and being sent off by Colin Thomas of Garnant – wrongly according to Dennis. Being robbed by the referee against Newport on the park, Huw Harries tormenting the Price brothers in Hendy, both on the field and in the bar. Watching Perris James side stepping at full speed. Playing in Felinfoel against a team containing two full Welsh internationals in Ossie Williams and Stan Williams and scoring three tries in an area covered with cow pats. Revelling in the space provided by Denzil Jones playing at outside half. Watching the Amman team being shocked by the ferocity of six Fijians playing for the 26th Field Artillery in Germany. Watching Wally Bowen being attacked by a player's mother in Trebanos and being unable to help, being doubled-up with laughter.

Place kickers are a breed apart and Amman has been lucky over the years. However, the one performance I recall vividly was Cen Davies's first game for the club on his return from playing for Llanelli, kicking 6 penalties in Pontardulais to take their ground record.

Ability to read games is a talent few people possess. Dai Price had it in abundance in his playing days and was one of the most knowledgeable talkers about rugby in the Amman Valley.

Having mentioned briefly Bertie Davies' talent for finding pubs open it would be remiss not to mention two successors of his who had similar talents.

Pat Brosnan and Brian Davies, were both second rows or props as the need arose, but were not up to the standard of Bertie as regards to pubs – both tended to go for the rundown, seedy ones.

Brian further excelled himself as landlord of 'Clwb-yr-Arabs' on the park as carnival organiser supreme over a period of 10 years and was also famous for the phrase 'one for the road'. He also had the ability to give appropriate nicknames to club members and is responsible for many brilliant nicknames both in the club and in the valley.

A successful club has successful stewards and nowhere was this more apparent than when Edgar Llewellyn was steward. A man of even temperament, he was an ideal steward with a marvellous sense of humour. Memories of Edgar behind the bar abound but two surface regularly: Raymond Morgan getting seriously drunk on rum & blackcurrant, which had no rum in it. He was refunded the money spent when he appeared the following night.

Peter Thomas (The Plough) being overcharged 25p per pint to help the striking miners. This was also returned a week later.

Adrian Jones was a talented scrum half and man of steel, the finest corner-flagger I have ever seen and compares favourably with all Amman scrum-halves. Who would choose between him and John Gwyn Jones, John Williams, Glyn James, Alan Rogerson, Al Thomas, Howard Jones and Hubert Jones as the best scrum half since the 1950s?

Full backs- Ieuan Evans, Con Mathias, Raymond Walters, Reggie Bevan, Malvern Evans, Ryan Bartlett, Colin Davies and Alan Davies. All have graced the Amman jersey with honour and bring back different memories.

I have been privileged to play with and watch many talented wing-threequarters and who would choose between Perris James, Gwyn Jones, Peter Williams, Carwyn Thomas, Dai Thomas, Ian Penman, Cen Davies, Dai Howells, Elwyn Owen and Dai Evans as the finest post-war wing in the valley.

Amman has always been lucky to be well-supported over the years two supporters come to mind firstly David Lewis from Glynmoch, who has watched the club continuously since being taken by the Cen Glynmoch fan club to watch his hero and secondly Aubrey Morgan who has probably seen more Amman games than anyone.

It has always been a source of wonderment to me that parochialism and rivalry can so easily turn to complete and utter loathing. No where is this exemplified more than in the rivalry between Amman and Brynamman, when the sight of a green jersey makes even the mildest Amman fan a raging psychotic.

It is a strange phenomenon how things can trigger memories. Walking on Gellywerdd recently, it came to mind that in past years very few Amman captains played down in the first half on the park. The reason maybe beyond comprehension to modern players but playing down in the second half and facing Gellyceidrim Tip and the Maclean tipper was worth five points to teams of the 1940s and 1950s.

The recent deaths of two Amman stalwarts of previous years, Denny Cochram and Danny Williams, brought back memories of front row players who have done the club proud over the years.

The aforementioned two, together with Iau Ward and Bobby Hunt, caused chaos in the West Wales League over a number of years. John Jones (Globe), Ryan Jones, Trevor Jones, Gareth Jenkins, Dai Lloyd, Hywel Evans and Darrell Campbell, Dai Williams and Martin "Chopper" Evans were all hookers of note and never took a backward step, although Martin Evans did show a distinct liking for the human ear when he was having a particularly rough time. Props such as Dennis Davies, Jarvis Styles, Islwyn Arnold, Gwyndaf Walters, Brian Lewis, Nev Anthony, Gethin James, Steve Hopkins, Evan James, Graham Bundock, Adrian Phillips, Alan James, Wyn Jones, Lennie Jones, Howard Davies and Ian Wagstaff made sure that Amman scrummages were always on top.

Having an eye test some time ago brought to mind a player who gave sterling service to the club, despite having a glass eye. A snooker player of note and a good darts player he thrived on challenges, the more money put down the better he played. He was Lyn John, who captained the Quins and played for Amman for many years.

Lyn and I were delegated to accompany Ryan Jones to Morriston Hospital after a blood bath at Vardre. Arriving at casualty, Lyn informed the sister that Ryan had a badly cut leg and that he himself couldn't see out of his "blind eye". Sister panicked seeing an empty socket and bells rang with theatres being prepared and doctors summoned. When she returned and was told he could now see – having returned his glass eye to its socket - she went bananas and if she had caught him would have probably have taken his head off.

Many more players and many more memories could have been included but enough is enough.

Memories – Thousands. Value -Priceless. Thanks for the privilege.

All rugby players know that what happens on tour stays on tour. However, to conclude this short narrative, the following questions need to be answered.

1) What is the true story of the Elephant?
2) Who lied to Howie Davies in Southend about the 6'9" American second row?
3) Where is the airline sterwardess's hat?
4) Why was a hot dog salesman in Hamburg chasing a member of the local constabulary?
5) Who vomited in the snooker table pockets in the sergeant's mess?
6) What is Emrys Timothy's connection with Mats and Candles?
7) Why was Gareth Jenkins in the West End in football kit?
8) Who swapped the false teeth of two committeemen in Germany?
9) What happened to the six chickens in Lincoln?
10) Who was Pegi?
11) Who taunted Manchester United fans about relegation during a tour to Manchester?
12) Why was Dan Davies (Tynywern) thrown out of Maidstone Cricket Club?

THE THOUGHTS OF A SCOT: IANTO "JOCK" PENMAN
By Ian Penman

My apologies in advance to any club members past and present if I forget any names and personalities; however, I am sure if you indicate Jones, Davies, Evans or Williams in the line up it will turn out okay.

I look back on my short time with "The Amman" as an absolute privilege to be involved with the club in any shape or form. The Welcome, The Support, The Advice and The Team "Spirit" (Buckley's Bitter) received was second to none I have had anywhere.

Ian Penman and Randall Williams at the 75th Anniversary Dinner

I arrived by accident at the Amman. I was only looking for training facilities but was advised the club would welcome anyone who was keen; at this time I had been playing semi-professional soccer in Scotland, so rugby was fairly new to me, but I duly turned up for training regularly on a Tuesday and Thursday night. Alan the captain took training and I was a bit puzzled when after 90 minutes of hard graft we went to the Half Moon (no clubhouse then) and had 5 or 6 pints of Buckley's, followed later by chicken curry and chips at the local restaurant in Ammanford. Perhaps Alan's training nutritional needs were light years ahead of his time.

In those days I could run and kick a bit so I was eventually coaxed into playing for the Quins I think at Cwmgorse? Eventually with players like Trevor Evans, Owen Jones, "Wee John" and the sylph like "Coch", the side was to become quite a force in the old West Wales League.

Incidentally, the team talk at half time was, and still is a mystery to me.

The social side was quite special. I was introduced to games like "Cardinal Puff", "Names Of" and songs that were never heard in a Welsh Chapel. I have special memories of Ikey Pike's classic rendition of "I'll be there".

A teaching post was impossible to find, so thanks to Trevor Evans, Ritchie Bundock and Coch, I was introduced to the seamy side of the construction industry, namely Davies Construction. One of these workers, whose name I forget, was always asleep in the tea shed but he was a left-footed full back for Llanelli when they had the great win over the All Blacks at Stradey Park.

Co-incidentally at that time, Davies Construction went into liquidation and I don't know if the names I mentioned had anything to do with it but lots of things went missing.

Randall Williams, Ian Penman, Gillian and Ieuan Thomas (Butch) at the 75th Anniversary Dinner.

Invitation Ticket to the Amman United Rugby Club's 75th Anniversary Dinner in 1979 at the Top Rank, Swansea.

75th ANNIVERSARY
AMMAN UNITED RUGBY FOOTBALL CLUB

CELEBRATION REUNION

Dinner Dance and Cabaret

featuring STAN STENNETT

TOP RANK SUITE, KINGSWAY, SWANSEA   FRIDAY, 16th MARCH 1979

7.30 p.m. for 8 p.m. ——— Ticket £6.50 ——— Dress optional

Socially, we had a memorable tour to Southend, where I was very impressed with the toilet facilities on the bus. Two plastic buckets and a hole in the floor or open the door and throw it out. We created quite a bit of damage on and off the park so I leave the rest to your imagination.

By now, the Sevens season was upon us. It was a game I had never played but with the players we had, we were almost unbeatable (not quite). One of my happy memories was scoring the winning try in the final of the play-offs at Ammanford, beating our old rivals Llandybie.

Any of the younger players reading this will think "Oh! No! Not the National Sevens Final again!" However, it was a magical, bitter and sweet day, rubbing shoulders with the top teams and international players, and the "Wee Amman" going through round after round to the final.

Ian Penman Seven-a-side team, back:5th.

It is all history now of course, but I would like to take this opportunity to thank everyone concerned at that time for the most wonderful day of my sporting life and the one and a half years of memories that will live with me forever.

I was with you all on the 75th Anniversary.

I hope to be there on the 100th Anniversary

It remains only for me to say, "I WAS THERE"

With deep affection

Yours aye

HAPPY MEMORIES AND THOUGHTS
By Jeff Thomas

On one important occasion, Napoleon Bonaparte said, 'An idea is the most powerful thing in the world'. How true this is when the idea turns itself into an institution of validity and vitality. As Captain Robert Falcon Scott was preparing to proceed on his first South Pole expedition, the Amman Valley pioneers were giving birth to Amman United Rugby Football Club.

It is with nostalgia and affection that we now recall its traditions, history and values. Rugby at this level is the lifeblood of our national game and the Amman has also provided a vital focal point for our community. It is essential that grass roots rugby continues to receive extensive support – after all, it has provided so many of us with such enjoyment and friendship.

I hope I will be forgiven for not dwelling too long on the finer points of the game or the successes which came our way during my playing era; after all, it is the people within the community who contribute to its success. Who better to start with than the collier captain, Dennis Davies – to me, as a young boy breaking into the team, he was an immense figure. His strength, courage and honest determination demanded that even the young and innocent followed him into battle; after one rather inauspicious team performance, Dennis was determined to restore some pride to his beloved Amman. As we once again paraded behind our try line, awaiting the conversion kick, he simply declared, ' We've lost the game, let's now win the fight'. Suffice to say the match ended gloriously and the fact that Dennis bought me an after-match drink was, according to some, testament that I had done my duty.

Sadly, Dennis passed away many years ago, as has another stalwart and back-row colleague of mine, John Rees – tall, fast and possessing a cunningly deceptive rugby brain, his humour and warmth endeared him to so many. He was excellent company on any sojourn, as indeed he was on our tour to Bradford in the mid 1970s. In our very first match, John requested that he be rested but volunteered to act as linesman. He was undoubtedly the best-dressed one of any era, as to save some time to pursue other interests, he turned out for duty in an immaculate pin-stripe suit and shining black shoes. I vividly recall the team hopelessly defending a high, hanging kick to our corner with all our players remarkably observing the event from within the opponent's half. As we awaited the inevitable try, we all witnessed what must have been an unique occasion in world rugby – John's excellent handling, eye for the ball and speed, only marginally handicapped by his attire, came to the rescue – he made a marvellous mark and the try was thwarted. I will leave it to your imagination to answer the question, 'What happened next'.

The highly revered 'Manora' twins always brought their influence to bear both on and off the park. I recall the highly talented Dai having to make a monumental decision in his mid-20s, having almost overnight lost his head of hair. A journey to Bristol was immediately made and a top-quality wig purchased, sufficiently endurable to withstand the rigours of rugby football - or so he thought. I recall playing on a windswept Cwmamman Park with ball in hand and the speedy Dai just outside me in prime position for a dash for the try line. Alas, as I was about to pass, Dai with both his hands on his head shouted, 'Kick the bloody ball, my wig's coming off!' The try was lost and very soon after, the wig also. It was exchanged for a sports car and, according to Dai, more than made up for his baldness with his female admirers.

John, his brother, was a mischievous lad, equally as busy off the park as he was on it. On a tour to the Manchester region, following a hard game and night, John busied himself with hoovering the hotel lounge carpet. Whilst he was at it, he brought a personal touch to the occasion and extended me the courtesy, whilst asleep, of treating my beard as an extension to the floor carpet! I survived, but not my beard, and to make matters worse, his swiftness of foot did not allow me any degree of retribution.

John must rank as one of the most exciting players to have ever donned the red jersey; with his mischievous swagger, he would go on his sweet path and with a sleight of hand that even the most hardened tackler would swallow; but that was before the rise of the Coach as a cultural phenomenon.

Speaking of coaches, one must mention the late Ieuan Evans, who was undoubtedly one of the outstanding coaches of his day at Llanelli, Swansea and the Welsh Youth team. He would occasionally spare some time to coach lesser mortals such as ourselves, only to be rewarded by an unfortunate accident as he was showered, fully clothed, by a bucket of cold water. Ieuan was not amused, convinced that it was a plot to ensure his absence from further 'task-master' training. This, of course, was not true; all appreciated his boldly pioneering methods and I fondly recall the humour and passion that was his hallmark – a truly great character.

One who played outside John Thomas for more than a decade at both Amman United and Llanelli was Cen Glynmoch – he was a fine player, strong, loyal, sincere and dedicated, traits he possessed both on and off the park. His fitness was supreme, despite his dedication extending to his prowess at the bar. Cen was a living proof that government health scares about alcohol unit consumption were desperate measures, doomed to failure, fundamentally dishonest and morally reprehensible!

Given that Howie is the book's editor, he deserves a mention. Howie was a great Clubman, although he did once transgress and failed to regularly appear at our training sessions. In his defence, Howie explained to Coach Al Thomas that he was a busy man, recently married and had to cut enough coal to ensure sufficient house warmth for the week, to which Al, rather unimpressed, replied 'Tell me Howie, where do you live, in a bloody power station?' Perhaps his absence from training was the reason he was not playing in one home match, and I vividly recall him watching, leaning on the perimeter barrier. We were not playing well and through a gap in the lineout, I spotted his dour face – instinctively I did not go for the ball and instead hammered my elbow into my opposite number's midriff and again looked for Howie. His face was a picture, genuinely beaming and excitedly speaking to his friends. Who said it's only tries that make people happy?

In so few words, I hope I have conveyed the happiness, the friendship, and the camaraderie that my era presented to so many, but it also gave so much more. It produced a world- renowned rugby administrator in the form of the brilliant and modest Vernon Pugh, Chairman of the International Rugby Board; a British Lion in the form of Trevor Evans, whose combativeness was easily the equal of his considerable skill. More importantly, it produced a second-class team more than capable of competing with the country's best at a time when Wales were a real World force.

Something strange has happened in Wales since those days. What was once clearly present in West Wales and was the perfect springboard for subsequent elevation to the higher echelons, has somehow vanished like the mist in the autumn sun - natural talent. I hope that the future structure of the professional set up will take one step back and not talk of rugby as if it has recently been invented. The future must enhance, not retard the progress of clubs such as ours. Club officials of today have extreme difficulties and challenges to cope with and I thank them for their continued diligence. Amman United Rugby Football Club became for so many of us an important focus for values such as sacrifice, constant endeavour, loyalty and solidarity. Let us be proud of the past and optimistic for the future.

WONDERFUL MEMORIES
By John Gwyn Jones.

Most promising player of the year 1975 John Gwyn Jones

Presented by President Marcus Roberts

When I reflect back to my playing years at Amman United, I can honestly say that the memories and experiences, and in particular the wonderful friends I made, will always remain with me as "The Good Old Days".

What makes a successful club are the characters within it, and in this respect, I could easily write a book about those great personalities that became household names within the ranks of the "Amman" Greats. To start with, Winston James was one of those who had the vision of feeding youngsters through the youth in preparation for senior rugby. He was responsible for luring me away from Brynamman to join Amman United, which was definitely frowned upon in those days. Winston was such a gentleman and had a nature about him that brought out the best in all of us. He was well supported by a group of elders – Brian 'Crow' Davies, Randall 'Coch', and Eurof Walters to name a just few. What was such a positive feature about the club, especially being a Brynamman exile, was the interest and encouragement the senior members of the club gave to the youngsters.

I recall my first "stay away" trip with the "elders" which turned out to be such a huge learning curve for me. I travelled with Brian 'Crow' Davies, Winston James and Jeff Thomas to Murrayfield for a Wales v Scotland International. Boy, did I grow up, over that weekend! I'll never forget the "Heads or Tails" challenge, which 'Crow' initiated. We all tossed a coin, and the odd one out would have to complete a task set by the others - guess who got caught out EVERY time! Yes! - Muggins.

The more I lost, the more determined I was for new challenges, and it wasn't until we were on our way home I was told how the "elders" had manipulated the game so that I lost every time! I certainly learnt the hard way, having to carry out tasks such as asking an attractive lady for a dance when she was already occupied with her boyfriend or buy the ugliest woman in the room a drink and many, many more! I am still waiting to have my own back!

One of the characters that had the greatest influence on me was Talley 'Bach' Davies. As a player in the youth team, I regarded 'Talley' as a bit of a hero, as he was a regular member of the 'All Whites' of Swansea team.

When the Western Mail newspaper headlines stated that 'Talley' had been placed on death row in an Italian prison, I should have been warned to stay away from him, but unfortunately, my mother always said I was easily led! Talley's presence, both on and off the field was huge. He was such a talented player and could feature prominently in any position. I suppose one of his great moments was when he had to move from fullback to scrumhalf for Swansea's match against the Baa Baa's, whereby he ended up making a fool of John Maloney, the Irish International. 'Talley's' downfall was probably his lack of discipline. He was one of those natural and gifted players who took rugby as a hobby to occupy his time on a Saturday. He would not compromise on enjoying the finer things in life - singing, drinking, telling stories and womanising! In this respect I learnt a lot from him.

Perhaps my influence on 'Talley' was to bring out the "Neil Diamond" in him, as we developed such a strong singing partnership. "Ble mae'r gitar" was often heard after a match! I could easily write a book on 'Talley', as he was such a dynamic character for whom everybody had the highest respect.

I will never forget that match we played in Dylan Thomas Country. On a freezing Saturday in January we had to travel to Laugharne for a Welsh cup match. That morning temperatures were well below zero, so we were surprised that the match was on. As it turned out, ours was the only match in Wales to be played that day. Playing up on a sloped hilltop, we took to the frozen field with no enthusiasm to play whatsoever. We must have looked like a bunch of wimps next to the Laugharnies, who were so eager to take us apart - there they were with their sleeves rolled up, as if it was a warm summer's day. It was clear what our plan was - as soon as we won a line out, I whisked the ball out to Piggy (Peter Griffiths - another character and great player) who thumped the ball as far into touch as he could. Whilst the Laugharne supporters ran down the slope to retrieve the ball. All of the Amman side headed for cover under the tin shed by the side of the pitch, and huddled together, whilst the Laugharnies were all lined up for the expected throw-in. This happened every time we won a lineout, and on one occasion, when we had to return to the pitch for the throw-in, Mike Mole refused to join us - he'd had enough!

As we played on, Mike ran on to the pitch to loud applause from all of us. However, he simply ran past all of us and made his way to the changing rooms. Minutes later, 'Talley Bach' moved aside for his opposite number to score, after which he said "Bugger it, let's join Mole and get under a warm shower as my balls are frozen solid!" So, off we all went, leaving a Laugharne side, along with the referee, totally confused.

One of the joys of playing away was to have a stop over, and that night, we had a great time on the bus, with the infamous "George," the bus driver. 'Talley Bach', pretending to be desperate for the toilet, pulled up the engine cover in the middle of the aisle of the bus and squatted with his trousers down to his ankles. George stopped the bus, grabbed the fire extinguisher and sprayed Talley's backside with frozen foam!

Talking about buses, I vividly recall when our bus broke down in Briton Ferry, which resulted in us being late for the kick-off.

We were playing Risca in another Welsh cup match and 10 minutes into the match we were 20 points down. Our skipper, Jeff Thomas gathered us together and said,"Bois Bach, we had better do something, otherwise it will be a 50 pointer." At the next maul, in front stand packed full of Risca supporters, Jeff let loose an almighty right hook, after which there followed a "free for all!" After calming things down, who was there with his arm around the referee, none other than, Jeff himself, uttering the words, "Well it's been a good game up till now ref, so there's no need for them to get punchy!"

Jeff was another Amman great, as he contributed so much to the club. I would describe Jeff as a competitive and committed player of immense stature. He was a player you'd always want to be in your side. His famous line when the game was lost was "well we've lost the match so let's win the fight."

I was fortunate to enjoy two great tours whilst playing for the Amman - one to Nottingham and the other to Manchester. On a Sunday afternoon, we went to watch a local match in Nottingham, which ended up with Alan 'Chico' Davies serving "free" beer behind the bar and all our players enjoying the after match food, which was meant for the visiting team. The Amman boys were never slow in coming forward! I could write a book about the escapades in the Hotel, but I would surely lose a lot of respect, as it was a written rule "Never bring tales back from tour!"

I must pay my respects to those great friends that I made over the years at Yr Aman - Dennis Davies, or big Den as he was known - what a character he was!

Then there were the formidable back row bunch made up of 'Butch', 'Sykes', John Rees, 'Dobbin', 'Mole', Keith Griffiths, Jeff Thomas, Phil Davies and 'Bruiser'.

Graham George I thank for taking many sucker punches on my behalf. Martin Rogerson and later on Darrel Campbell both were great hookers. My fellow half-backs, 'Hardrock', Terry Bach, 'Piggy' and Viv Madge, and wonderful backs such as Cen Glynmoch, Rowland John,' Talley Bach', 'Basher' and Dai 'Clough' Evans on the wing, to mention just a few.

There is no doubt in my opinion that Yr Aman yw y gorau..Y Gorau..Y Gorau.. And I hope that the future of the club remains to be prosperous and full of great characters that further enhances the great name of Amman United.

The club is very proud of its contribution over the years to the success of Welsh rugby and celebrating its Centenary is indeed an outstanding achievement.

Roll along Amman United…Roll Along..

THE AMMAN UNITED RUGBY FOOTBALL CLUB BADGE

By Eurof Walters

Argent: On Base, A castle in gold on scarlet with twin towers and Portcullis raised, surmounted by a raven with wings displayed.

The presence of the Right Honourable Lord Dynevor as President of the club since its early years made the task of designing a club crest comparatively easy

On being approached by the committee, he approved the project in principle with the proviso that a sample be prepared for his inspection prior to an order being placed for badges.

During a meeting in the Half Moon Hotel, Garnant in October 1950, he showed pleasure when shown the sample badge, designed in conjunction with the College of Heralds. His approval of the design was immediate and the crest has been the Amman blazer badge and logo ever since.

The castle represents Dynevor Castle and the Dynevor Estate of which large tracts of land in the Amman Valley form part, including Cwmamman Park.

The two turrets are representative of two castles close to the hearts of the people of Cwmamman, namely Dynevor Castle and Carreg Cennen Castle.

A raised portcullis signifies welcome and is synonymous with the ready acceptance by the people of Cwmamman of strangers passing through or coming to stay within its environs.

Ravens, though not with wings displayed, form part of the Dynevor crest and are also present in significant numbers on parts of the old Dynevor Estate.

Commemoration of the inaugural "Smoker" held in the Raven Hotel to celebrate formation of the club, is also signified by the presence of the bird ready to fly.

The scarlet backdrop represents the colour of the jersey worn by Amman United players, with the gold signifying the high esteem which the club has generated over the years in Welsh rugby circles.

Both Major Gilbert Davies and Mr Phil James had long association with the upkeep and the running of the Dynevor Estate and their long service with the club was also a factor in the design.

A Tribute to the Amman United
By Eric Jones (Twyn)

In 1950, having played a game of rugby, I was enjoying an after-match chat and drink with some friends at a Llanelli pub. This being a town steeped in rugby tradition, the walls of the pub were decked with photographs of well-known players. In the middle was a sketch of Billo Rees with a caption saying, 'The greatest outside-half Australia has ever seen'; this intrigued me and started me on the road of inquiry. I spoke to many people who had seen him play and the verdict was always the same – he was great. The words of one student and critic of the game sums him up – 'I have watched the game for 70 years, I have seen great players who were a joy to watch and thrilled us but Billo was SOMETHING SPECIAL; he was the GREATEST".

This made me think of all the great players that the Amman United Rugby Club has produced and gave me the idea of putting together a team of the greatest Amman players. Oh! What a team! If they could have only played together with Master Carwyn James at the helm.

AMMAN UNITED 'GREATS' XV
Coach: Carwyn James
Full Back: Joe Rees (Plough)
Wing: Jack Elwyn Evans – Shane Williams
Centres: Claude Davey - Ted Ward
Outside half: Billo Rees
Scrum half: D M Davies (Dai Cender)
Front row: Emrys Evans – Iau Ward – Eurig Thomas
Second row: Tom Evans – Evan Phillips
Back row: Trevor Evans – Will Davies – Bryn Llewellyn

Amman United 'Greats' Team Profile

Coach: Carwyn James (Amman United, Llanelli and Wales)
An excellent player but an incomparable coach. What he could have planned with the team above, the talent is inconceivable!

Joe Rees (Amman United, Swansea and Wales 13 caps 1935 - 1937)
A Welsh Captain and a very polished, immaculate player with an uncanny sense of position. The ball always seemed to fall into his safe hands and returned to touch with long accurate kicks, from the left or right foot. He was also a sound tackler – a complete full back.

Jack Elwyn Evans (Amman United, Llanelli and Wales 1 cap 1924)
A good all-round wing, whose excellent club form won him a Welsh cap; he later joined rugby league.

Claude Davey (Amman United, Swansea, Sale and Wales 26 caps 1930 – 1938)

A very strong, fit and durable player, a thrustful runner in attack, able to test the best defence to the limit. He was the famous crash-tackler of the 1930s, a centre to be feared by all.

Ted Ward (Amman United, Ammanford, Neath, Llanelli, Wigan, Wales Rugby League and Great Britain 3 caps 1946 - 1947)

A very good all-round centre, exceptionally good handler of the ball and never believed in passing to the wing unless he had a 50 – 50 chance, otherwise taking the tackle himself. A world-class goal kicker, able to kick penalties up to 60 metres. Ted broke the rugby league world record as points scorer.

Shane Williams (Amman United, Neath and Wales 11 caps)

A beautiful runner, good pace, always well balanced when moving left or right. Above average ability as a ball handler with excellent acceleration. A joy to watch, the game comes alive when he gets the ball.

Billo Rees (Amman United, Llanelli, Swinton, and Great Britain Rugby League 16 caps 1926 – 1929)

Short, stocky and strong with wonderful ball skills, could side step off either foot with tremendous speed. One of the greatest outside- halves of all time.

DM Davies (Amman United, Neath, Broughton Rovers, Warrington, Huddersfield and Keighley)

Dai Cender was an outstandingly talented player, excellent service, tackled well with a tremendous fast break from the scrum. Dai was a master at throwing a dummy, coupled with all the confidence in the world to go with it.

Emrys Evans (Amman United, Llanelli, Wales, Salford, Wigan and Wales Rugby League 3 caps union 1937 – 1939 and 1 cap league)

Very strong, durable and fast, he played for Wales as a wing-forward and played prop forward in league. During the summer, Emrys took part in athletics and was an above- average sprinter.

WD (Iau) Ward (Amman United, Aberavon and Swansea)

A good all round player; when hookers were 12 stone, Iau was 14 stone; the weight and strength was a big bonus. Iau knew his way around the dark corridors of the front row.

Eurig Thomas (Amman United, Aberavon and Welsh Trialist)

A well-built prop whose club form won him a Welsh trial.

Tom Evans (Amman United and Neath)

A very strong and abrasive player and was Captain of the Neath Invincible team of 1928/29. A forward who never took a step backwards. Tom was an A.B.A heavyweight champion of Great Britain.

Evan Phillips (Amman United, Llanelli and Welsh Reserve Ireland 1926)

A very fast, athletic and skilful player with a tremendous work rate; could play second row or flanker.

Trevor Evans (Pantyffynon Youth, Welsh Youth, Amman United, Swansea, Wales and British Lions 10 caps 1975 –1977, 13 appearances British Isles team in New Zealand 1977 and 1 test cap)

His record speaks for itself, an outstanding flanker.

Will Davies (Amman United, Swansea and Wales 4 caps 1931 – 1932)

Will Sgili, an outstanding back row forward, tremendously strong, an asset to any team.

Bryn Llewellyn (Amman United, Llanelli and Welsh Reserve)

A very talented player, fast and very committed. Played for the Amman as a teenager while still at school. Was a pilot during the war and was awarded the Distinguished Flying Cross for bravery.

TREVOR PRYCE EVANS
By Iwan Gabe Davies

Born Chorley, Lancashire, 26 November 1947
Career: Amman Valley Grammar School; Pantyffynon Youth; Welsh Youth; Amman United; Cambridge City; Cambridge County; Swansea; Carmarthen County; Barbarians; Wales B; West Wales; Wales and British Isles.
Flanker in 10 matches, against France 1975, 1976; England 1975, 1976; Scotland 1975, 1976; Ireland 1975, 1976, 1977; Australia 1975: Scored 2 tries. Uncapped matches included New Zealand 1975; Argentina, Tonga and Japan.
A British Lion and winner of ten caps for Wales during the Golden Years of the 1970s, Swansea flanker Trevor Evans took his first steps in senior rugby with Amman United in the 1966-67 season when he was 19 years old.

Although Trevor's roots are in the area, he was born in Chorley, Lancashire in 1947, before his father moved the family back to Garnant ten years later.

He attended Amman Valley Grammar School and played for Pantyffynon Youth and gained a Welsh Youth cap -" It was against France. We lost and I got dropped." - before moving to play for the Amman - "It was a big stepping stone moving from youth into playing with the big boys. I was fortunate to have gained the experience from the older players who looked after you. Dennis Davies was a legend. He wouldn't say much but he would always look after the younger players and (Randall) Coch was another "minder".

The games were very competitive and physical and I learnt a lot with the Amman. One of the important things I picked up is how teams protect the players around them".

At the end of that season, Trevor was commissioned into the Royal Engineers for three years, spending 9 months in the Libyan Desert extending an airfield for the Royal Air Force outside Tobruk.

Although he played no representative rugby for the army, he played for Cambridge City RFC; including the "Town versus Gown" matches against Cambridge University. Whilst with Cambridge City, he played alongside the legendary English and British Lion scrum- half Dickie Jeeps. "I don't know how old he was then but he could still make a break"

In 1970, under the guidance of the ex Amman United player, the respected Wales Youth, Llanelli and Swansea coach Ieuan Evans, Trevor joined the All-Whites.

Ieuan's approach to 15-man rugby resulted in an attractive game and successful era for Swansea.

Ieuan Evans played another crucial part in Trevor's early career by advising him to move from the second- row to blind-side flanker whilst playing for Pantyffynon Youth. This move was a resounding success for Trevor, who transformed his career and brought fame to his rugby clubs, school and the valley. After joining Swansea, he never looked back and played there from 1970 to 1978 and captained Swansea in season 1976-77.

Two memories of his playing days with the All Whites stand out in his mind.

"I remember playing against Llanelli; it was during broken play when the ball was kicked ahead up the field and as I chased in pursuit, I suddenly felt someone tugging my shirt. As I turned, I instinctively ducked, as it was not unknown to be 'ambushed'. To my surprise and relief, I saw the diminutive Llanelli centre John Thomas (nicknamed Manora) who was from Glanamman and an ex-Amman United player. By now we had both nearly stopped running and John said to me, 'Trev, any chance of a lift home after the game?' Okay, I replied and with the transport arrangements finalised, John and I rejoined our team-mates and got on with the serious matter of playing in a local derby".

Another abiding memory is playing against the Harlequins.

"We were attacking the Harlequins' line from broken play and as I took a pass, I also took a short arm tackle from Bob Hiller, the England and British Lions full back". Bob Hiller was a famous character nicknamed "Boss", who had struck up a close friendship with Maesteg born Ray "Chico" Hopkins during the successful 1971 Lions tour to New Zealand.

"It was embarrassing enough landing on my backside in this manner but the final indignity was leaving the pitch for stitches in my lip, while hearing a lone voice shouting, "Good tackle, Bob!"

I met Ieuan Evans our coach in the first-aid room with the Harlequins' doctor.

I was annoyed to say the least and in between stitches and in the heat of the moment, I made it quite clear that before the end of the game, I hoped someone would return the compliment. As I left the first aid room, my annoyance was still obvious and I was still repeating my misgivings. By the time I returned to the pitch another Swansea player had been taken off and, as this was the time before substitutes were allowed, I ended up on the wing.

Within two minutes, we put the ball high in the air and off I went to chase it with the other Swansea three-quarters. Bob Hiller waited courageously (or foolishly) for the ball to return to earth. As he took the ball, he started to crouch, possibly in an endeavour to lessen the impending impact. The result was a clash of our heads and it was Bob's turn to land on his back. Unfortunately, he had sustained a gash under his cheekbone; he left the field and headed to the first-aid room. Apparently, as he opened the door, the Harlequins doctor said, " Hello, Bob, I expected you before now."

In 1975, Trev skippered Wales 'B' before making his debut in the same season alongside Graham Price, Ray Gravelle, Steve Fenwick, Charlie Faulkner and John Bevan in a stunning 25-10 victory in the cauldron of Paris' at "Parc des Princes" on 18 January 1975.

France v Galles 1975

Wales B v Tonga 1974 Trevor Evans Captain

A narrow defeat to Scotland in Murrayfield, in which Trevor scored a try, robbed Wales of the Grand Slam in 1975.

However they were not to be denied that next season with Trevor again scoring a try against the Scots in a 28-6 victory; then they beat France 19-13 in a titanic Grand Slam decider at Cardiff Arms Park.

Wales v Scotland 197? Trevor scoring a try

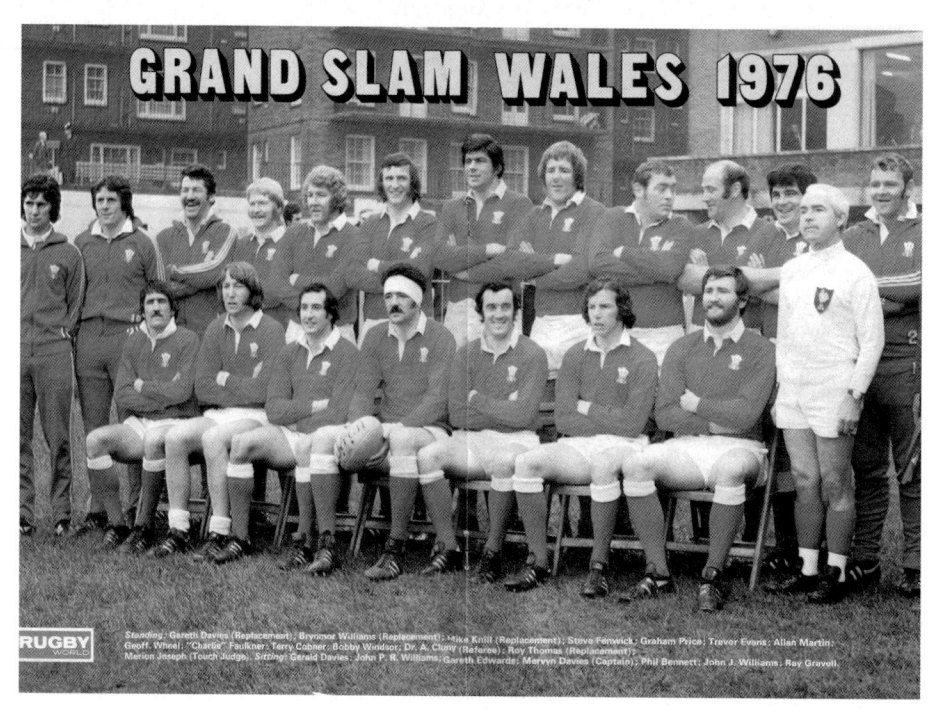

Due to a dislocated shoulder, he only played once in the 1977 Triple Crown season against Ireland. Trevor reached the pinnacle of his playing career when he was selected for the British Lions tour of New Zealand later that year.

Expectations were high for the 1977 team after the Lions had recorded historic series victories over the All Blacks in 1971 and South Africa in 1974.

Trevor remembers the tour was soured by relationships with the media. "The press didn't have as much access to us as they wanted and they started being critical of John Dawes (who was coach). After we lost the midweek game to New Zealand Universities, the first loss of the tour, just before the First Test, the knives were out."

Trevor made his first test appearance in the opening test in windy Wellington. The game was a controversial one for him. It was an evenly contested match with both sides giving very little away but the deadlock was broken when Grant Batty intercepted Trevor's pass to Scottish full-back Andy Irvine for the diminutive winger to sprint away to score a vital try. In the end, it was this try which eventually settled matters as the All Blacks triumphed 16-12.

He was blamed for the defeat, but Trevor gives for the first time his version of events. " I remember Terry Cobner over-ran the ball and I took the pass only to be immediately tackled. In that instant I couldn't see the surrounding players but when I heard Andy Irvine call for the ball, I flicked the ball out and the rest is history! What was most disappointing was reminding Andy afterwards that he had called for the ball and he replied, " I don't remember calling for the ball". Andy was too nice a person to categorically deny it but did not have enough backbone to admit it.

The game was to be Trevor's first and last Lions test match and the series was eventually lost 3-1.

He appeared in 13 matches for the 1977 British Lions in New Zealand and was captain on four occasions. Trevor skippered the midweek side and he remembers causing some controversy when he went for the toss-up with the referee and the opposing captain some time before the kick-off.

"The wind was swirling all over the place so, after winning the toss, I told the referee I wanted to wait until kick-off before choosing which way to play. He told me I would have to decide now and their captain supported the referee's view. In reply to their sportsmanship, I turned my back and as I walked away I said, "Get stuffed!"

Within a year, due to a recurring knee injury, he would retire from rugby altogether. His involvement in the game since his retirement has been limited and his energies have been taken up as a successful businessman.

Trevor has returned to rugby in 2003, having accepted the invitation to be the President of Amman United Rugby Football Club.

Wales v New Zealand 1977

Telegram from Marlene, Good Luck

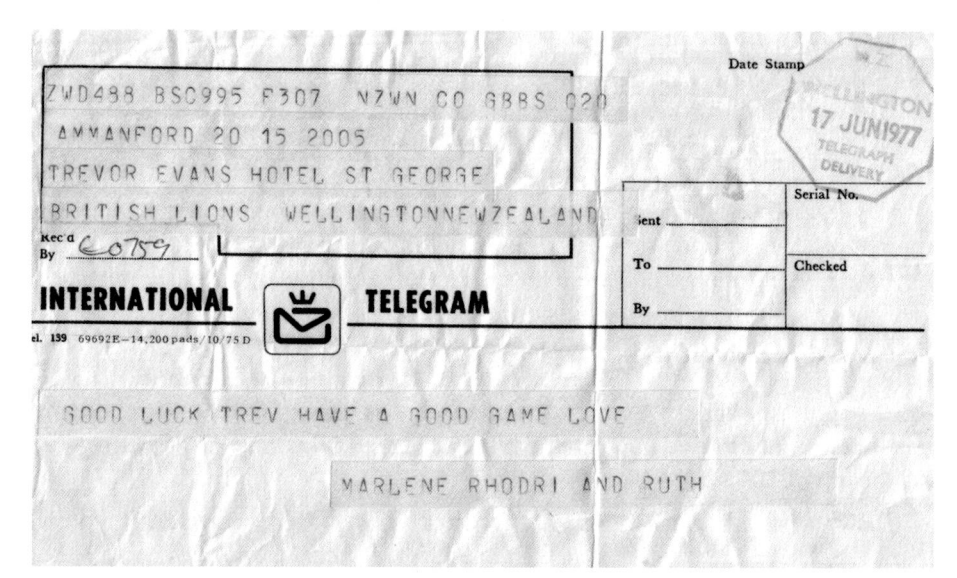

TEARAWAY TREVOR EVANS AND HIS MEN SHOCK TOURISTS

WEST WALES 14   ARGENTINIANS 12
Attendance: 14,000

The Pumas showed signs of tour strain at Stradey Park on Tuesday, October 12, 1976. This was their fifth game in 14 days and they just could not raise a match-winning effort against the lively West Wales pack. It was a keen disappointment for the tourists just four days before facing Wales in the Test. Most people felt the Argentinians would be back to their best following their surprise 24-9 defeat by the Midlands and North of England team at Leicester on the previous Saturday. But even with a much strengthened side, the Pumas were thrown off their game by the tenacious West XV.

Wing J. J. Williams, centre Steve Fenwick and Wales 'B' lock Barry Clegg had to withdraw because of injuries, their places being taken by Andy Hill, Phil Phillips and Phil May. All played their parts admirably in helping their side, captained by Swansea flanker Trevor Evans, who was in great form, become the first Welsh team to defeat the South Americans.

With Hugo Porta, their star fly half, back in action following injury at Aberavon, the Pumas looked geared for another special effort; but this time they could not establish a stable forward platform and the underdrive of Glyn Shaw and his fellow front row men upset the tourists' scrum pattern. This was the factor which paved the way for the West's exciting victory.

Nevertheless, the Pumas were 6-4 in front at the interval and had they snapped up a corner try when Adolfo Travaglini burst over just before half time, the balance of power may have swung in their favour. But the referee ruled a forward pass to Travaglini and the West were saved.

Neath wing Elgan Rees suffered an eye injury after five minutes and was replaced by Bridgend skipper Lyndon Thomas. While the West were reduced to 14 men they snatched the lead with a smart try by full back Clive Griffiths, and though the tourists forged in front 6-4, a rousing rally brought the West 10 points in a seven-minute spell at the start of the second half. The Pumas never recovered and for the first time in four games in Wales they failed to register a try.

THE TEAMS

WEST WALES: C. Griffiths (*Llanelli*); E. Rees (*Neath*), P. J. Phillips (*Maesteg*), R. T. Bergiers (*Llanelli*), A. Hill (*Llanelli*); D. Richards (*Swansea*), S. Williams (*Llanelli*); G. Shaw (*Neath*), E. R. Thomas (*Llanelli*), P. D. Llewellyn (*Swansea*), P. May (*Llanelli*), G. A. D. Wheel (*Swansea*), G. Jones (*Bridgend*), H. Jenkins (*Llanelli*), T. P. Evans (*Swansea, capt.*). Replacement: L. Thomas (*Bridgend*) for Rees.

ARGENTINIANS: M. Sansot; J. M. Gauweloose, G. B. Varela, A. A. Travaglini, D. B. Varela; H. Porta, A. M. Etchegaray (*capt.*); M. Carluccio, J. G. Braceras, A. J. Risler, E. Branca, J. Fernandez, J. Carracedo, J. R. Sanz, C. M. Neyra.

Referee: D. I. Burnett (*Ireland*).

Scorers: For West Wales, Clive Griffiths, Trevor Evans, Andy Hill (tries), Phil Phillips (1 con.).   For Argentinians, Gonzalo Beccar Varela (1DG, 1PG), Martin Sansot (2PG).

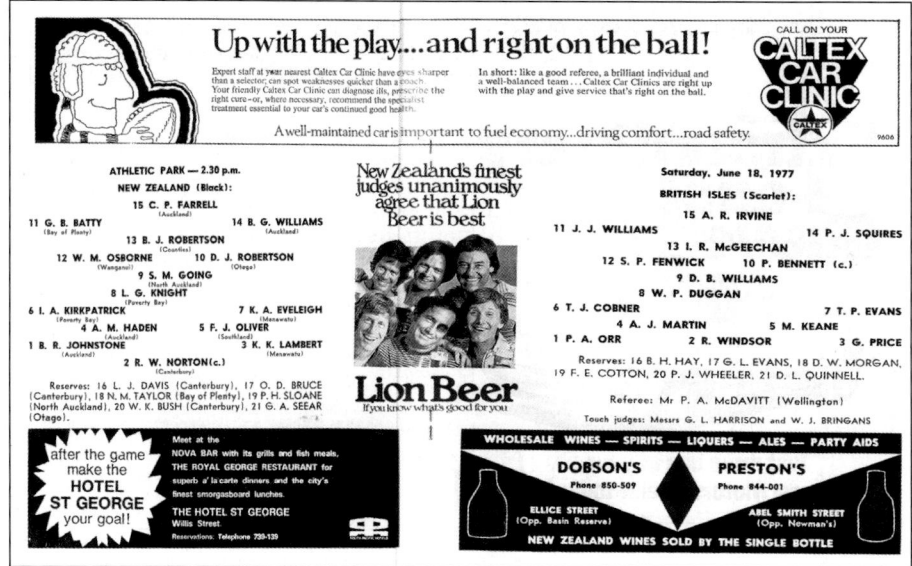

British Lions v New Zealand 1st Test 1977

British Lions v New Zealand juniors 1977 Trevor Evans Captain

Barbarians v Australia 1976

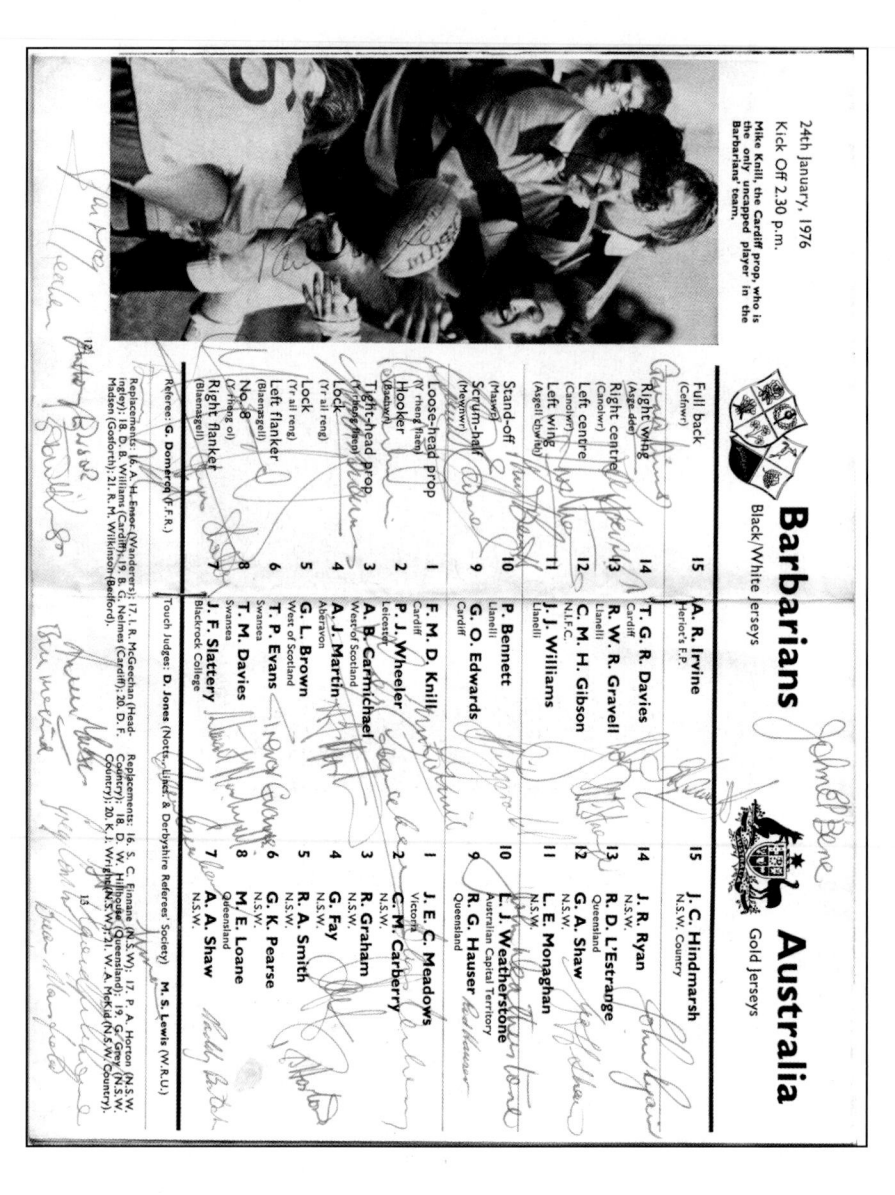

24th January, 1976
Kick Off 2.30 p.m.

Mike Knill, the Cardiff prop, who is the only uncapped player in the Barbarians' team.

Barbarians
Black/White Jerseys

Full back	15	**A. R. Irvine** Heriot's F.P.
Right wing	14	**T. G. R. Davies** Cardiff
Right centre	13	**R. W. R. Gravell** Llanelli
Left centre	12	**C. M. H. Gibson** N.I.F.C.
Left wing	11	**J. J. Williams** Llanelli
Stand-off	10	**P. Bennett** Llanelli
Scrum-half	9	**G. O. Edwards** Cardiff
Loose-head prop	1	**F. M. D. Knill** Cardiff
Hooker	2	**P. J. Wheeler** Leicester
Tight-head prop	3	**A. B. Carmichael** West of Scotland
Lock	4	**A. J. Martin** Aberavon
Lock	5	**G. L. Brown** West of Scotland
Left flanker	6	**T. P. Evans** Swansea
No. 8	8	**T. M. Davies** Swansea
Right flanker	7	**J. F. Slattery** Blackrock College

Referee: **G. Domercq** (F.F.R.)

Replacements: 16. A. H. Ensor (Wanderers); 17. I. R. McGeechan (Headingley); 18. D. B. Williams (Cardiff); 19. B. G. Nelmes (Cardiff); 20. D. F. Madsen (Gosforth); 21. R. M. Wilkinson (Bedford).

Touch Judges: **D. Jones** (Notts., Lincs. & Derbyshire Referees' Society) **M. S. Lewis** (W.R.U.)

Australia
Gold Jerseys

	15	**J. C. Hindmarsh** N.S.W. Country
	14	**J. R. Ryan** N.S.W.
	13	**R. D. L'Estrange** Queensland
	12	**G. A. Shaw** Queensland
	11	**L. E. Monaghan** N.S.W.
	10	**L. J. Weatherstone** Australian Capital Territory
	9	**R. G. Hauser** Queensland
	1	**J. E. C. Meadows** Victoria
	2	**C. M. Carberry** N.S.W.
	3	**R. Graham** N.S.W.
	4	**G. Fay** N.S.W.
	5	**R. A. Smith** N.S.W.
	6	**G. K. Pearse** N.S.W.
	8	**M. E. Loane** Queensland
	7	**A. A. Shaw** Queensland

Replacements: 16. S. C. Finnane (N.S.W); 17. P. A. Horton (N.S.W.); 18. D. W. Hillhouse (Queensland); 19. G. Grey (N.S.W. Country); 20. K. J. Wright (N.S.W.); 21. W. A. McKid (N.S.W. Country).

SHANE WILLIAMS
By Iwan Gabe Davies

Amman Juniors, Amman United, Neath and Wales

Towards the end of the 2002-03 season, Bridgend visited Neath for a vital Welsh league championship match.

The two were the only teams in contention for the title.

Televised live on BBC Wales, midway through the first half, the talented Welsh All Blacks winger Shane Williams received the ball inside his own half.

The home crowd gasped in anticipation hoping he would weave some magic to tilt the game in Neath's favour only to see him boot the ball aimlessly into touch on the full.

Rugby legend Jonathan Davies berated him from the commentary box saying a player of his talent should have looked to use his speed and skill to open up the opponents' defence.

A few minutes later, as if stung by the former maestro's criticism, Shane took the ball at speed about ten yards from the Bridgend line and ghosted through five helpless defenders to score a breathtaking try.

It was reminiscent of a try scored by that British Lion and Irish genius Mike Gibson, against Wales at Cardiff Arms Park in the 1970s.

The try was the defining moment of the game.

The tide was turned in Neath's favour and he made sure of victory in the second half with a sparkling try after some neat interplay by his team-mates.

He is one of the most exciting players in Wales during what is the darkest period in its history, yet there is no place for him in a national team that struggles to win a solitary Six Nations match against weak Scottish and Italian teams.

Out of favour with Wales' Kiwi coach Steve Hansen, the winner of 11 caps and with 12 tries scored, he has received scant reward for a player whose obvious talents have been confined largely to the Welsh domestic game.

"I must admit it is frustrating after the 2002–03 season went so well for me. I have played some good rugby and scored over 20 tries.

"But there's nothing I can do about it except keep playing the way I am and hopefully I'll be able to get back in the squad. There's no disagreement between Hansen and myself as far as I know. He has said he would like me as an utility player and wants me to play as a winger and practise as a scrum-half to be something like England's Austin Healey; although I joined Neath as a scrum-half, I would prefer to be known as a winger."

Shane's roots are in the Amman Valley. Born in Glanamman on 26 February 1977, he attended Glanamman Primary School and Amman Valley Comprehensive and still lives in Glanamman and is a fluent Welsh speaker.

Once a keen football player for Cwmamman United, he then changed his allegiance to rugby and began playing for the Amman Juniors in 1987 and then Amman United Youth.

He played 50 games for the Amman at scrum-half for two seasons before his talent was spotted by the then Neath Coach Alun Edmunds (who also coached at the Amman) and who took him away from Cwmamman Park to the bright lights of The Gnoll.

Within a short time he was playing against some of the world's finest players in the Heineken Cup but he admits the transition was a difficult one.

"The first thing I noticed was that the pace of the game had quadrupled and I realised I had a lot of work to do on my fitness."

After shining in one game in the Heineken Cup against Perpignan and scoring three tries, the visitors were so impressed with him that the French club asked if he would sign for them. But he turned them down, like so many other clubs wanting to add a star player like him to their squad.

Lyn Jones, Neath's charismatic and respected coach, is one of the reasons he stays at Neath.

"Anyone who has been in contact with Lyn knows he is an exceptional coach and he's done a brilliant job at Neath. He's quite unique in his ways. He's got a lot of respect throughout the squad and he's still just one of the boys. He never criticises his players."

Shane tips him as a possible future Welsh coach. It was with Jones's advice, recognising his elusiveness and talent for changing a game, that Shane moved to the wing.

He was soon hitting the headlines and secured a place in the Wales A squad before running on to make his full international debut as a substitute against France at the Millennium Stadium in 2000.

The man who gave him his chance at international level was the Great Redeemer, Graham Henry. Although it wasn't a fairytale first cap, with Wales going down to a heavy 36-3 defeat, it still holds fond memories for Shane.

"I loved it. I was so proud to just be sitting on the bench but to get onto the field and hear the cheering, I just wanted to do it again."

By this time, Coach Henry's honeymoon period with the Welsh rugby public, who had held him in adoration the year before, was already in decline.

Famous victories over France in Paris, England at Wembley and South Africa (the first ever win against the Springboks and the inaugural match at the Millennium Stadium) in 1999 placed Henry and Wales on the crest of a wave that came crashing down soon after.

Shane Williams being presented with his first Cap by Sir Tasker Watkins

By the spring of 2002, after an ignominious defeat by the Irish in Dublin, Henry was gone forever, the scapegoat for a catalogue of disastrous defeats.

But Shane remembers the New Zealander with a great deal of affection.

"I thought a lot of him and got on really well with him. He did me a lot of good.

"He was treated so unfairly and I really felt for him. He brought a lot to the Welsh game and we'll never know now how good a coach he really was."

A series of injuries have led to Shane being an outcast on the international scene. Although playing exceptional rugby, he finds himself absent from Hanson's Welsh set-up. Shane said his omission wasn't due to anything personal. " I don't really know him and I've only spoken to him a few times. It's still early days."

Shane is pleased with the new provincial set-up for the 2003-04 season and playing for the Neath/Swansea side. He said, "I'm looking forward to it and I think it will be a good thing for the Welsh game. From now on players need to be at the top of their game all the time. To be honest, I didn't care who we merged with. I have really enjoyed my rugby with Neath and they're a good bunch of lads. Fortunately, a large percentage of the players are staying and I'll be hoping to stay for at least a year. And I'm looking forward to playing with players like Scott Gibbs and Colin Charvis."

Shane has enjoyed celebrity status since his first appearance in the Welsh jersey; his good looks and unassumingly modest nature have won him a legion of fans from attractive young women to elderly ladies and he remembers being kissed by an adoring grandmother in a supermarket. Graham Henry attacked the media when Shane first burst onto the scene after he accused them of hyping him up to be the David Beckham of Welsh rugby. "When I first started playing, I started getting a lot of fan mail, not only from women, but lot of kids. I've also had letters from people in America and Japan who write to say how well they thought I was doing."

Although he may not be as famous as Beckham, he has done some modelling work.

His face was used to promote "Welsh Milk" in an advertising campaign run by Dairy Crest throughout Wales.

The obvious talents of the Amman United boy should ensure he shines in the new Osprey provincial team set-up to start in the 2003 season and that this will lead to a few more Welsh caps.

Shane Williams scoring a try against Japan

Dairy Crest advertisement - Welsh Milk 2001

Shane Williams scoring a try against Japan 2000

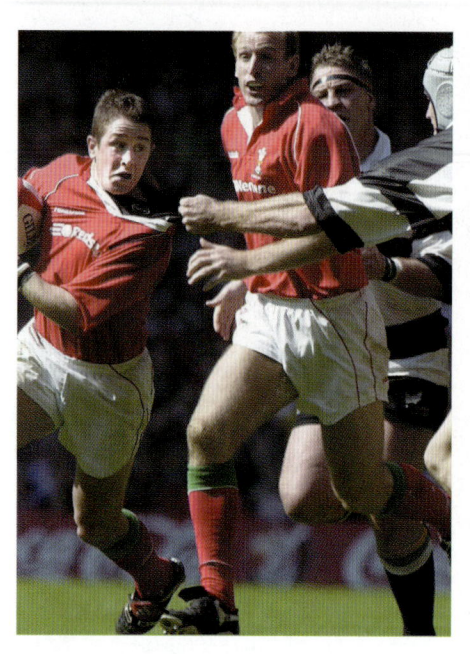

Shane Williams v Barbarians 2001 Breaks through to score, Pat Lam in background on the ground

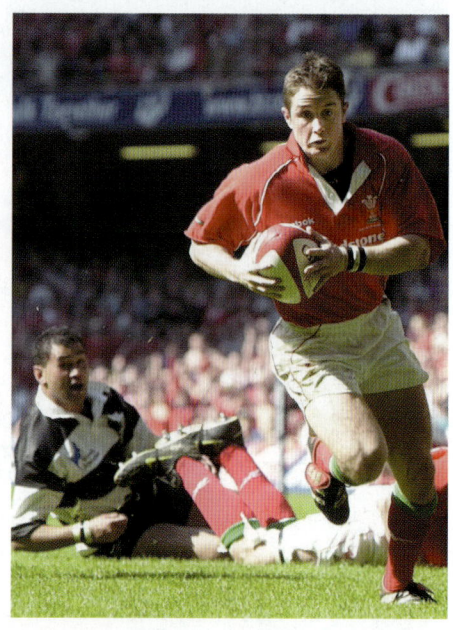

Shane Williams v Barbarians 2001

Shane Williams v Barbarians 2001 Scores try

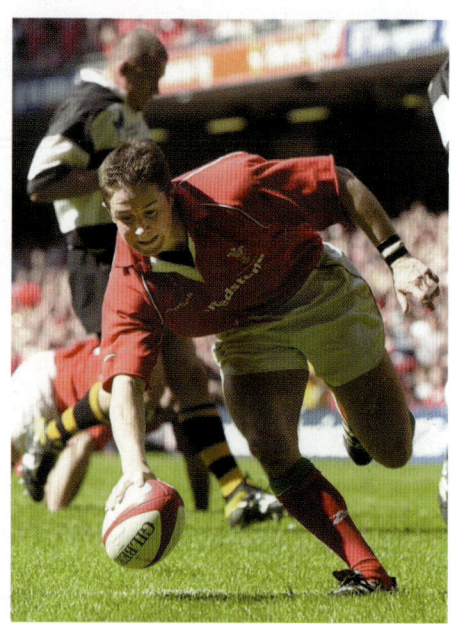

PROFILE OF DAVID JONES
By Howard Gabe Davies

David Jones was born in Llanelli on 9 January 1950 and raised in Tircoed, Glanamman. He was educated at Glanamman Primary School, Amman Valley Grammar School and Birmingham College of Art.

Whilst at the College of Art, he met his wife Jane and the couple now have two children, Philippa, 18, and Guy, 13, who plays for Walsall RFC under-13s.

David started work as a photographer with the Merthyr Express, then the Western Mail and is now with the Press Association based in Birmingham.

He can be seen at Cardiff's Millennium Stadium taking photographs at rugby internationals which are used in newspapers all over the world.

David has also been seen by Amman members at the Commonwealth Games in Kuala Lumpur and also at the South Africa v British Lions game at Newlands, Cape Town.

His travels have also taken him to St Helena in the South Atlantic, Romania and to Northern Ireland during the height of the Troubles.

In 1987 he won the Newspaper Photographer of the Year award for the pictures he took of the infamous Milltown Cemetery Attack in Northern Ireland.

In 1989 and 1990 he won the Newspaper Sports Photographer of the Year.

David was the only photographer allowed on the Earl of Spencer's estate during the Princess of Wales's burial and his photographs were seen all over the world.

He played flanker for Amman Valley Grammar School, Amman United, Carmarthen County and Ammanford. David followed in the footsteps, as a player, of his father Bowen, who played for New Dock Stars and his Uncle Ritchie Bundock, who played for the Amman.

Voted Player of the Year with the Amman in 1973, he was then, in his own words, "surplus to requirements" the next season and subsequently went to play for Ammanford.

Anrhydedd i'r Ffotograffydd o Lanaman

Mae cael eich dewis yn **Dynnwr Lluniau Chwaraeon y Flwyddyn** ddwywaith, ac yn **Dynnwr Lluniau Newyddion y Flwyddyn** hefyd yn gryn gamp. Ond dyna un mesur o'r llwyddiant a ddaeth i ran **David Jones,** mab i Mr a Mrs Bowen Jones, gynt o Lanaman (ond sydd bellach yn byw yn Waun Sterw, Rhyd-y-fro).

Un o fois Glanaman yw David, 'boi nêt' yn ôl rhai oedd yn ei 'nabod e, a fu yn flaen asgellwr da i dîm yr Amman United. Wedi bod yn ddisgybl yn ysgol Ramadeg Dyffryn Aman, aeth i Goleg Celf Caerfyrddin cyn mynd ymlaen i Goleg Celf yn Birmingham.

Dechreuodd ar ei yrfa fel ffotograffydd gyda'r Merthyr Express, a threuliodd gyfnod hapus wedyn yn Solfa, Sir Benfro. Bellach mae wedi setlo yng ngogledd Birmingham ers dros bum mlynedd, ond mae'n dweud mai yng Nghymru y buasai'n dewis gweithio. Roedd gofyn symud y tu allan i Gymru i gael yr her yr oedd ei angen arno. Eto daw ef gyda'i wraig a'i blant ar wyliau yma mor aml ag sy'n bosib, ac mae'n dal i gefnogi Amman United. Bu'n ffotograffydd i'r Western Mail a'r Echo am flynyddoedd, a nawr ef yw cynrychiolydd y Press Association yng nghanolbarth Lloegr.

Ddechrau mis Medi ymgymerodd David Jones ag un o'r swyddi pwysicaf a gafodd erioed fel ffotograffydd. Galwodd pennaeth asiantaeth newyddion y Press Association arno i fynd i dynnu lluniau o'r fangre lle y claddwyd y Dywysoges Diana, ar dir ystâd Althorp yn Sir Northampton. Ef oedd yr unig dynnwr lluniau a gafodd rwyfo allan â'i offer mewn cwch bach i'r ynys dawel honno. Rhyw 60 - 80 troedfedd ar draws yw'r ynys fechan sydd wedi ei hamgylchynu gan lyn a'i daear yn garped trwchus o flodau amrywliw. Dywedodd David iddo allu arogli'r blodau wrth iddo gerdded yn ofalus ar hyd y llecyn prydferth a thynnu ei luniau. O fewn dwy awr roedd ei luniau i'w gweld ar y teledu, ac ymhen deuddeg awr wedyn 'r oedden nhw ar dudalennau blaen bron i bob papur newydd led-led y byd.

Bu'n tynnu lluniau o'r Dywysoges Diana sawl gwaith cyn hynny, ond dyma un o'r pethau mwyaf ac anhygoel iddo, meddai, o gofio y byddai'r miliynau'n gweld ei waith. Er cymaint fu ei lwyddiant cyn hyn, caiff David Jones o Lanaman ei gofio am byth bellach fel yr un a dynnodd y lluniau hanesyddol hynny.

Mae darllenwyr Glo Mân a'i holl gyfeillion am ei longyfarch, ac am ddymuno'n dda iddo ef a'i deulu i'r dyfodol.

(Ymddangosodd portread o David Jones a'i gyfweliad â Sian Gwynedd yn **Y Cymro,** Medi'r 17eg. Diolch i'r **Cymro** am ganiatâd i addasu peth o'r hanes).

● Tîm yr Amman United, 1969-70. *David Jones - yr ail o'r chwith yn y rhes gefn.

AMMAN UNITED'S WELSH INTERNATIONALS

Joe Rees
Born 3 June 1897; died Swansea 12 April 1950
Career: Amman United, Ammanford, Swansea
Full Back in 12 matches against England 1920, 1921, 1922, 1923, 1924; Scotland 1920, 1921; France 1920, 1923; Ireland 1920, 1921, 1923: Scored 2 con 1pg – 7 points Joe Rees, a school attendance officer, was the brother of Billo Rees, the Wales and Great Britain rugby league international. Joe captained Swansea in 1922 – 1923.

Jack Elwyn Evans
Born Brynamman 1897; died Denbigh 15 July, 1941
Career: Brynamman, Amman United, Swansea, Llanelli
Centre 1 match against Scotland 1924
After retiring as a collier Jack Elwyn Evans became the steward of Mansleton Social Club. He signed for Broughton Rangers RLFC and made his debut for them against Widnes on 30 January 1926.

David Benjamin Evans
Born Llandybie 3 September, 1899; died Port Talbot 23 June, 1977
Career: Amman United, Llanelli, Swansea
Full Back 1 match against England 1926
For many years "DB" was a colliery fireman but later became an area manager for an insurance company.

William Guy Morgan
Born Garnant, 26 December 1907; died Carmarthen, 29 July 1973
Career: Christ College Brecon, Welsh Secondary Schools, Cambridge University, Guy's Hospital, Swansea, London Welsh, Barbarians
Centre in 8 matches, against: France 1927, 1929, 1930; Ireland 1927, 1929, 1930; England 1929; Scotland 1929: Scored 3t 1dg – 13 points
Guy Morgan was the son of a Garnant doctor and was also the nephew of Teddy Morgan and W Ll. Morgan, won four Blues in 1926-29 and captained Wales on four occasions. He also made forty-five appearances for Glamorgan Cricket Club. In May 1941 he changed his name by deed poll to W Guy Stewart-Morgan. He was a schoolmaster at Radley for thirty-two years.

Claude Davey
Born Garnant 14 December 1908
Career: Ystalyfera County School, Swansea University, Welsh Secondary Schools, Cwmgorse, Amman United, Swansea, Sale, Aylesbury, Reading, London Welsh, Rosslyn Park, Barbarians, Lancashire, Berkshire
Centre in 23 matches against France 1930, 1931; England 1931, 1932, 1933, 1934, 1935, 1937, 1938; Scotland 1931, 1932, 1933, 1934, 1935, 1937, 1938: South Africa 1931; New Zealand 1935 Scored 5t – 15 points.
A schoolmaster and electrical engineer. Claude Davey was renowned for his ferocious tackling. In October 1931 he scored a try for Swansea against South Africa. He captained Wales on eight occasions and London Welsh from 1945-47.

William Davies
Born Cwmgorse 14 February 1906; died Cwmgors 5 October, 1975
Career: Cwmgors, Amman United, Swansea
Forward in 4 matches against South Africa 1931; England 1932; Scotland 1932; Ireland 1932 Scored 3 points
At school and in his early days at senior level Sgili Davies, who was a colliery official, had played at scrum-half and centre. He scored the Welsh try against the victorious Springboks at St Helens in December 1931. His son Billy played at forward for Swansea.

Emrys Evans
Born Gwaun Cae Gurwen 24 April 1911 died Bristol 23 June, 1982
Career: Cwmgors, Amman United, The Army, Llanelli
Forward in 3 matches against England 1937; Scotland 1939; Ireland 1939.
Employed in the haulage industry, Emrys Evans played in two service internationals. In September 1939, he scored two tries in his debut for Salford RLFC against Rochdale Hornets. After the war, he rejoined the club before moving to Wigan RLFC, and gained one cap for the Wales RL team.

Gwynfor Evans
Born Treherbert 17 August 1918
Career: Clydach Boys School, Pontardawe Technical School, Amman Quins, Vardre United, Clydach, Swansea, and Cardiff. Glamorgan Police, Welsh Police, British Police, Barbarians
Flanker in 12 matches against England 1947, 1948, 1949; Scotland 1947, 1948, 1949; France 1947, 1948; Ireland 1947, 1948, 1949,; Australia 1947 Scored it – 3 points
A police officer in the Cardiff City Force, Gwyn Evans served in Italy and the Middle East during the Second World War. He was chairman of the South Wales Police RFC 1971 – 1979.

Carwyn Rees James
Born Cefneithin 2 November 1929 died Amsterdam 10 January, 1983
Career: Gwendraeth Grammar School, Welsh Secondary Schools, Aberystwyth University, Amman United, Cefneithin, Llanelli, London Welsh, Devonport Services, Royal Navy, Barbarians
Stand-off/Centre in 2 matches Australia 1958; France 1958
Carwyn James taught at Llandovery College and Trinity College, Carmarthen. At the time of his death he contributed to the rugby column of The Guardian which often contained brief comments of acute observations, A great nationalist, and a lover of Welsh literature, he stood as the Plaid Cymru candidate for the Llanelli seat in the 1970 General Election, polling 16.8% of the votes. During national service, he learnt Russian. Possibly, his greatest achievement on the sporting front was preparing, in his capacity as coach of the British Isles XV of 1971 and the Llanelli team of October 1972, for their respective defeats of the All Blacks.

Trevor Pryce Evans
Born Chorley, Lancashire 26 November 1947
Career: Amman Valley Grammar School, Pantyffynon Youth, Welsh Youth, Amman United, Swansea, Wales B, Barbarians.
Flanker in 10 matches against France 1975, 1976; England 1975, 1976; Scotland 1975, 1976; Ireland 1975, 1976, 1977, Australia 1975; Scored 2t – 8 points
British Isles 1977 Tour New Zealand 1 cap
Trefor Evans, who captained Swansea in 1976/77, was an estate agent in the city. He appeared in 13 matches for the 1977 British Lions team in New Zealand.

Shane Williams
Born Glanamman 26 February 1977
Career: Amman Valley Comprehensive School, Amman Juniors, Amman Youth, Amman United, Neath and Wales.
Wing in 11 matches against France, Italy, England, Scotland, Ireland, Manu Samoa, South Africa 2000; Japan (1 + 2) 2001; Romania 2003.
Shane played all his rugby at scrum-half until converted to wing-three-quarter by Neath. In 18 months Shane went from being the scrum-half for Amman United to playing for Wales as a substitute against France.

John Howells	Malvern Evans	Peter Gerrard	Huw Harries	David Thomas	
Ian Wagstaff	Jeff Thomas	Jeff Price	Rhys Harries	Huw Marshall	
Graham Bundock	Adrian Phillips	Aled Bartlett	Andrew Price	Chris Hughes	
Alwyn Davies	Ryan Williams	Matthew Brayley	Stephen Phillips	Steffan Edwards	
Ioan Cunningham					

HONOURS LIST

British Lion
Trevor Evans
British Isles Tour to New Zealand 1997

British Lions Coach
Carwyn James
British Isles tour to New Zealand 1971

Welsh Internationals
Joe Rees	1920-1924	12 caps
J Elwyn Evans	1924	1 cap
D B Evans	1926	1 cap
William Guy Morgan	1927-1930	8 caps
Claude Davey	1930-1938	23 caps
Tom Day	1931-1935	13 caps
Jim Lang	1931-1937	12 caps
Will Davies	1932	4 caps
Emrys Evans	1937-1939	3 caps
Gwyn Evans	1947-1949	12 caps
Carwyn James	1958	2 caps
Gwyn Evans	1947-1949	12 caps
Trevor Evans	1975-1977	10 caps
Shane Williams	2000-2003	11 caps
Nathan Brew	2003-	1 cap

Barbarians
William Guy Morgan	1927
Claude Davey	1934
Gwyn Evans	1948
Trevor Evans	1976

Welsh 'A'
Trevor Evans
Shane Williams

Welsh Under 21s
Alwyn Davies (Captain)
Mathew Brayley (Captain)
Ioan Cunningham
Nathan Brew

Combined Services Under 21s
Gavin Lewis

Welsh Reserve Internationals
Evan Phillips
Sgt. Emrys Griffiths
D J Rees
Eurig Thomas
Billo Rees
Bryn Llewellyn
Dick Thomas
Edryd Jones

Cambridge Blue
William Guy Morgan

Oxford Blue
Owen Jones (captain)

British Universities
Stephen Phillips

Services International
Nevin Anthony

Welsh Rugby League Internationals
Billo Rees
Ted Ward
D M Davies
Rees Rees
Evan Phillips
Emrys Evans

Great Britain Rugby League Internationals
Billo Rees
Ted Ward

English Rugby League Internationals
Billo Rees

Honours at Schools and Youth Level

Welsh Schools Intermediate Group (Under 16)
Peter Gerrard	1952	Ammanford Secondary Modern School.
Clive Williams	1957	Amman Valley Grammar School.
Jeff Price	1978	Amman Valley Comprehensive School.
Rhys Harries	1980,81	Amman Valley Comprehensive School.
Adrian Phillips	1984	Amman Valley Comprehensive School.
Chris Hughes	1994,95	Amman Valley Comprehensive School.
Ryan Williams	1998	Amman Valley Comprehensive School.
Ioan Cunningham	1999	Amman Valley Comprehensive School.

Welsh Schools Rugby Union Senior Group
William G. Morgan	1924,25,26	Christ Collage, Brecon.
Deveraux Morgan	1926	Ammanford County School.
Claude Davey	1927	Ystalyfera County School.
Darrell Griffiths	1945	Ammanford County School.
John Howells	1952	Ammanford Grammar School.
David Thomas	1965	Amman Valley Grammar School.
Ian Wagstaff	1967	Neath Grammar School.
Jeff Price	1980,81	Amman Valley Comprehensive School.
Rhys Harries	1983	Amman Valley Comprehensive School.
Huw Marshall	1983	Amman Valley Comprehensive School.
Graham Bundock	1984,85	Amman Valley Comprehensive School.
Adrian Phillips	1987	Amman Valley Comprehensive School.
Aled Bartlett	1988	Amman Valley Comprehensive School.
Andrew Price	1989	Amman Valley Comprehensive School.
Alwyn Davies	1994	Ysgol Gyfun Ystalyfera.
Chris Hughes	1996,97	Amman Valley Comprehensive School.
Ioan Cunningham	1999	Amman Valley Comprehensive School.

Youth Internationals
Peter Gerrard	1955	
Malvern Evans	1956	
Huw Harries	1958	
Trevor Evans	1966	Pantyffynnon Youth
Jeff Thomas	1967	Llandybie Youth
Chris Hughes	1998	Llanelli Youth
Mathew Brayley	1999	
Stephen Phillips	1999	

Welsh Youth under 19 F.I.R.A.
Steffan Edwards	1998
Ioan Cunningham	2003

Club Officials

Patrons
Mr Dudley Folland

Club Presidents
D T Jones	1903-1911
Rt. Hon Lord Dynevor	1911-1971
Marcus Roberts	1971-1988
Tommy D Williams	1988-2002
Trevor Evans	2002-to date

Life President
Bertie Davies

Past Chairmen
Rees Dukes	1903-1904
E Ceidrim Rees	1904-1912
David Thomas	1912-1914
James Enoch James	1914-1919, 1932-39
F W Gunning	1919-1926
Ivor Rees	1926-1930
Bertie Davies	1952-1962
Percy Rees	1950-1951
Phil James	1962-1974
Eurof Walters	1974-1983
David Worsfold	1983-1990
Edgar Morris	1990-2003

Club Secretaries
David Thomas	1903-1910
Sid Herbert	1910-1913
Will Hay	1912-1926
Harry Slocombe	1926-1931
DB Evans	1932-1936
James Davies	1936-1939
Tom Ellis Howells	1945-1948
Sid Davies	1948-1950
D Percy Thomas	1950-1954
Ieuan Evans	1954-1956
Egwad Rees	1956-1959
Wally Bowen	1959-1964
Nevin Anthony	1964-1979
Will Styles	1979-1990
Martin L Jones	1990-2003

Club Treasures
Willie Camber Thomas	1903-1906
Evan Bassett	1906-1909
Anthony Rees	1909-1912
Billy Morgan	1912-1914
Will Jenkins	1914-1919
Joe Bevan	1919-1939

John Thomas	1941-1944
William Meurig Jones	
Gwynfor Lewis	1939-1941
Tom Ellis Howells	1944-1945
Jack Davies	1945-1949
Sidney Davies	1949-1953
Brian Lloyd	1958-1968
Lyn Evans	1954-1955
Cyril Lewis	1968-1973
Ken James	1973-1979
John Rees	1979-1982
Dai Rees	1982-1983
P R Owen	1983-1988
Rowland John	1988-2001
Heddwyn Morgan	2001-2003
Raymond Phillips	1988-2001

Past Life Members

Billy Jones	Tom Ellis Howells	Meurig Jones
Joe Rees	Percy Rees	Phil James
D B Evans	D Percy Thomas	Lewis James
Emrys Evans	H M Fuller	Harold Davies
Joe Bevan	D Emlyn Davies	Cis Jones
Will Davies	T Hughes Williams	Raymond Morgan
Evan Bevan	W A Hay	Jack Evans
Claude Davey	Bertie Davies	Elwyn Treharne
Jack Elwyn Evans	Gareth Jenkins	Will Styles
David Thomas		

Present Life Members

Nevin Anthony	Clive Brooks	Shane Williams
Eurof Walters	Martin L Jones	
Hywel Williams	Trevor Evans	

Amman United Captains

1903-2003

1903-1904	Billy Jones	1953-1954	Gwyn Jones
1904-1905	D J Rees	1954-1955	Geoff Hitchings
1905-1906	Emrys Griffiths	1955-1956	Pat Brosnan
1906-1907	Phil J Rees	1956-1957	Evan James
1907-1908	Willie Jenkins	1957-1958	Ieuan Jones
1908-1909	Jim James	1958-1959	Mel Griffiths
1909-1910	Evan Bevan	1959-1960	Randy Rees
1910-1911	Dick (Bach) Thomas	1960-1961	Glyn James
1911-1912	Gilbert Davies	1961-1962	Huw Harries
1912-1913	Evan Bevan	1962-1963	Dennis Davies
1913-1914	D Benjamin Rees	1963-1964	Glyn James
1914-1915	World War 1	1964-1965	Huw Harries
1915-1916	World War 1	1965-1966	Alan Thomas
1916-1917	World War 1	1966-1967	Alan Thomas
1917-1918	World War 1	1967-1968	John Williams
1918-1919	Will Thomas(Maesteg)	1968-1969	David Lloyd
1919-1920	Gilbert Davies	1969-1970	Owen Jones
1920-1921	Garfield Phillips	1970-1971	Gordon Thomas
1921-1922	J Henry Griffiths	1971-1972	Hywel Evans
1922-1923	Tom Evans	1972-1973	Hywel Evans
1923-1924	Ike Lloyd	1973-1974	Gordon Thomas
1924-1-25	Reg. Davies	1974-1975	Gordon Thomas
1925-1926	Gomer Griffiths	1975-1976	Jeff Thomas
1926-1927	Nathan Rees	1976-1977	Jeff Thomas
1927-1928	Sammy Evans	1977-1978	Graham George
1928-1929	Sammy Evans	1978-1979	Graham George
1929-1930	Freddie Bevan	1979-1980	Keith Griffiths
1930-1931	Will Davies	1980-1981	Malcolm Davies
1931-1932	Jim Quick	1981-1982	Malcolm Davies
1932-1933	Eddie Bevan	1982-1983	John Gwyn Jones
1933-1934	Ivor Jones	1983-1984	Darrel Campbell
1934-1935	Les James	1984-1985	Mike (Mole) Evans
1935-1936	Cliff Harry	1985-1986	Jeff Price
1936-1937	Mal Bevan	1986-1987	Clive Williams
1937-1938	Bertie Bowen	1987-1988	Clive Williams
1938-1939	Ivor Jones	1988-1989	Clive Williams
1939-1940	World War 2	1989-1990	Stephen Phillips
1940-1941	World War 2	1990-1991	Stephen Phillips
1941-1942	World War 2	1991-1992	Darrel Campbell
1942-1943	World War 2	1992-1993	Darrel Campbell
1942-1944	World War 2	1993-1994	Huw Marshall
1944-1945	W Ward	1994-1995	Nick Griffiths
1945-1946	W H Thomas/W Ward	1995-1996	Dyfed Llewellyn
1946-1947	Jack Davies	1996-1997	Graham Watkins
1947-1948	Eddie Slocombe	1997-1998	Karl Worsfold
1948-1949	D Cochran	1998-1999	Steve Mackey
1949-1950	Gwilym Ward	1999-2000	Graham Bundock
1950-1951	Bobby Hunt	2000-2001	Shaun Davies
1951-1952	Vince Jones	2001-2002	Shaun Davies
1952-1953	Glyn John	2002-2003	Alun Rees

Club Coaches

1967-1969	Alan Thomas	1988-1989	Adrian Jones-Malcolm Davies
1969-1970	Ryan Bartlett	1989-1992	Peter Griffiths
1970-1973	Alan Thomas	1992-1993	Peter Griffiths-Clive Williams
1973-1974	Unknown	1993-1994	Andrew Bateman
1974-1975	Ian Wagstaff	1994-1995	Phil John- Nick Griffiths
1975-1977	Huw Harries	1995-1996	Lyn Evans
1977-1980	Colin Thomas	1996-1997	Phil John
1980-1982	Colin Davies - Clive Brooks	1997-1999	Alan Edmunds-Owain Lloyd
1982-1983	Colin Davies	1999-2000	Adrian Phillips - Nick Griffiths
1983-1986	Clive Brooks	2000-2001	Adrian Phillips- Neil Bundock
1986-1987	Don Davies	2001-2002	Phil John- Neil Bundock
1987-1988	Colin Mathews	2002-2003	Phil John-Pat Nolan

Team Managers

1997-2000	Peter Griffiths	2000-2003	Lyn Roberts

Presidents of the Welsh Rugby Union

1983-1984	Eirwyn B Davies	1991-1992	Ieuan Evans

Chairman of the General Committee of the Welsh Rugby Union
1993-1997   Vernon Pugh

Chairman International Rugby Board
1997-2003   Vernon Pugh

Welsh Rugby Union Selection Committee Member
Will Hay

Welsh Rugby Union District Members
Bertie Davies
T E Howells
Ieuan Evans

Welsh Rugby Union Referees

H M Fuller	Ryan Bartlett
Owen Jones	Eddie Bevan
Joe Bevan	Rowland Jones
Terry Thomas	Colin Thomas
Freddie Bevan	Martin Howells

Chairman of the Welsh Youth Rugby Union
E B Davies
Ieuan Evans

Coach of the Welsh Youth Rugby Union
Ieuan Evans

Coach of Llanelli Rugby Club
Carwyn James
Ieuan Evans

Coach of Swansea Rugby Club
Ieuan Evans

British Isles Captain
Trevor Evans

Welsh Captains
Joe Rees
William Guy Morgan
Claude Davey

Harlequins Secretaries (Formed 1947)

Sid Davies	Glan James
Egwad Rees	Keith Morgan
Amman Rees	Tom Ellis Howells
Wally Bowen	Nevin Anthony
Hywel Williams	Martin Howells
Martin Luther Jones	Alan Arnold
Ken Davies	

Harlequins Captains (Quins formed in 1947)

1947-1948	Gareth John	1975-1976	Martin Jones
1948-1949	Gareth John	1976-1977	Terry Thomas
1949-1950	Gareth John	1977-1978	Terry Thomas
1950-1951	Unknown	1978-1979	Dr Alan Jones
1951-1952	Unknown	1979-1980	Vivian Madge
1952-1953	Unknown	1980-1981	Clive Williams
1953-1954	Unknown	1981-1982	Mike Mackey
1954-1955	Lyn John	1982-1983	Mike Mackey
1955-1956	Wally Bowen	1983-1984	Keith Williams
1956-1957	Nevin Anthony	1984-1985	Keith Williams
1957-1958	Nevin Anthony	1985-1986	Anthony Jones
1958-1959	Nevin Anthony	1986-1987	Keith Williams
1959-1960	Raymond Walters	1987-1988	Martin Howells
1960-1961	Keith Hughes	1988-1989	Martin Howells
1961-1962	John Bartlett	1989-1990	Duncan Calow
1962-1963	Erith Price	1990-1991	Duncan Calow
1963-1964	John Bartlett	1991-1992	Shaun Davies
1964-1965	Keith Morgan	1992-1993	Shaun Davies
1965-1966	Vince Morgan	1993-1994	Shaun Davies
1966-1967	Ken Davies	1994-1995	Shaun Davies
1967-1968	Ken Davies	1995-1996	Mike Evans
1968-1969	Ken Davies	1996-1997	Mike Evans
1969-1970	Clive Brooks	1997-1998	Mike Evans
1970-1971	Clive Brooks	1998-1999	Anthony Jones
1971-1972	Clive Brooks	1999-2000	John Worsfold
1972-1973	Clive Brooks	2000-2001	Paul George
1973-1974	Martin Jones	2001-2002	Stuart Davies
1974-1975	Martin Jones	2002-2003	Richard Davies

Youth Secretaries

1949-50	D P Thomas	1963-65	Peter Williams
1950-54	E B Davies	1968-71	Ray Edwards
1954-59	Vivian Williams	1971-79	Winston James
1959-61	Aneurin Evans	1979-83	David Worsfold
1961-63	Ieuan Evans	1983-03	J V Williams

Youth Captains

1949-50	Jeff Jones	1975-76	Martin Howells
1950-51	Irfon Walters	1976-77	Andrew Evans
1951-52	Unknown	1977-78	Mike Evans
1952-53	Ryan Jones	1978-79	Mike Francis
1953-54	David Price	1979-80	Mike Francis
1954-55	Unknown	1980-81	Brian Davies
1955-56	Glyn James	1981-82	Huw Williams
1956-57	Unknown	1982-83	Royston Davies
1957-58	Huw Harris	1983-84	Shaun Davies
1958-59	Martin Jones	1984-85	Steve Mckay
1959-60	Martin Jones	1985-86	Paul Jones
1960-61	John Bartlett	1986-87	Nick Griffiths
1961-62	Unknown	1987-88	Gary Davies
1962-63	Unknown	1988-89	Gary Davies
1963-64	Barry Perry	1990-91	Gareth Morgan
1964-65	Gordon Thomas	1991-92	Karl Nottingham
1965-66	No team	1992-93	Karl Worsfold
1966-67	No team	1993-94	Karl Worsfold
1967-68	No team	1994-95	Carl James

Youth Captains continued

1968-69	Ryan James	1995-96	Stephen Morris
1969-70	Glyn Rees	1996-97	Emyr Timothy
1970-71	Martin Rogerson	1997-98	Steffan Edwards
1971-72	Eric Jones	1998-99	Stephen Phillips
1972-73	John Gwyn Jones	1999-00	Tristan Manning
1973-74	Brian Knight	2000-01	Nick Davies
1974-75	Vivian Madge	2001-02	No team

Junior Rugby Secretaries (U8s to U16s)

1973-1978	Eifion Rogers	1998-	Hywel Roberts
1978-1980	John Francis	1998-2001	Micheal Mangam
1989-90	Alan King	2001-2003	Gerwyn John

Amman Utd Players Represented Carmarthenshire County Which includes under '21' Games

Ieuan Evans	Vivian Rees	Adrian Phillips
Ryan Bartlett	Aled Bartlett	Geoff Hitchings
Glyn John	Kendrick Lewis	Darrel Campbell
John Thomas	Shane Williams	E Walters
Gwyn Jones	Mal Evans	Elwyn Davies
Carwyn Thomas	Gary Davies	Nick Griffiths
P James	Allan Jones	Evan James
David Thomas	Justin Power	Andrew Price
John Williams	Dennis Davies	Paul A'hearne
C L Davies	Alan Davies	K Davies
Peter Williams	John Howells	Sean Howells
Huw Harries	Steve Morris	G James
Con Mathias	Lyn Stephenson	Kevin Morris
Roy Evans	Sean Davies	Elwyn Owen
K Barnett	Denzil Jones	John Williams
David Jones	Karl Worsfold	Alan Rogerson
Vince Jones	Hubert Jones	J Butt
Graham Bundock	Richard Dunn	John Rees

The highest record of caps received by a County player is held by Darrel Campbell with 22 caps previous record holder was Ieuan Evans another Amman Player.

Playing Record

West Wales League Champions
Season 1935-36
Season 1991-92

Section Winners (Introduced in 1975-76)
Amman Utd 1986-1987
Amman Utd 1991-1992

West Wales Rugby Union Welsh Brewers League Bowl
Amman Utd 1991-1992

The Eurof Davies Memorial Cup
(Most points scored during the season)
Amman Utd with 457 points 1971-72 season
Played 18 won 18
Points for 457 points against 86

Most points scored by a player in a season is held by Alan Davies with 304 points in 1991-92
Previously held by Ryan Bartlett with 240 Points Season 1971-1972
First player to score 100 points for the club DW Evans 1930

Other Achievements

C C Evans Cup Competition	Runners Up 1962
Bertie Davies Cup Final	Winners 1968-69
Bertie Davies Cup Final	Winners 1971-72
C C Evans Cup Final	Runners Up 1985-86
C C Evans Cup Final	Winners 1986-87

Sevens Competitions
Welsh Rugby Union National Sevens District 'F'
Winners 1966
Winners 1967

Welsh Rugby Union National Sevens Finals
Runners-Up at Aberavon 1967
Beat Ebbw Vale 15-4
Beat Bridgend 6-3
Beat Neath 10-8
Lost Cardiff College of Education (UWIC) 10-11

Group F Winners	1969
Group F Runners- Up	1970
Group F Runners- Up	1972

Rhandirmwyn Sevens Winners 1968

Amman United RFC Committee

Back Row: Brian Davies, Nigel Pawson, Darrel Campbell, Heddwyn Morgan, John Vince Williams,
Front Row: Eric Jones, Rowland John, Edgar Morris (Chairman), Martin Jones (Secretary),
Ken Davies.

Amman United RFC Trustees 2003

Peter Williams, Eurof Walters, Martin Luther Jones.

Amman United RFC Life Members 2003

Back Row: Shane Williams, Eurof Walters, Martin Jones, Hywel Williams,
Front Row: Clive Brooks, Trevor Evans, Nevin Anthony,

Amman United RFC Centenary Book Committee 2003

Standing: Alan Thomas, Lyn Roberts, John Vince Jones,
Seated: Eurof Walters, Howard Gabe Davies, Martin Luther Jones.

VERNON PUGH QC 1945-2003
By Jeff Thomas

When great men die, one tends to remember where you were on hearing of it. I was sitting quietly at home reminiscing with an old school friend. The telephone rang; it was my mother who had heard of Vernon's death whilst listening to Radio Cymru.She simply said, "Ma Vernon wedi marw. Pam ma dynion da yn gorfod dioddef fel hyn?" (Vernon has died. Why should good men suffer in this way?). I knew that at that time she was shedding a tear or two, as my friend and I did. We did so proudly, sincerely and with feeling, as thoughts of yesteryear flew back. We did so because we knew the person, not the lord and master of rugby union.

The obituaries have said so much of his greatness as a barrister and rugby administrator and the respect in which he was held worldwide. I am sure, however, that the respect in which he was held in the Amman Valley meant just as much to him, if not more – that respect abounded long before his name became synonymous with World Cups, development of the game in lesser known countries, the worldwide move to professionalism, the expansion of the Five Nations Tournament to embrace Italy or the forging of the Heineken Cup and Parker Pen Shield in Europe. For the people who knew him and grew up with him in the Amman Valley, all these achievements were merely "icing on the cake" He had made his mark on us long before then. Oh yes, from the days of playing tennis together at Wimbledon, cricket at Lords, football at Wembley and rugby at the Arms Park - an act of embroidery of course, as those famous sporting venues should be replaced by the roadway in front of the Glynmoch council houses, the field behind the Glynmoch council houses or when time allowed, Grenig Park, following a sprint along the Valley railway line. One instinctively followed him; even then he was the natural leader, an example being his organisation of a group of teenagers to prepare Grenig Park as a football pitch, giving birth to Glanamman Juniors AFC, long before the advent of grants and officialdom.

If there was one man destined for greatness, we knew it would be Vernon and he did not disappoint us. How many have said, "I was in school with Vernon Pugh, I played rugby with Vernon Pugh, I'm from the same village as Vernon Pugh." We were not name dropping, we were just proud to have known him. And he so humbly returned such compliments, a chance street meeting led to lunch, and the presence of the world's top rugby players and administrators in a Cardiff Hotel World Cup time would not prevent him spending time in one's company. His humour, warmth and sense of fun had not deserted him. Dennis Gethin, former Secretary of the Welsh Rugby Union, was so right when he said, "Despite all his achievements, he remained that valley boy from Glynmoch."

Indeed, it could be argued that his place of birth and his humble coal mining background contributed so much to his success; he was brought up to respect but not to accept the superiority of others; his father's principled ideology instilled in Vernon an innate determination for fairness and equality. It led him to produce a damning critique of the players and administrators who had joined an international squad to celebrate the centenary of the rugby board of South Africa, then still ostracised because of apartheid. He also produced an unsolicited addendum recommending wholesale reform of the Welsh Rugby Union, in what had become a commercial era; by the same token, he fought and prevented tycoons and entrepreneurs such as Kerry Packer and Rupert Murdock from establishing control of the sport. He was furious with the Rugby Football Union for brokering a unilateral deal with BskyB television, a stance that saw England temporarily expelled from the Five Nations, and he penalised New Zealand by stripping them of their co-host status, alongside Australia, for the 2003 World Cup after they failed to comply with certain commercial strictures. Vernon may not have enjoyed those battles, but he was prepared to fight them on the basis of principles and fairness. This, allied with his prodigious intellect, made him a formidable campaigner. He possessed an outstanding memory and could articulate at length to the finest detail. It was remarkable to be in his presence and to observe his brain working, accepting nothing at face value and establishing the truth with remarkable energy and accuracy. Little wonder that he did not grub around for votes come re-election time, always topping the poll by virtue of his reputation for getting things done. He was a rare man in rugby and gave the game dignity and credibility.

I know that Vernon seized upon many opportunities to help those who were less fortunate than himself and that his legal business was no bar to finding time to represent those he knew, often at no cost to the persons concerned. The service of others has been his trademark and his warm, generous nature was to be seen in so many ways by so many people. The recipients of that generosity will grieve for him; the broadsheet obituaries only tell part of the story.

His courage was exemplified two weeks before his death by his attendance at his daughter's wedding in London and then, just two days before it, he was at Chepstow Races, fighting to the last breath. How I would have been privileged to be present, just helping in some small way, as he had done to others in all his formative and working life.

I conclude by simply saying, "To the world he was a barrister, a rugby administrator. To his family and those who really knew him, he was the world."

Obituary

Vernon Pugh **The man who brought much needed reform to Welsh and international rugby union**

Paul Rees
Saturday April 26, 2003, The Guardian

Vernon Pugh, who has died aged 57, was international rugby union's most influential figure and a leading QC on planning and environment issues.

At the start of 1993, he was coaching a junior club, Cardiff Harlequins, but that April, the Welsh rugby union's general committee was overthrown. This followed the leak of Pugh's 1989 report into Welsh involvement in the centenary celebrations of the then South African rugby board.

Pugh was hired by the WRU to find out why so many Welsh players and administrators had gone to South Africa. In an unsolicited addendum, he concluded that the governing body was ill-equipped to run the game in a commercial era, and recommended wholesale reform. The WRU never published the addendum, nor did it make its member clubs aware of its existence. When the South Wales Echo published it in February 1993, clubs forced the WRU's general committee to hold an extraordinary meeting. New elections followed a vote of no confidence.

Pugh refused to stand until two hours before nominations closed. He topped the poll as national representative and was elected the general committee's first chairman - a position he held until 1997. He became one of Wales's two representatives on the international rugby board, and was its chairman within 12 months.

The chairmanship was in those days awarded on a rotational basis, with the eight foundation unions (England, Wales, Scotland, Ireland, France, South Africa, New Zealand and Australia) taking it in turns to hold the position for a year. Pugh persuaded the IRB's council to change the system and in 1996 he became its first elected chairman. He had served two three-year terms and was planning to stand down after the World Cup this autumn, before he was diagnosed with cancer last September.

As chairman of the board's amateur committee, it was Pugh who announced in August 1995 that rugby union was becoming open and abandoning its most cherished principle, that of not paying anyone for playing a part in the game. He was later accused of not giving unions enough time to prepare, but he had announced a review of amateurism in March that year. After the World Cup, which was held that summer in South Africa, reports appeared suggesting that the Australian mogul Kerry Packer was trying to tempt the cream of the world's playing talent into joining a professional circus. Pugh described amateurism as a dam which could no longer hold water.

He was a pioneer. He helped set up the Heineken Cup, a tournament competed for by the leading clubs and provinces in Europe; he was instrumental in securing Italy's place in the Six Nations Championship; he worked assiduously to get rugby union accepted back into the Olympics; he established the international Sevens circuit to broaden the sport's popularity in a version of the game more readily understandable to neutrals than 15-a-side; and he had a vision of rugby union as a game of international appeal rather than one which had significance in only a few countries. He persuaded China to join the IRB and believed that the sport's future depended on getting a toehold in countries with large populations, such as the US.

It was one of the reasons why he arranged an inaugural contest between the hemispheres last November: he saw it as a means of raising money for emerging nations, but his illness allowed vested interests to prevail and the game was called off.

Pugh was born in Glynmoch near Ammanford. His father was a miner and a self-educated socialist who took his three teenage sons down a pit, telling them when they reached the surface: "I never want to see you near a place like this again."

Pugh was educated at Amman Valley Grammar School, the University College of Wales, Aberystwyth, and Downing College, Cambridge where he gained his LlB. He was called to the bar in 1969 and achieved his ambition of becoming a QC before the age of 40.

He played in the centre for Pontypridd and Cardiff HSOB. His passion was coaching - he took charge of Welsh Universities at the same time he became the board's fulltime chairman - and he longed to see Wales as a major force in the world game again.

"Vernon was the greatest administrator Wales has produced," said the former WRU secretary Dennis Gethin, a contemporary of Pugh's at Cambridge. "There has been no better one in the world in my time, but I suspect he would have given it all up to become the coach of Wales."

Pugh turned down a high court judgeship because he would have had to give up his IRB position. His sharp intellect meant many regarded him as aloof and arrogant, but far from arrogance, he was warm and convivial among friends and disarmingly polite to those who crossed him. He was a radical for whom too much tradition was dangerous: his aim was to turn the IRB into a business and he wanted to hand over the chairmanship to a chief executive rather than someone on a union's committee.

A keen soccer player in his youth, Pugh was an avid racegoer and was at the Cheptsow meeting two days before his death, having attended the wedding of his daughter Nerys 11 days before. He died at a hospice in Penarth.

He is survived by his wife, Dorinda, and their three daughters, Non, Nerys and Nia.

Glanville Vernon Pugh, lawyer and rugby administrator, born July 5 1945; died April 24 2003
Guardian Unlimited © Guardian Newspapers Limited 2003

CONGRATULATIONS
From Glanmor Griffiths Chairman Welsh Rugby Union to Amman United Rugby Club in their Centenary year

It is a great achievement for any sporting institution to reach 100 years of age. By the time Amman United was formed, the Welsh Rugby Union itself had been going for 12 years and both bodies have grown in stature since the early days of the 20th century.

Much has changed over the years, but the solid support given to the WRU and our national sport by the great men and women who have served Amman United for a century has never wavered. For that, and much more, I offer the sincere thanks of the WRU.

It has always been a personal pleasure for me to visit Amman United - one of only two 'United' clubs in membership of the WRU. The other one is in Gwent - Pontypool United.

I was always curious to know why the club incorporated the name 'United' into its title. Looking back, it proves how far sighted the committee men of that era were because Amman United was formed as an amalgam of a number of clubs from the villages of Garnant and Glanmman back in 1903.

In a move that must sound strangely familiar to everyone involved in Welsh professional rugby in 2003, the view was that it was better to form one strong side to represent the area than to have a number of weaker units. Perhaps Amman United should claim to be Welsh rugby's first 'Regional' club ahead of the likes of Llanelli Scarlets, the Celtic Warriors, Gwent Dragons, Cardiff Blues and Neath/Swansea Ospreys.

The amalgamation of those village teams certainly made a difference and it wasn't long before Amman United were able to boast the first of their 10 Welsh international players. That distinction went to Joe Rees in the first championship match played by Wales after the First World War, against England at St Helen's, Swansea on 17 January, 1920.

Rees was by then playing full back for Swansea and took part in a huge upset as Wales won 19-5. Both Rees and the Newport centre Jerry Shea, who scored 16 points, were carried off shoulder high by excited fans - no doubt including some Amman United members amongst them.

Rees went on to steal another 'first' for his village club when he became Amman United's first Welsh captain. Unlike his debut, defeat to England at St Helen's on 19 January, 1924 marked an end to his captaincy and his Test career.

But there were more great Amman United products to follow him into the Welsh jersey - J Elwyn Evans, David 'DB' Evans, Claude Davey, Tom Day, Jim Lang, Will Davies and Emrys Evans.

The Llanelli centre Elwyn Evans actually made his one and only appearance for Wales in the very next game after Rees' career came to an end, against Scotland in a rather ignominious defeat in Edinburgh. After that, he headed north to Broughton Rovers.

The Swansea full back David Evans was the next to win a coveted cap when he played in the draw against England in Cardiff in 1926 before the thirties brought the 'golden age' for Amman United products as Davey, Day, Lang, Davies and Evans all appeared for their country.

Davey led Wales on eight occasions in his 23 appearances and became revered for his tough tackling and no-nonsense approach at centre. Just imagine how proud everyone must have felt at the Amman Hotel when the Swansea back row man Will Davies marked his international debut against the 1931 Springboks with a try in a game that also saw Davey and Day figure in the Welsh line-up.

Davey was at the heart of Wales' first win over England at Twickenham in 1933 and then central to that 13-12 triumph over Jack Manchester's All Blacks in Cardiff in 1935 - with Lang also in the Welsh side.

Davey was also captain, and Lang was in the side, when the Llanelli flanker Evans made his Welsh debut at Twickenham in 1937. It was the first of his three caps, although he had to wait until 1939 to taste victory over the Scots and the Irish

After that, there was a big gap before the rampaging Swansea back row forward Trevor Evans burst onto the international scene to earn 10 caps, a Grand Slam in 1976 and a British Lions tour to New Zealand in 1977.

And that brings us right up to date with the Neath wing Shane Williams, the latest player off the Amman United production line to star for his country. With 10 tries in 10 Tests, he has made the most of his limited opportunities and surely has much more to offer at the highest level.

But you should never rank a club by its international caps alone. What about the 20 Welsh Secondary Schools players the club has produced, the three Under 21 caps and five Wales Youth internationals.

Amman United, along with so many other great clubs in Wales, has a rich tradition of grooming youngsters for stardom with recent junior internationals like Matthew Brayley, Ioan Cunningham, Alwyn Davies and Steffan Edwards being the latest examples.

But the club's success has not been restricted to the playing field. Perhaps what marks out Amman United for even richer praise is its contribution to the administration of the game in Wales.

How many clubs can boast two Presidents of the WRU and a man who rose to the highest chain of office in the world game.

Eirwyn 'EB' Davies was a tireless worker for the Wales Youth Union and became President of the WRU in 1983/84. The charismatic Ieuan Evans followed him in 1991/92 after a distinguished career as coach to the Wales Youth team, Swansea and Llanelli.

Ieuan also went on to chair a committee that reviewed the whole structure of the game in Wales and made a huge contribution to the General Committee. And then came Vernon Pugh, the man I succeeded as chairman of the WRU and who so tragically died of cancer a few months before his beloved Amman United was able to honour him as their chief guest at their centenary celebrations.

With his brother, John, Vernon launched his playing career at Amman United. He went on to play for his college at Cambridge University, Pontypridd and finally settled at Cardiff High School Old Boys. He must have had mixed feelings when his team were drawn against Amman United in the WRU Challenge Cup in 1974, especially when his home village side came up trumps with a 13-10 win to seal a once in a lifetime game against Llanelli in the next round.

The name of Vernon Pugh will forever be etched into the history of Welsh rugby for his many achievements in a brilliant career with the WRU. He presided over a difficult period in Welsh rugby, but was instrumental in creating new wealth for our game via TV and sponsorship deals and gave Wales a powerful and authoritative voice on the Five Nations and IRB committees.

He had a brilliant mind and a great love for rugby and will be sorely missed by the rugby world, but especially in Wales.

He was the driving force behind some of the most far-reaching development in the history of the game, both at home and abroad, as he over-saw the worldwide move to professionalism, the enlargement of the World Cup, the establishment of the Heineken Cup for European club rugby and the reintroduction of rugby to the Olympic movement.

The first chairman of the WRU General Committee, he also became the first elected chairman of the International Rugby Board and a Director of Rugby World Cup. From Amman United to the top of the world in the game he loved so much.

As our own chief executive, David Moffett, put it after Vernon's untimely death: "Vernon Pugh become one of the most powerful and dominant rugby administrators in the world game. He helped to take the IRB into a new era and his sharp mind was responsible for turning the Rugby World Cup into an outstanding financial success. He will be remembered as one of the outstanding rugby administrators of his age, a rare breed who was able to combine his lifelong passion for rugby with a brilliant career as a sporting administrator."

And so back to Amman Untied, loyal servant to Welsh rugby for 100 years and members of the WRU since the 1910/11 season. In this, their centenary season, they will be found playing in Division 4 south-west after previous appearances in Divisions 7-5.

Stalwarts of the West Wales Rugby Union, whose proud champions they were in 1936, Amman United represents the bedrock of Welsh rugby. I salute the current players, coaches and committee members of all ages, I thank those of previous eras for their contributions and I look forward to a second century of glory for this great club.

CONGRATULATIONS ON ONE HUNDRED YEARS

It is a personal pleasure to offer my sincerest congratulations to Amman United RFC on reaching its Centenary Year. It is a great achievement and with it there will be happy recollections from many stalwarts of the Club and the exciting matches that the Club has participated in. I was Secretary of Ammanford RFC when they celebrated their Centenary Year in 1987-88 and I know the pride that was felt by all in reaching that milestone in the Club's history.

I am equally sure that your special year will be celebrated in style. The name of Amman United, "Yr Aman," is synonymous with all that is good in Welsh Rugby. Whilst its latter playing records have not been successful as in the past, the club, nevertheless still offers formidable opposition to opponents.

My first visit and recollections of Amman United was being taken by my father as an eight year old to watch Ammanford play Cwmllynfell at Cwmamman Park in 1959. It was a horrible wet night but what struck me was the size of the crowd at the game. It was huge. How times have changed now and club treasurers would welcome a return to those heady days!

Down the years Amman United has been blessed by excellent administrators namely Nevin Anthony, the late Bill Styles, and the present Secretary Martin Luther Jones . These are names that ran parallel during my time at Ammanford. Despite the obvious rivalry that existed between the Clubs the first person to offer his help when I became Secretary of Ammanford was Bill Styles. A big man in all ways and someone for whom I had a lot of respect. Amman v Ammanford meant the keenest of rivalries but a great bond of friendship exists between the clubs. Games are hard, long may it flourish, but we are friends afterwards. Minor matters such as blood relationships or friendships are non-existent during the matches and one story written by Bill Styles in a letter of congratulations to Ammanford RFC in its Centenary Year told of one diminutive player en-route to the field who reminded an opposing giant sized forward – "Don't forget we are related," – to which the reply came – "Not until after the bloody game we're not."

I have to thank the Club Officials for the opportunity in contributing a few lines in this Centenary Book. On behalf of the District 'F' I wish you well for the future knowing that the solid foundations built over one hundred years will stand you in good stead.

Diolch am y cyfle I fod rhan o ddathlu'r Camlwyddiant Clwb Rygbi Yr Aman wrth gyfrannu'r geiriau hyn. Ar rhan Clybiau Ardal 'F' mae'n bleser I ddymuno'r gorau I'r Clwb wrth fynd I'r ganrif nesaf, Pob hwyl a phob llwyddiant.

Brian Fowler
Welsh Rugby Union District 'F' Representative

CANMLWYDDIANT CLWB YR AMMAN

Ym 1947, yn fachgen ifanc yn fy arddegau cynnar, roeddwn yn un o'r miloedd a dyrrodd i Barc Y Strade i weld gem derfynol Cwpan Gorllewin Cymru rhwng Clwb Rygbi'r Aman a Chlwb Rygbi'r Tymbl. Anlwcus y buont y tro hwnnw ond dyna fy nghysylltiad cyntaf a Chlwb Rygbi'r Aman. Heddiw, dros hanner canrif yn ddiweddarach, mae'n bleser mawr gennyf ddymuno penblwydd hapus i'r Clwb, a phawb syn gysylltiedig ag ef, ar ddathlu can mlynedd o chwarae rygbi.

'Nol yn y pum degau cynnar, roeddwn yn aelod o dim Ieuenctid Cefneithin a chwaraeau'n gyson yn erbyn Ieuenctid Yr Aman. Roedd hwn yn gyfnod llewyrchus iawn i rybgi yn y cwm wrth i rai o chwaraewyr y ddau dim, a thimau eraill o'r cwm, gynrychioli Ieuenctid Cymru ar lefel ryngwladol.

Yn bersonol, yr adeg a saif yn fy nghof yn bennaf am y Clwb, yw'r adeg honno rhwng '66 a '72 pan dringodd Yr Aman i'r brig wrth chwarae rygbi saith bob ochr, nid yn unig adran "F" ond drwy Gymru gyfan. Pwy all anghofio'r dewiniaid hynny John a Dai Thomas, yn mesmereiddio'r gwrthwynebwyr a'u talentau disglair, a'r dilynwyr brwdfrydig yn atseinio'r lle i'r gorchymyn "Give me an "A"......."A" "A", give me an "M"......."M" "M" ac yna, diweddglo enfawr, "What have we got ? Amman!

Ond, beth bynnag yw llwyddiant y Clwb ar y cae, rhaid cofio'r bobl gweithgar y tu ol i'r llenni sy'n cadw bwrlwm y Clwb yn fyw. Ymysg y rhain, gellid olrhain yr anfarwol Bertie Davies a Ieuan Evans (Llywydd Undeb Cymru '91-'92), y ddau wr tawel a gweithgar, Colin Thomas (Adran 'F') a Nev Anthony, ac yn awr yn y presennol, Martin Jones, yr ysgrifennydd, sydd a'r awenau yn ei ddwylo.

Diolchaf am y cyfle o allu rhannu'r ychydig atgofion yma dros yr hanner canrif ddiwethaf ar yr ychlysur o ddathlu eich canmlwyddiant. Hyderaf os bydd y gem yn cael ei chwarae yng Nghymru mewn canrif eto, fe fydd rygbi yn Yr Aman. Dymunaf pob llwyddiant ar gyfer y dyfodol i'r Clwb a'r dilynwyr. Daliwch ati i feithrin yr ieuanc er mwyn diogelu'r gem a sicrhau bydd dilynwyr yr Aman yn y flwyddyn 2003-2004 yn medru dweud, yn ol geiriau'r gan, "R'yn ni yma o hyd."

Dymuniadau gorau

Lance Roderick,
Adran "F"
Undeb Rygbi Cymru

ATGOFION RHEOLWR Y TÎM
Gan Lyn Roberts

Ers ei sefydlu yn 1903 mae Clwb Rygbi Yr Aman wedi cyfrannu llawer at hanes y gymuned, ac i'r gêm rygbi yng Nghymru.

Mae'r berthynas rhwng y clwb a'r gymuned wedi bod yn briodasol dros y ganrif. Roedd poblogrwydd y clwb ar ei fwyaf yr adeg yr oedd diwydiant tun a glo yn denu miloedd o bobl i weithio yn yr ardal.

Dros y blynyddoedd mae'r clwb wedi bod yn feithrinfa, yn datblygu chwaraewyr talentog sydd wedi cynrhychioli timoedd Llanelli, Abertawe, Castell Nedd a Aberafan thimoedd Cenedlaethol Cymru.

Gan ddechreu gyda Joe Rees hyd at Shane Williams yn fwyaf diweddar. Y chwaraewr mwyaf profiadol yn hanes y clwb yw Trevor Evans yn cynrhychioli'r Llewod ar ei daith i Seland Newydd yn 1977.

Mae'r Aman hefyd wedi cael ei bendithio gyda llawer o gymeriadau gweithgar a lliwgar. Yr hen Bertie, Dennis Davies, Phil James, Huw Harries, Colin "Talley" Davies, John Bach Monora ac yn fwy diweddar Darrel Campbell, Clive "Bruiser" Williams a Mike Mole i enwi dim ond ychydig.

Mae'r pwyllgorau, chwaraewyr a'r teuluoedd sydd wedi bod yn ganolog i ddatblygiad yr Aman hefyd wedi bod yn amlwg yn y gymdeithas, yn cynnwys prifathrawon fel Peter Williams, Alan Thomas ac Owen Jones.

Mae'r byd rygbi wedi elwa o swyddogion sydd wedi cael eu meithrin yn yr Aman, yn eu plith y diweddar Ieuan Evans, cyn Lywydd Undeb Rygbi Cymru a Vernon Pugh, Cadeirydd Bwrdd Rygbi Rhyngwladol.

Ar yr adeg hyn mae llwyddiant ar y maes chwarae wedi bod yn bring iawn. Yr Aman yn gwneud ei gorau i ddal ei lle yn y gyngrhair genedlaethol. Ond efallai y peth mwyaf pleserus yw gweld tîm o fechgyn lleol, sydd wedi datblygu trwy adran ieuenctid y clwb yn cadw traddodiad rygbi Yr Aman yn fyw.

Rwy'n hyderus iawn bydd dyfodol yr Aman yn dod â llwyddiant unwaith eto. Mae nifer o chwaraewyr fel Stephen Phillips a Ryan Williams yn tynnu sylw'r clybiau enwog ac mae gan Ioan Cunningham y cyfle i ddatblygu yn chwaraewr o'r safon uchaf.

Gyda'r gefnogaeth ffyddlon, rwy'n siwr bydd dyfodol disglair ar ei ffordd unwaith eto i Glwb Rygbi Yr Aman.

Cofiwch,

Yr Aman Yw Y Gorau!

CANEUON YR AMAN

Roll along Amman United, roll along
To the top of the league where you belong.
With a little bit of luck
We will win the silver cup.
Roll along Amman United, roll along.

We're Amman United, we come from the West,
We're some of the latest and some of the best.
We are respected wherever we go
For we are the Amman United.
Down by the sea, down by the sea,
Where the water melons grow,
I long to be
Down by the sea.
And when I do,
My mother will say,
Have you ever seen a cow with a green eye-brow
Down by the sea,
Zee la zee ba, zee la zee buzza,
Cor y bela, cor y bela,
Ching, ching y buzza,
Yr Aman yw y gore, y gore, y go-o-re

Song made famous in the Amman by Nev Anthony in the late 1960s

Wanted Man - Artist: Frankie Laine

Words and Music by Bob Hilliard and Lee J. Pockriss

SPOKEN: Bullet in my shoulder. Blood runnin' down my vest. Twenty in the posse and they're never....gonna let me rest

Till I became a wanted man I never even owned a gun
But now they hunt me like a mountain cat
And I'm always, always, always on the run

I killed poor Jed Kline (?) in bad Laredo fight
Killed him with my bare hands for the girl I loved that night
Jed's brother's out to get me

He's comin' with a gang
But I'd rather shoot it out, by God
Than let 'em watch me hang
Bullet in my shoulder!!
BLOOD runnin' down my vest
Twenty in the posse!!
And they're never gonna let me rest
Till I became a wanted man I never even owned a gun
But now they hunt me like a mountain cat
And I'm always (always), always (always), always on the run

She had spangles on her red dress
She had laughter in her voice
When he tried to put his hands on her
My heart left me no choice
But was she really worth it?
Well, I guess I'll never know
She'll be drinking someone else's rye
When I'm six feet below

Bullet in my shoulder!!
BLOOD runnin' down my vest
Twenty in the posse!!
And they're never gonna let me rest
Till I became a wanted man I never even owned a gun
But now they hunt me like a mountain cat
And I'm always (always), always (always), always on the run

A wanted man
A wanted man
On the run

Montage of Amman Players and Administrators

278

279

280

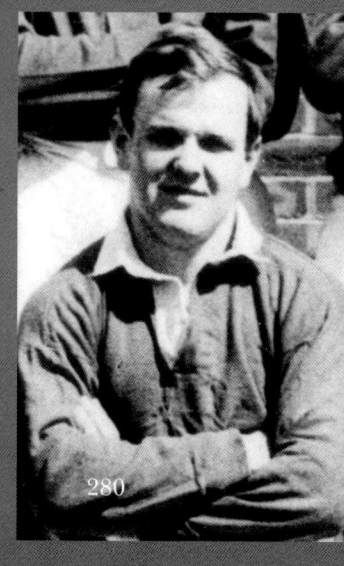

Pobol y Cwm as shown on the C4 Channel

Arial view of Cwmamman Park